CONSTITUTIONALISM
AND
THE CHANGING WORLD

CAMBRIDGE
UNIVERSITY PRESS
LONDON: BENTLEY HOUSE

NEW YORK, TORONTO, BOMBAY
CALCUTTA, MADRAS: MACMILLAN
TOKYO: MARUZEN COMPANY LTD

CONSTITUTIONALISM
&
THE CHANGING WORLD

Collected Papers

BY

C. H. McILWAIN

*Eaton Professor of the Science of Government
in Harvard University*

CAMBRIDGE

AT THE UNIVERSITY PRESS

1939

PRINTED IN GREAT BRITAIN

CONTENTS

Preface   *page* vii

I   The Historian's Part in a Changing World   1

II Sovereignty   26

III A Fragment on Sovereignty   47

IV Whig Sovereignty and Real Sovereignty   61

V   Due Process of Law in Magna Carta   86

VI Magna Carta and Common Law   127

VII Who was "Rossaeus"?   178

VIII The House of Commons in 1621   183

IX A Forgotten Worthy, Philip Hunton, and the
    Sovereignty of King in Parliament   196

X   The Transfer of the Charter to New England
    and its Significance in American Constitu-
    tional History   231

XI The Fundamental Law behind the Constitu-
    tion of the United States   244

XII Liberalism and the Totalitarian Ideals   259

XIII Government by Law   266

XIV The Reconstruction of Liberalism   283

XV The Tenure of English Judges   294

Index   309

PREFACE

OF the fifteen papers selected to be reprinted here, some are recent, others are old, but all, with one possible exception—and that, I think, only apparent—have some connexion with the history of constitutionalism or the bearing of that history upon our present problems. History may offer no solution for these problems, but it is safe to say that no solution which ignores history is ever likely to be either lasting or satisfactory.

The paper on "Sovereignty" (Number II) first appeared in *Economica* in November, 1926; the one entitled "A Fragment on Sovereignty" (Number III) is reprinted from *Political Science Quarterly* of March, 1933; Number VI, "Magna Carta and Common Law," was included among the papers published for the Royal Historical Society in 1917 under the general title "Magna Carta Commemoration Essays"; Number VII, "Who was 'Rossaeus,'" is from *Politica* of November, 1936; Number VIII, "The House of Commons in 1621," from the *Journal of Modern History*, June, 1937; Number IX, on the political ideas of Philip Hunton, from *Politica*, February, 1935; Number X, "The Transfer of the Charter to New England," from the *Proceedings of the Massachusetts Historical Society*, volume 63, December, 1929; Number XIII, "Government by Law," from *Foreign Affairs*, January, 1936; and Number XIV, "The Reconstruction of Liberalism," from *Foreign Affairs*, October, 1937. The dates and places of the original appearance of the others are indicated in the various articles themselves.

To the fifth paper in the collection, "Due Process of Law in Magna Carta," I have added a note to indicate a revision that now seems to me to be necessary. It may be thought that I should have done the same for Number VI,

"Magna Carta and Common Law." I am fully conscious that this paper is antiquated now. I am allowing it to be reprinted just as it was, because I still adhere to its general conclusions, because the principles with which they deal, inadequately treated elsewhere in this volume, are essential in all historic constitutionalism, and finally because I take some satisfaction in the thought that this paper may possibly have had something to do with the appearance since 1917 of a number of more thorough studies of the same general subject.

I wish to express here my thanks to the editors and publishers of the periodicals in which these papers originally appeared for their kind permission to have them reprinted as a collection.

C. H. McILWAIN

Belmont
Massachusetts, U.S.A.
December 1938

THE HISTORIAN'S PART IN A CHANGING WORLD[1]

Probably never since this Association was founded have men and women of our profession been asking themselves as earnestly and as anxiously as they are asking now, the old questions, so often asked before, whether we, as historians, have anything practical to offer to our own country and to the world in times of crisis like the present, and if we have, how we can make our particular contribution most effectively.

Each one's answer to these pressing questions must be his own personal answer, based on his own individual experience, if it is to be anything vital to him or any practical help to others. But if this is true, each one must also see that his answer can never be more than a tentative one. He must realize how very narrow the range of his vision must be; how infinitely small a part of the whole varied experience of our race, which is history, can be mastered in one short span of life or even in many. All history should be a lesson in humility to us historians, but there is no more striking lesson than the present world crisis, in many of its most important aspects wholly unpredicted, if not unpredictable, even at the opening of this twentieth century.

To one in a boat at sea the horizon seems to recede into infinity on every side, but if he is a seaman, he knows he is only looking over the brim into nothingness.

In a troubled time like our own, in thinking of our inherited institutions and ideas, one sometimes feels as old

[1] Presidential Address delivered on 30 December, 1936 at the annual meeting of the American Historical Association held at Providence, R.I., U.S.A.

Thomas Fuller did in 1655 on the completion of his *Church History of Britain*, when, as he says in his preface, "An ingenious Gentleman some moneths since in Jest-earnest advised me to make hast with my History, for fear (saith he) lest the Church of England be ended before the History thereof."

In this period of perplexity, we naturally wonder what service history can render in solving the problems of our country and of the world. We are asking ourselves how we, as historians, can do our part and what that part may be. No words seem more aptly to express this mood or to make clear our own present doubts and fears and hopes, than the moving preface of an English pamphleteer of 1643 who signed himself "An Earnest desirer of his Countrie's Peace":

When a Patient lies sicke under the destroying paroxismes of a Fever, every stander-by will be telling his Medicine, though he be no Physitian: O then let no Sonne of this State account it presumption in me, for putting in my judgement, and speaking that which I conceive might, if not remove, yet mitigate this fatall distemperature of our common Mother: at another time perhaps it might be censurable, but in this exigence laudable.

For whether we like to admit it or not, we know we are to a large degree the creatures of habit, and the makers of history are no exception; they always have been and always will be guided in their actions rightly or wrongly by what they conceive to be the results of past experience, by the "lessons of history"; at least they will attempt to justify these actions or to secure popular assent to them by an appeal to the past. "It is these lessons of history that we want", I once heard it said by an eminent professor of pedagogy, and we do want them; but I was glad it was pedagogy and not history he professed, for he added that it was only the lessons, not the history, that we needed. In the schools, two or three weeks, he thought, would be enough for the history itself. This certainly is "to make haste with our history", and perhaps it is this very widespread unthinking haste of to-day that best indicates the most helpful contribution we can make as students of history. Some "lessons of history" we know will always be drawn, some "lessons of history" will always be acted on. Our part is to see that these really are the lessons *of history*.

It is not as easy a part as it might seem at first sight. Especially in times like this we are in a hurry lest the institutions we study "be ended before the History thereof". We are anxious—too anxious—to find a short cut.

In this connection we are often told that each generation will rewrite its history of the past. Even if it does not wholly reconstruct this past, it will make its own choice of the parts to be noted, and these parts will be precisely those which are uppermost at the time when the history is written. One scarcely needs to be told that this is so, but some have told us more. They have not only admitted the fact that this is done. They have said it ought to be done. At times they have implied, if they have not actually said, that what is out-of-date now ought to be eliminated from history. Others have put it a little differently, perhaps a little less crudely. It is humanly impossible, they say, even to approximate in our words the complex of innumerable facts and forces that made the life of any part of the past. The historian at most can make only a selection, and a woefully inadequate one at the best. This is too true, though one might question whether it is any more true of some parts of the past than of the actual present.

But again these defeatists, for they are defeatists, would tell us more. Because it can never be done perfectly, it should not be attempted at all. At times they seem even to make a merit of our obvious, but unfortunate, defects. Why not admit that all our histories are after all little better than fiction, little more than impressionistic pictures? And isn't it better so? The writing of history, they tell us, is only an "act of faith". One convincing proof of the inadequacy of this phrase of an eminent predecessor on this rostrum is the tale of his own distinguished contributions to history.

Styles change in history as they do in women's garments, but sometimes the latter revert too. When some of us were youngsters we were taught to look up to the aims and aspirations of Leopold von Ranke as a guide. Now this is all changed. We find ourselves as professed historians engulfed in the general wave of pessimism, economic, political, and intellectual, which has been sweeping over the world since the Great War. Because we now know we can never achieve the full objectivity which Ranke preached, we are told that we should never make an effort to do so. Let us rest content with the subjective. It is all we can ever reach, all that can have any truth or value for us. Objective truth is a chimera. History is only an "act of faith". This intellectual weariness is no new thing in the world. Plato spent his life in combating it among the Sophists. To-day the world is again in a sophistic mood—I am using the word, of course, without any modern sinister meaning. There is a general distrust of reason. Behaviourists would have us believe that blind animal instinct alone determines human destiny, and fervid nationalists are setting up the menace of a particular tribal culture against the historical verdicts of universal human reason. Such subjectivism usually ends in a complete scepticism. As Gorgias said in the Socratic dialogue, even if there were an objective truth, we could never recognize it. History is a vain quest. Let us frankly admit that we are only drawing imaginary portraits and vistas that never were on sea or land. No doubt it is a good thing thus to know our own limitations. In the past, without question, we have known too many things that were not so, and we shall never know more than a little of what is so. Some distrust of ourselves is not a bad thing. As one result, we shall probably be spared some further excursions into prophecy under the name of the "philosophy of history".

But with all due deference to the considerations just recited, the historian is after all faced with the brutal fact that some things did actually happen in the past, and that some record of these happenings sometimes survives. And if these things happened, they had definite historical causes and results of which we often have some account remaining, even if incomplete.

How, in common sense, dare anyone say that we can know absolutely nothing positive about these past transactions, even if we cannot know all, even if we can know but little? And why should we be content merely to tint our picture with the colours that suit the changing taste of our own time? I am impressed by the sober words of the late Professor Tout in the opening part of his great work on English medieval administrative institutions. They seem to reflect more of the general aims and purposes of Ranke than of some later ones. "We investigate the past," he says, "not to deduce practical political lessons, but to find out what really happened."

We may not agree unreservedly with the first half of this sentence, but what serious historian can question the second? And if we investigate the past "to find out what really happened", knowing all the time that we can never truly find out anything whatsoever, why should we waste our time? Why not turn at once to historical romance? Too much of our written history even now is actually historical romance, and there may be a danger that much more will be. Biography seems to be turning that way, and already there are more than hints in certain parts of the world that all past history must be rewritten for a present purpose. In these days of propaganda, propagandist history is not likely to be neglected. Just let me give you a short extract from one interesting older example of it.

The author, John Aylmer, later bishop of London, is particularly bitter against the French—the date of the book, 1559, is significant—and asks, "Are they Giaunts, are they conquerours, or monarks of the world? No good Englishe men they be effeminate Frenchmen: Stoute in bragge, but nothing in dede.... They be your slaves and tributaries." They are in fear of the English, he says, "and it is no mar-

vaile, for we have thorow Gods help ever had the better of
them.... When durst these meacockes mete us in the field?
or if they did: went they not weepynge awaye?... We have
a fewe hunting termes and pedlars French in the lousye lawe,
brought in by the Normanes, yet remayning: But the language and customes bee Englyshe and Saxonyshe." "We
live in paradise. England is the paradise and not Italy, as
commonly they call it." And here in the margin the author
has added, "God is English"!

You laugh, but how much more fantastic is this than some
things written or taught or promoted in our own time? If
such is the rewriting of one's history for his own generation
—or his own nation—then some of us may prefer, with
Professor Tout, to stick to the more humdrum task of trying
"to find out what really happened", even if we know in
advance that we can never find it all out. And few serious
students of the history of English institutions, I think, would
venture to deny that this more patient method in Professor
Tout's own hands has actually resulted in a truly measurable
increase in our positive knowledge of "what really happened".

There is, of course, a sense in which each generation not
only does, but undoubtedly should, rewrite past history for
itself. For example, no one could deny that our modern
concern in the material things of life—whether that itself be
good or bad—has led to an appreciation of their importance
in the past, fuller and probably more just than the views of
some of the older historians. But when this leads, as it sometimes does, to a treatment of some past periods on the assumption that these same material or economic factors must have
been just as prominent then as they are now in the political
or intellectual development of the time—when this is done,
we get in the name of history a distortion in place of an
interpretation.

When kept within proper limits, this general kind of
revision has, it is true, resulted in a very great enrichment of

our history; but it is a mistake to think of it as the only kind; indeed, it is the principal contention of this paper that the most valuable of the newer interpretations of that history are now to be found in a quarter not only different from this, but almost directly opposite to it. The most serious defects in our existing histories of past institutions—the kind of histories with which I am most familiar—lie, not in any undue suppression of modern modes of thought and action, but rather in their untimely intrusion. Thus the chief advances made in the recent study of these institutional developments have come from a recognition of such defects. And I venture to predict with some confidence that any further improvement we may ever be able to make over our predecessors in this study in the years to come, any firm building we may succeed in erecting on the foundations they have laid, is likely to be in large part the result of a still clearer recognition of these defects and of a still further application to history of the canon which Sir Edward Coke once laid down for law: *contemporanea expositio fortissima est.*

Infractions of this rule naturally come oftener in some kinds of history than in others and are far more frequent for certain periods. For contemporary or recent history the danger is slight, for there familiarity with present-day conditions forms the necessary basis of all accurate historical judgments; and even in ancient history the faults are likely to be of a very different kind. You will notice that most of the illustrations of our retrogressive modernism come from the institutional development of the Middle Ages and after. This is the period from which we can trace our own familiar institutions in a continuous development. It is the stage of growth immediately behind us, in which were laid the foundations on which our social and political fabric still stands. Thus it is just because these institutions are so peculiarly our own and yet during their earlier growth so fundamentally different in character from what they have now become, that the temptation is so great to slur over the historical stages in their evolution. Probably for no other period is it so necessary or so difficult to observe in our thinking and writing the caution of Maitland when he says, "We shall have to think away distinctions which seem to us as clear as the sunshine; we must think ourselves back into a twilight. This we must do, not in a haphazard fashion, but of set purpose, knowing what we are doing."

Actual changes like this in our attitude toward particular historical problems have, however, not as a rule come about wholesale, or from any "set purpose". They have usually come piecemeal, because someone has been steeping himself in the thought and motives of some past epoch by extensive and careful reading of the records or writings of the time, and one day wakes up to find—usually to his utter amazement —that this thought or these motives and institutions are not at all the ones he has been reading about all these years in the standard modern books. Then he gets to work. If I may be pardoned a personal allusion, I can never forget the shock— it was really consternation rather than mere surprise—when I suddenly realized that men like Lambarde or Fitzherbert in Elizabeth's time, when they spoke of a parliament, were thinking of something in many ways very different from what I had learned. It is a little shocking to find the actual makers or the contemporary recorders of the past saying or doing or thinking something entirely different from the thing we have always had in mind, or, what is worse, have even been teaching to others as history.

But such shocks do not commonly arise out of the consciousness that our received notions of earlier historical developments fail to square with modern conditions. On the contrary, nine times out of ten it is just because these notions are too modern that the historian finally discovers that they do not fit the actual facts, that they furnish no explanation at all, or an obviously inadequate or even a distorted explanation of past movements and actions.

To see if this is true or not, it might be profitable to look at a few specific instances of revisions made in recent years in the field of our own earlier institutions which historical scholars have accepted generally as improvements. It is most interesting to compare, for example, the older traditional conception of these institutions in England just after the Conquest with the one now prevailing. The former is concisely stated in Freeman's *Growth of the English Constitution*, first published in 1872, and still survives in some of our textbooks; the latter is brilliantly set forth in Professor Stenton's *First Century of English Feudalism*, which appeared in 1932. To Freeman, apparently nearly as much as to Bishop Aylmer in the sixteenth century, all "the language and customes bee Englyshe and Saxonyshe". The words of our greatest modern master in this field are strikingly different. They were written by F. W. Maitland in 1895, or just before. He admits, as everyone must, that the Conqueror could not and did not "sweep away English law and put Norman law in its stead", nor ever intended to do so; but he sees, nevertheless, "one indelible mark" which the Conquest "has stamped for ever on the whole body of our law". He continues:

It would be hardly too much to say, that at the present day almost all our words that have a definite legal import are in a certain sense French words....Earl was not displaced by count, sheriff was not displaced by viscount; our King, our Queen, our lords, our knights of the shire are English; our aldermen are English if our mayors are French; but our parliament and its statutes, our privy council and its ordinances, our peers, our barons, the commons of the realm, the sovereign, the state, the nation, the people are French; our citizens are French and our burgesses more French than English....In the province of justice and police with its fines, its gaols and its prisons, its constables, its arrests, we must, now that outlawry is a thing of the past, go as far as the gallows if we would find an English institution.

The date of the final conquest of French over English in the courts Maitland significantly puts rather in 1166 than 1066, at the time of Henry II's Assize of Clarendon instead of the Battle of Hastings, and he goes on to warn us that this fundamental change in language must be the index of much more. These may be only terms of law, but they touch life in all its phases. For "Language", he says, "is no mere instrument which we can control at will; it controls us. It is not a small thing that a law-book produced in the England of the thirteenth century will look very like some statement of a French *coutume* and utterly unlike the *Sachsenspiegel*." When we pass from these more general matters to specific events of this period, the difference appears even more marked between the old interpretation and the new. Let us take the famous Salisbury oath of 1086, which brings up "perhaps the obscurest question in Anglo-Norman history", as Professor Stenton says. Speaking of it in his *Norman Conquest*, Freeman attacks certain "ingenious writers", because—to quote his own words—"they have picked out, as the act by which a Feudal System was introduced in England, the very act by which William's far-seeing wisdom took care that no Feudal System ever should grow up in England". These "ingenious writers" are chiefly lawyers, and in speaking of them Freeman says he is tempted to refer to St Luke xi. 52, which, by the way, reads as follows: "Woe unto you Lawyers: for ye have taken away the key of knowledge: ye entered not in yourselves, and them that were entering in, ye hindered." Following the Peterborough Chronicle, Freeman seems also to accept its statement that some 60,000 freemen took that oath in that unique "Gemót of Salisbury", which destroyed feudalism for ever in England.

To Professor Stenton, on the other hand, the same transaction appears simply as an application on a large scale of the normal and widely extended feudal institution of liege homage, and he says "its authority was in accordance with the strictest feudal principles". Furthermore, in his view it was not all the freemen who took the oath at Salisbury, nor even the mere knights, but only "the leading mesne tenants, men with military resources of their own, and the personal influence which birth and experience gave.... And the social custom of the time regarded such men as barons 'whosesoever men they were'." Such a feudal and aristocratic interpretation is a far cry from Freeman's glowing Germanic democracy.

Another important institution of the same period furnishing a similar illustration of the change in historical treatment is the county court and the membership of that court under the Norman kings. Even Bishop Stubbs seemed to regard attendance at the court as a privilege or honour so much cherished in twelfth-century England that King Henry I found it necessary in a writ which still survives to restore the frequency and regularity of its meetings after a period of interruption. A more recent view is somewhat different. Attendance at these courts was no honour that members prized or communities sought for. Instead, this attendance was a nuisance to those members and a burden of service upon those communities which should not be exacted any oftener than precedent warranted. The well-known writ of Henry I for holding the county and hundred courts, it is thought, is not then, as Stubbs and his predecessors assumed, an order for the holding of these courts oftener than before; it is a command that they should meet less often. The amount of suit at court shall not be increased for the local communities; as the contemporary author of the so-called Laws of Henry I puts it, they are "not to be worried further by any wearisome burdens" (*nec ullis ultra fatigationibus agitari*). The grievance redressed here is not too little representation, but too much. Like changes have taken place in our modern accounts of the nature of the central assembly, the Great Council or *Magnum Concilium*. It is now usually thought of as essentially a meeting of tenants-in-chief in response to a royal summons to acquit their lands of a strictly feudal obligation, the obligation of counsel. This has diverged pretty far from Freeman's conception of a great national assembly at whose meetings "the whole people had an acknowledged right to attend". What was formerly considered a national privilege turns out to be only a feudal burden.

Such revisions of Anglo-Norman history all tend in one direction, and they may be considered sound or unsound, but no one can deny that they are momentous. They amount to a fundamental change in our notion of the whole of the social and political institutions in operation in that important period. They modify our ideas respecting almost every side of men's life at the time.

None of them, however, seems to have been prompted by any feeling that earlier historians had neglected the forces of the present in their treatment of the past. The changes noted above in our ideas about Norman England have come almost invariably from an enlarged estimate of the importance of feudal relations in the life of that period; and yet, if there is one thing conspicuous by its absence in the life and thought of our own time, it is feudalism. What really produced this great change, then, was no reading in of modern modes of thought or action, but a reading out. It has resulted from no attempt, conscious or unconscious, to rewrite this part of the past in our own terms, but rather from a realization, born of careful research into the records of the time, that those records actually tell a story different from the one we have hitherto accepted as history.

Turning from the twelfth to the thirteenth century, we find similar changes of emphasis or of interpretation. One of these, at least, seems to have won the assent of historical scholars generally.

In 1853 Sir Edward Creasy described the Great Charter of King John as "a solemn instrument deliberately agreed on by the King, the prelates, the great barons, the gentry, the burghers, the yeomanry, and all the freemen of the realm". Of the famous words of its thirty-ninth chapter, "except by the lawful judgment of his peers, or by the law of the land", he said, "I believe that the trial by peers here spoken of means trial by jury. The words will bear this meaning; it is certainly impossible to give them any other satisfactory meaning." The clause guarantees "full protection for property and person to every human being who breathes English air". This is a fair statement of the opinion of historians pretty generally in 1853, and no doubt it is law, for this identification of the feudal trial by peers and our trial by jury is made in many of our own state constitutions. But good law may be pretty bad history. Needless to say, no reputable historian accepts this view to-day, though it lives on in Fourth of July orations and no doubt will for years to come. Less generally accepted perhaps, but no less significant, is an apparent change in the attitude of historians toward the annulment of Magna Carta by Pope Innocent III. It has been usual to see in it something of a papal attack on the independence of an English Church. Even as late as 1914 Mr McKechnie could say that "the conception of an English Church that was something more than a mere branch of the church universal, began to take clearer shape", when English churchmen found that John was receiving sympathy and support from Rome. If there is any contemporary evidence that can be fairly interpreted in this sense, I do not know what it is. The reasons for the revocation given in the bull itself seem ample; they are chiefly the compulsion under which John's promises had been extorted and the surrender of royal authority which these promises involved. The first of these grounds is too obvious to need comment, the second is far more interesting constitutionally; but on either ground it is hard to avoid the conclusion that the Pope could scarcely have given any other decision than he did; while the belief that Langton and John's other clerical opponents saw in it any attack on their national Church looks like just another of these anachronisms we have been tracing, which it is the business of the historian to disprove.

Since this paper was finished another illustration has occurred to me to insert, because it is a comparatively recent one—just eight years old, in fact.

For about three hundred years, and possibly longer, if we

took the trouble to trace it back; at least from the time of Queen Elizabeth, when John Manwood wrote the first comprehensive treatise on it; there has been one accepted doctrine on the relation of the law of the forest to the common law of England in the later Middle Ages. From the sixteenth century to the twentieth it has been held with hardly a dissenting voice that medieval Englishmen living within the boundaries of a royal forest were subject to a single law and a single jurisdiction, that of the King's justices of the forest; and that they were wholly exempt from the ordinary jurisdiction of the county courts in which the common law of the realm was normally administered. This is the doctrine of Manwood and of Blackstone, and it has been asserted recently in dogmatic form in the editor's note to the French translation of Stubbs's *Constitutional History*.

But in 1928 a doubt was expressed by Miss Elizabeth Wright in an article in *Speculum*. She had been reading the records of many cases in those forest courts, and noted that none of them dealt with anything beyond the vert and the venison, the beasts of the chase and the covert which protected them. She also knew, of course, that an English *foresta* of the thirteenth century was by no means the same as a "forest" in our usual modern sense. It often included great stretches of open country inhabited by hundreds of Englishmen who were living and tilling their fields in much the same way as the dwellers beyond the purlieus of the forest. Suppose then— and it was no improbable supposition—that one of these men in the forest should murder another, or commit the crime of homicide, or theft, or arson. There are no such cases included in the surviving pleas of the forest. Were these men of the forest then never guilty of these offences committed so often elsewhere, or were they free of all the heavy penalties inflicted for such breaches of the king's peace everywhere else in England? It seemed hardly likely. But under the accepted theory only one other alternative was possible: that these offences if committed within a forest were punished by the

King arbitrarily and without judicial process of any kind. That seemed equally improbable. But if none of these things were actually true of the thirteenth century, then the orthodox theory must be all wrong; men living in a forest must have been subject to two laws and two jurisdictions; the common law must have run in the forests as everywhere else for the matters coming within its scope; there was not one law in the English forests, there were two, not an exclusive jurisdiction of the forest justices, but a concurrent jurisdiction of these and the itinerant justices in the county courts. Could that be true? That doubt demolished at one blow a constitutional doctrine orthodox for three hundred years. For verification was easy. We have in print records of several eyres of the justices in the early thirteenth century. Among these, in four of the counties where forests were extensive Miss Wright found a number of cases in which men living in a forest were tried in the county court for breaches of the peace, and she found other cases of writs of *novel disseisin* for lands within the forest boundaries.

Here was no "act of faith", nor any interpretation of the past in light of modern conditions. This significant revision of our ideas concerning the scope and extent of our common law in its most important formative period grew out of a doubt, and that doubt was generated by extensive examination of the actual cases of the time. It is a typical instance. When we have enough like it we shall know better than we do now "what really happened" in thirteenth-century England.

I return now to a few further heresies that to-morrow may or may not be accepted as orthodox history.

Historians have thought and apparently still often think they find a sort of national declaration of independence of the canon law of the Universal Church in the famous declaration by the barons at Merton in 1236, *Nolumus leges Angliae mutari* —"We are unwilling that the laws of England be changed." This nationalistic explanation seems still to be the one generally accepted, and a good deal of eloquence has been expended on these patriotic barons. But a revisionist with contemporary evidence in mind must have his doubts. No man in England in 1236, noble or non-noble, layman or ecclesiastic, would have dreamt of challenging the Church's exclusive right to define legitimacy—the particular question then at issue—or to determine it in a particular case in its own courts. The barons do not say they repudiate canon law; they do not even say they repudiate the church's definition of legitimacy; they claim for themselves no jurisdiction over legitimacy generally; they only say that in determining a right of succession to English land, which is a proprietary right, the King's courts will follow the ancient English land law relative to succession in cases of illegitimacy in preference to any other rule. It might be added that although the Statute of Merton, of which this is one of the sections, is always printed among the Statutes of the Realm, it antedates any surviving statute roll, and how it originally got the name and authority of a statute must be considered now a question of much greater doubt, since the recent notable investigations of Messrs Richardson and Sayles into the history of the early statutes.

Other instances of the same thing will no doubt occur to you. This same antedated nationalism that formed our traditional estimate of the Statute of Merton and inspired McKechnie's criticisms of Innocent III's revocation of Magna Carta has also suggested similar modern objections to the arbitration of St Louis in 1264, in which he declared that the Provisions of Oxford of 1258 were void even though enacted with Henry III's formal assent, because they were an infringement of the King's royal authority. It has not always been sufficiently noticed that this constitutional objection of St Louis is the same that Innocent III had made against parts of Magna Carta, nor has enough weight been given to this and to other contemporary evidence for the existence at this time in England of a constitutional principle which seems to forbid even the King himself, much more any of the King's subjects, to "blemish" the rights of the crown, and renders null and void even a royal act which attempts it. If such a principle was in existence then, St Louis' decision, like Innocent III's, was probably the only one that could be justified then or now, in view of all the circumstances of the case.

Similarly, of course, these considerations must affect our estimate of Simon de Montfort and his work. We may admire as much as before the nobility of his character and aims and recognize the great significance of his acts and proposals, but we are less likely now to call this nobility patriotism or to defend those acts as constitutional. In the same way, and for much the same reasons, important recent historical research into the origins of English representation has made it impossible any longer to refer to him, as the German historian Pauli did, as "The Founder of the House of Commons".

What the retrospective nationalism of the older histories has done in this way for the work of Simon de Montfort, retrospective constitutionalism has done for the administration of King Edward I. He was the hero of Stubbs's great constitutional epic. Now he is regarded rather as a champion of prerogative than of constitutionalism; but to think of him thus, as a man of his own time rather than of a later time, is in no way really to detract from the nobility of his character or the true greatness of his designs. If one thing in his reign more than another might serve to illustrate our changing historical views, it is what I could now probably speak of without risk as "the Myth of the Model Parliament".

So we might go on to the revaluations of the great ordinances of 1311 and the Statute of York which repealed them and enacted what Stubbs, in his constitutional enthusiasm, regarded as the provision establishing the share of the commons in legislation. We might pass to the great ecclesiastical statutes of the middle of Edward III's reign, the Statutes of Provisors and Praemunire, and Maitland's classic exposure of their nationalistic interpreters and the naïve *non sequitur* that they had proved the existence of an opposition to papal authority among the English clergy because they had been able to show an opposition to the clergy among the English laity.

When we reached the Tudors in a survey of this kind it might seem at last that we had come to a period in which historical revision was to take a more modern form, something possibly almost like a rewriting in terms of our own day. For so far as there has been any recent revision in the historian's conception of this epoch it has seemed to incline to a softening of the old accepted phrase "Tudor absolutism" as a characterization of the time. At last we might seem to need a little more modern constitutionalism instead of reactionary antiquarianism if we were to reach a just estimate of the period. Like most such sweeping phrases, "Tudor absolutism" does cover a multitude of sins, not only past but present. In the reign of Henry VIII, at least, there is plenty of oppression, much injustice, at times intolerable cruelty. There can be no doubt of that, but can we properly call it a despotism? Strictly, it was not. The King had great power, and at times he greatly abused what he had, but he certainly did not legally have *all* power: there were limits to what he could legitimately do. His mere will was not law. It is impossible to characterize the Tudor reigns as an absolutism or a despotism in any proper sense of those terms.

Bishop Aylmer has been quoted for his fantastic chauvinism, but when he could forget that, he was a remarkably keen observer, and he might be quoted again in this connection:

But to what purpose is all this? To declare that it is not in England so dangerous a matter to have a woman ruler, as men take it to be—If on the other part, the regement were such as all hanged upon the King's or quene's will, and not upon the lawes written; if she might decre and make lawes alone, without her senate; if she judged offences according to her wisdom, and not by limitation of statutes and laws; if she might dispose alone of war and peace; if, to be short, she were a mer monarch, and not a mixed ruler, you might peradventure make me fear the matter the more, and the less defend the cause.

That is a very remarkable statement of constitutionalism to be written in 1559, and there is plenty of other contemporary evidence in support of it which I cannot stop to cite. Clearly we must temper our phrase, "Tudor absolutism". But is this because it is too modern to fit the facts, or because it is not modern enough? The answer to that question depends on another—whether despotism or absolutism is itself a medieval or a modern form or ideal of government. Without doubt it is modern, not medieval. In fact, in sixteenth-century England medieval constitutionalism was fighting for its life against the new, the more modern despotic tendencies, but it survived there. In sixteenth-century France the same battle was going on, but the outcome was different; there modern absolutism replaced an older constitutionalism, to last till the Revolution of 1789; the "tempered monarchy" of earlier times gave way before the personal rule of the Bourbon kings. What we still chiefly need, then, even for Tudor England, if we are to comprehend it better, is a more thorough understanding not so much of its modern innovations as of its great medieval heritage.

Need I cite more examples of such anachronisms as these? Because they were political liberals, St Thomas Aquinas must now be made over into a modern Whig and Cardinal Bellarmine into a democrat; because they believed in a restricted royal prerogative, men like Sir John Eliot and Sir Matthew Hale have to be turned into preposterous parliamentary Austinians. This is about the last and the worst case of this kind of procedure. Lessons may be got in this fashion, no doubt, but they will not be the lessons of history. The quickest and the surest way of finding the present in the past, but hardly the soundest, is to put it there first.

The illustrations above have practically all been taken from the earlier history of our own constitutionalism in the mother country, but further illustrations, equally pertinent, will no doubt occur to you from historical fields other than the constitutional and from other lands than England.

Let me add just one or two short illustrations from one of these other fields, intellectual history. There are few past developments in that field that leave a modern reader more cold, or that probably should leave him more cold, than the heated arguments of the sixteenth century over the question whether the references in the Apocalypse to the coming of Antichrist were or were not prophetic statements concerning the Pope applicable to the controversies of the post-Reformation period.

It is a sign of some progress that we are no longer interested in such a question as a matter of theology or of practical life. But when we read the books that were poured out to prove that point, when we consider that the greatest Catholic apologist of the later sixteenth century felt it necessary to devote one whole book of his *Disputationes* to a refutation of such arguments, how can any historian of the thought of that period neglect them, or if he does, how can he escape the just charge of being superficial? To-day these things are as dead as a door-nail, but they were living once, and any historian who ignores them because unrelated to our modern life simply writes himself down as one whose historical work is completely negligible.

Or take the dry discussions in the Synod of Dort over *supra* and *infra* lapsarianism between the Remonstrants and the rigid Calvinists. Nothing could be more foreign to our modern life and thought and no doubt we ought to be thankful for it, but they were no unimportant matters to Episcopius and the other leaders, and they can therefore be no more unimportant now to any serious historian of that intellectual epoch.

But here someone may object. He may say, as Glaucon said to Socrates in Plato's *Republic*, that this rehearsal thus far has been all negative. If it is true that some measure of objective history can really be reached, as has been maintained, then one ought to be able to point to something positive in that history, something not completely vitiated by the fallacies we have been tracing.

It is with a good deal of hesitation that I would venture to put forward one or two general political principles that do seem to accord with the words and actions of men throughout the earlier part of our constitutional history and yet have persisted to our own time or almost to it—principles, therefore, that may possibly survive the tests by which we have ventured to discard some others. Probably the best way to suggest these principles here is in the form of a commentary on one of the texts that expresses them best. It is the well-known line of Bracton in which he says, "Rex non debet esse sub homine, sed sub Deo et lege"—"The king ought not to be under a man but under God and the law." It would be hard to fix on any sentence outside Scripture more quoted in our later constitutional struggles than this, but the way it has usually been quoted is rather amazing. How many times we have all seen the last part of this maxim repeated, "under God and the law"! But how often do we ever see a quotation of the first part—*non sub homine*, "not under a man"? Yet Bracton himself put both these parts together, and he put *non sub homine* first. Some English royalists of the seventeenth century quoted the first part of Bracton's sentence and stopped there; many more on the parliamentary side repeated the last part and began with it. Practically none, to my knowledge, made use of both parts of Bracton's statement, and this is probably not surprising. It is always a favourite trick of propagandists to quote half a sentence and carefully omit the rest. But how shall we explain the fact that sober historians in later times have in this case done the same thing and kept on doing it? Why have we all gone on for ages repeating the words, "under God and the law", and as regularly omitting, "not under a man"? If we could answer those two questions satisfactorily, we might find that we had incidentally answered some others of very general historical significance and possibly even of some practical importance to the world to-day.

The King, Bracton says, should have no man over him, but

he should have over him the law. In ignoring the former part of this statement we are no doubt assuming that it does not fit our modern conditions, that it is untrue for us. That assumption might be questioned; but historians seem to have assumed even more than this, and the present argument is addressed to historians. In virtually suppressing this first part of Bracton's explicit statement, "not under a man", we appear also to condemn him, tacitly at least, of a misunderstanding of the political conditions in his own day. We reason, I take it, somewhat as follows: Bracton has said that the King should be under the law. This can mean one thing only; namely, that others either stand over the King to impose a penalty on him if he breaks or exceeds this law, or have at least an authority, independent of him, to oppose his acts. It can mean nothing less than this; therefore, our author's assertion which contradicts it, that none should be over the King and none equal with him, must be just a slip. It cannot be coupled with the words *sub lege*; it is obviously untrue, and therefore Bracton must have been in error in making it. I have called this an assumption. It looks more like presumption. We in the twentieth century are venturing to tell the ablest English constitutionalist of the thirteenth that he is all wrong about his own country and his own times, that we know more about it than he did. Suppose, then, we should adopt the more modest alternative, at least as a temporary hypothesis, should assume that the discrepancies in Bracton may after all be more apparent than real, and should set to work seriously to examine the institutions and ideas of Bracton's time for contemporary indications as to the accuracy of his statements or the possibility of reconciling seeming contradictions in them.

There is no need to bring evidence to show the general acceptance of the second part of Bracton's maxim, *sub Deo et lege*, either in his own time or by modern historians. It is generally admitted, though hardly sufficiently to account for all the facts of the sixteenth century. The part requiring proof is the first part, *non sub homine*. Yet, what Socrates says of

justice in Plato's *Republic* may be equally applicable here—
"what we were looking for has all this while been rolling
before our feet and we never saw it". For what but a constitutional doctrine like Bracton's could have led Innocent III
to quash a king's charter because it contained a loss or surrender of royal right (*regalis juris dispendium*); what but this
could have been in the mind of St Louis in 1264 when he
declared that King Henry III "should have full power in his
realm and government free of control" (*plenam potestatem et
liberum regimen habeat in regno suo*); or on what other principle
can we account for parliament's repeal in 1322 of an ordinance
already assented to by the King, ostensibly of his own "free
will"?

There are many other evidences of the existence and the
continuance of this constitutional principle of Bracton's, and
one of the most interesting comes late in the fifteenth century,
in the very heyday of the so-called "Lancastrian constitution"
and from the greatest of Lancastrian "constitutionalists",
Sir John Fortescue. In the famous and oft-quoted phrase by
which he characterizes the existing English monarchy, *regimen
politicum et regale*, Fortescue couples together *politicum* and
regale, just as Bracton did the two like parts of his maxim; and
if Bracton's two statements contradict each other, so do
Fortescue's. We must, in fact, condemn practically all medieval authorities as muddle-headed if there is not justification
for every part of Bracton's dictum.

The explanation of all this confusion is simple enough. We
historians have been confusing two things that contemporaries
were always careful to distinguish, *restriction* and *control*. They
held that the King's authority was legally restricted, or
bounded, or "limited" in its extent—*sub Deo et lege*, a *regimen
politicum*, as Fortescue put it; but it does not follow that they
did not, or that they should not believe that his rule was at the
same time "free"—*non sub homine*, in Fortescue's terms a
regimen regale, a *regimen liberum* in St Louis'.

One part of Bracton's sentence has to do with the extent,

the other with the manner of royal government. The confusion of these two is no mistake of contemporaries; it seems to be our own, and probably no similar lack of discrimination has ever caused more serious misrepresentations of history than this unfortunate failure to distinguish medieval *limitation* from modern *control*.

To the end almost of the sixteenth century English constitutional history is not fully clear without some reference to this old distinction. In 1587, in Cavendish's case, Elizabeth bowed when the judges ignored her express command to transfer an office from one man to another—the command was *ultra vires*; but in 1575 the intrepid Peter Wentworth had been sent to the Tower for even discussing the exercise of the Queen's authority as "supreme governor"—that was an attempt at *control*.

Even the process by which this older notion of limitation gradually grew into something more, in the development of a real control by a representative parliament becoming more and more conscious of its power—even this, in its full historical significance, is likely to escape us if we have no appreciation of the older ideas and institutions out of which the new ones grew. *The Winning of the Initiative by the House of Commons*, as Professor Notestein has so aptly termed this great change, can never have much real meaning for us if we allow ourselves to forget that this initiative did, after all, have to be *won*.

In Bracton's line, "Rex non debet esse sub homine, sed sub Deo et lege", we have, apparently, at least one positive principle of lasting importance, a faithful summation of medieval politics; and in the later modification of it we might find a considerable part of the modern. Consideration of it seems to point to the fact that we must distinguish pretty carefully in our history between autocracy and despotism; it seems to indicate that the medieval King was an autocrat, was absolute in the sense of having no superior, but was anything but despotic, in that his *jura regalia* left off where the rights of his subjects began. He was in fact limited but not controlled.

When we look for survivals of such principles in later times, after the initiative had been won, we must substitute the modern "government" for the medieval King, but a modern historian might find some illustration of this same old principle in the solidarity of the English cabinet; and even the American historian may wonder whether our bills of rights which embody this principle may not be a surer safeguard of liberty than an overextension of checks and balances which violate it in making government innocuous only by making it ineffective, and by splitting it up do little else than render it irresponsible.

As historians, our real task is with history, not with its application; but when troubles come upon us, the question will always emerge—it will not down—whether it belongs to the historian, even if not strictly *as* a historian, to find in all these facts and developments, assuming them to be accurate, any lessons of value that may be practically useful. I sincerely believe that it does; but like that other "earnest desirer of his countrie's peace" already referred to, if I tried to urge any such lessons for our present troubles, I should be "telling my medicine" only as a bystander, and not as a physician. If there are any practical inferences to be drawn from this jumbled survey, therefore, I leave them for you to draw.

II

SOVEREIGNTY

One of the most famous definitions in all modern political philosophy is Bodin's definition of sovereignty: "Majestas est summa in cives ac subditos legibusque soluta potestas."[1] The indefiniteness of the last word of this definition contains within it most of the controversies and much of the misconception that have marked the discussion of this important subject from Bodin's day to ours.

Potestas, power, here may mean *auctoritas*, authority, a power based upon positive law; *de jure*, not merely *de facto*; as *potestas* is used in the Roman *Lex de Imperio*,[2] or in the famous phrase of Justinian's Institutes in reference to it, "omne suum [i.e. populi] imperium et potestas";[3] and this is the meaning of Bodin himself. But, on the other hand, *potestas* conceivably might have another meaning here: it might be taken as the equivalent not of *auctoritas* but of *potentia*, a power *de facto* instead of *de jure*; actual might rather than lawful authority.

It is clear that in any state a *potestas* may exist of either or of both of these kinds, and that if there are several of each kind one of these will be "the highest". It is possible also, at least temporarily, that the highest *de facto* power may be different from the one whose claims are the highest *de jure*. But in Bodin's view it is also a characteristic of sovereignty that it is not only supreme, but single and undivided: there can be but

---

[1] *Jo. Bodini Andegavensis, De Republica Libri Sex*, Bk. 1, ch. 8, p. 78 (Lyon and Paris, 1686). The Latin version of his great work, written ten years after the first edition in French, may be regarded as containing Bodin's matured views on this question.

[2] As in the *Lex de Imperio Vespasiani*, discovered in the fourteenth century in Rome. Text in Girard's *Textes de Droit Romain*, 5th ed. pp. 107–8.

[3] Inst. 1, 2, 6.

one sovereign. If so, is this the *potestas* highest in actual might
—*potentissima*; or is it the one with the highest authority?

There can be no question in my mind that it is the latter, and
the latter alone. The correlative of sovereignty is obedience.
The sovereign, as Austin says, is the person who is obeyed.
But we may obey one armed with a pistol as well as one armed
with a warrant. "It is not wisdom, but authority that makes
a law", Hobbes declared.[1] But the essential weakness of his
whole theory was that this "authority" must be more than
a mere *potentia*: it has to be obeyed, and obeyed not from mere
compulsion, but on the whole willingly; and Hobbes could
find no better way to give a *de jure* character to his *potestas* than
the unhistorical compact. We are not so much interested in
the failure of this solution as in its recognition of the existence
of a problem to be solved. Supreme might will secure
obedience. No one doubts that, nor needs be told how or
why. But surely he is under no necessity of identifying this
might with sovereignty. It is significant that the motto even
of those coming nearest to doing so is that might *makes* right,
not that might *is* right. Obedience rendered to a power
without right will be rendered only so long as it is compelled.
Such a power to be really sovereign must have some right to
receive obedience, and in the long run this right will be one
conceded by those who obey. In a body of pirates this
obedience may be rendered to a chief because he is the
strongest or the most cunning, but in any society worthy the
name of a state, higher and more permanent considerations
than these must be present to warrant the acceptance of the
domination of some over others. Might will be taken as right
only in the lowest forms of political life. Some such idea as
this was in the mind of St Augustine when he put his famous
question: "Without justice, what are kingdoms but robber
bands enlarged?" For him kingdoms (*regna*) might exist
without justice, but never a true commonwealth. For, as he

[1] *A Dialogue...of the Common Laws of England*, English Works, edited
by Molesworth, VI, p. 5.

said, *res publica* is *res populi*, and the higher political life of man requires not merely *any* association, but an association of a people in consent to law, as Cicero said.[1]

In every such association by consent to law the highest constituted authority must exist by law, even though it be, as Bodin said, *legibus soluta*. Sovereignty is the highest authority, not the greatest might. The only modern political philosopher who has been able consistently to identify might and right is

[1] This interpretation of the *Civitas Dei* is not accepted by most of the modern authorities. Dr Carlyle, Sir Frederick Pollock, and the late Dr Figgis, for example, all hold the view that St Augustine was too much of a realist not to see that a state even without justice was a state none the less. An examination of the words of St Augustine in their full context has convinced me that this view is untenable. It is true that for him mere *regna* might be little more than enlarged *latrocinia*; associations held together by *any* bond, however base, if it were only an aim which they cherished in common. But to me he seems to imply much more. Justice and justice alone is the only possible bond which can unite men as a true *populus* in a real *respublica*. The great empires before Christianity were therefore for St Augustine *regna* of the former sort; but they were not true commonwealths, because there was no recognition of what was due to the one true God, and without such recognition there could be no real justice, for justice is to render to each his due. They were, however, *regna* and entitled to admiration and respect, because in the time before the introduction of the new law by Christ, as St Paul might have said, "When the Gentiles, which have not the law, do by nature the things contained in the law, these, having not the law, are a law unto themselves" (Rom. ii. 14); "and the times of this ignorance God winked at" (Acts xvii. 30). But since the coming of Christ and the new law—i.e. in St Augustine's own day—there could be no true justice without the rendering to every one his due; and, he asks, "quae igitur justitia est hominis quae ipsum hominem Deo vero tollit, et immundis daemonibus subdit?" If so, the great pagan empires might have been *regna*, they might have been bound together by some *pactum societatis*, and they would be *regna* if bound together *aliquo societatis vinculo*; but they never could be true *populi*, and their associations and their governments could never rise to the true height of a *res populi* or *respublica*; for a *populus*, in Cicero's phrase, meant "non *omnem* coetum multitudinis sed coetum *juris consensu* et utilitatis communione sociatum"; one united *consensu juris*, and under a *jus* that must include the law of God as well as the law of men, whose justice therefore could not be complete if it ignored the just claims of the one true God.

Spinoza, and he is able to do so only because he recognizes the existence of no rights whatever other than those based on *potentia*. For all others the *potestas* must have a basis in right of some kind outside itself. This means that those subject to it are so because they recognize in it a right to require their obedience. No such right can be permanently maintained without consent, though the reasons for that consent may be various. Hume recognized this. "A man's natural force consists only in the vigour of his limbs, and the firmness of his courage; which could never subject multitudes to the command of one. Nothing but their own consent, and the sense of the advantages resulting from peace and order, could have had that influence."[1] Why do multitudes subject themselves to the command of one? If it is not on account of his might, it must be on account of some right believed by the multitude to be in him. His dominance must be, as Rousseau said, something "légitime et sûre", not resting on mere force, but in itself "un droit sacré".[2]

We are not concerned with the kind of title deeds the multitude demanded in evidence of this right to govern, whether by a supposed law of God or of nature, by compact, or by ancient custom. These may be considered as the source of the principles, but the important thing is that an *auctoritas* based on any one of them is such by virtue of the positive law of the state; just as Gaius tells us that all states employ laws partly common to all mankind and partly peculiar to themselves,[3] but none the less, it is their being part of the *jus civile* that gives any of them binding effect in a state.

The upshot of this is that "sovereign power" as distinct from any other power is the highest *legal* power in a state, itself subject to no law. And this being so, the term "sovereign" has no proper application beyond the domain of law.

---

[1] *Of the Original Contract.*
[2] *Du Contrat Social*, Bk. 1, Introduction and ch. 1.
[3] Inst. 1, 1, 1. The text of Gaius is defective here, but is supplied from the Institutes of Justinian 1, 2, 1 and from the Digest, 1, 1, 9.

It is a purely juristic term and it should convey a purely juristic idea. It has no proper meaning if carried beyond the sphere of law and into the sphere of mere fact. Sovereignty is authority, not might. The sovereign power is the highest legal authority *qua* legal not *qua* actual. In a state of mature development actual power and legal authority might be identical or nearly so, but they seldom are and for various reasons. But in any case the important thing to note is that the only really "sovereign" power is that made so by law. Lord Bryce attempted to reconcile this with the facts by splitting sovereignty up into two varieties, one legal, the other political. The "legal" is to him "the person (or body) to whose directions the law attributes legal force, the person in whom resides as of right the ultimate power either of laying down general rules or of issuing isolated rules or commands, whose authority is that of the law itself"; the "practical", "the person (or body of persons) who can make his (or their) will prevail whether with the law or against the law. He (or they) is the *de facto* ruler, the person to whom obedience is actually paid."[1] Now this, if it means anything, means merely that the only sovereign truly so called is what is here styled the "legal" sovereign. The so-called political sovereign, if we examine him closely, is no sovereign at all. He has no authority. He has no lawful title. It means equally that the real, the only sovereign—the one Lord Bryce calls "legal"—will at many times and in many places have only the form of power, not the substance. Sovereignty it will be found can be squared with fact only by a liberal use of legal fictions. In some cases it will itself tend to become little more than a legal fiction. But fictions are not uncommon in other branches of law than this; and, Bentham notwithstanding, many of them may be defended as useful and beneficent. It is to be noted that Bodin's definition says that sovereignty is a power *legibus soluta*: it is not free of influence or compulsion of a non-legal character and it need not be. Parliament may be the sovereign

[1] *Studies in History and Jurisprudence*, II, pp. 505, 512.

and yet be controlled by the electorate or by "public opinion", or by a dozen other non-legal forces, determinate or indeterminate, good or bad, that may be called superior to it without being legally above it. These forces are not sovereign nor are the persons exercising them the real sovereign, in any sense that has any definite meaning. They belong to the realm of the practical. Practically, the supreme power of Parliament may be a fiction, a thing non-existent because controlled by other and stronger forces outside itself, but its commands are recognized as legal commands none the less. The fact is that this untenable distinction between "legal" and "political" sovereignty is simply the nineteenth-century form of an ancient confusion of thought.

The Germans have made a useful distinction between what they choose to call the sovereign and the sovereign organ, *Träger der Staatsgewalt*, or *Staatsorgan*; but political thinking would be made clearer if it were understood that in any society which has advanced to the political stage, the highest organ is the true sovereign and the only one, because it is the highest body legally able to make rules for the subjects, and itself free of the law.[1] It may be, nay it must be, controlled by the people who set it up, but their control over it is not through laws; for they can make none except through it, without altering the whole constitution of the state. They control it politically not legally. Now this is a legalistic conception,[2] and if this highest organ is to be called sovereign,

---

[1] It is certainly in this sense, as compared with Rousseau's idea, that Bodin uses the term *la souveraineté* or *majestas*. "Bodin kennt keine Staats-, sondern nur eine Staatsorganssouveränität" (Rehm, *Geschichte der Staatsrechtswissenschaft*, p. 224).

[2] "Um diesen wichtigen Punkt zu erledigen, muss man vor allem sich vor Augen halten, dass die Souveränetät ein *Rechtsbegriff* ist und auch in der naturrechtlichen Literatur stets als solcher gedacht wurde. Die Unabhängigkeit der Staatsgewalt von jeder anderen Autorität wurde immer als *rechtliche*, nicht als faktische Unabhängigkeit aufgefasst" (Jellinek, *Allgemeine Staatslehre*, 2nd ed. p. 462). "Souveräne Gewalt ist demnach nicht staatliche Allmacht. Sie ist rechtliche Macht und daher durch das Recht gebunden" (*ibid.* p. 468).

it must be in the legal sense only. From the practical point of view it is a sovereign only by a fiction; and the greater the actual power of the people in a state, the more obvious the fiction is likely to be. But fictions such as this have played a great and valuable part in the steady and orderly development of private law, and this one has played an equally valuable part in public law. For by it alone, to take one striking instance, the ancient English monarchy has been enabled to continue within a state that was gradually developing first into an oligarchy and later into a democracy. It is largely to the credit of one of the most transparent fictions in political history that these great changes have been brought about largely without violence or bloodshed. The King remains "the sovereign", but his sovereignty became a fiction long ago. Why not admit that the Parliament, too, "reigns but does not rule"? It is the fact that in the self-governing colonies the actual power of Parliament is about what the King's is in England. Colonial self-government has made it a fiction just as cabinet government made the sovereignty of the King. It was a refusal to recognize this that lost the thirteen colonies, and only a tacit acceptance of it that saved Canada for the Empire a half century later. It might be better both theoretically and practically frankly to admit the existence and character of these fictions. In reality they constitute England's greatest contribution to politics in modern times, the limited monarchy. Thus they have secured change without violence. The fictional character of the King's sovereignty has long been understood. We need an equally clear appreciation that the sovereignty of Parliament is to all intents and purposes the same in kind at least, if not in degree. And this in no way detracts from the excellence of the British constitution. Rather it is a fuller recognition of it. For it is precisely in states of the highest and most uninterrupted constitutional development that these factors will be found in their most striking and extreme form. It is only in absolute monarchies or oligarchies or in democracies small enough to be pure democracies, that the actual fact and the legal theory will be likely ever entirely to coincide. Rousseau would not have admitted this, but it was because he ignored the most important phenomenon of modern politics, representation. Wherever representative institutions exist, unless the so-called representatives are in law and in fact mere *mandatarii* instead of true representatives, this adjustment of fact and theory must be made. Rousseau settled it by denying the possibility of representation, and Lord Bryce has simply brought up afresh the old seventeenth-century difficulty caused by the fact that the actual power and the constituted authority are not always the same. The old method of evading this difficulty was by an imaginary compact which merged all wills in that of the constituted authority; the newer one is hardly preferable.

The results of this confusion of the sovereignty of the government and the *Allmacht* in the state have been by no means all of a theoretical kind. They are found in the sinister inference of Austinianism that "what the sovereign permits he enjoins", and they have in fact led to an exaggerated *étatisme* which would deny legitimacy to all associations within the state which do not originate in or receive the imprimatur of "the sovereign". From such a denial of the legitimacy of these associations to the actual crushing of them is usually not a long step. The mistake is made of assuming as *de jure* everything which is habitually done and everything that may actually be done by "the determinate person or body of persons" in the state whom Austinians call the "sovereign"; of demanding as a legal claim of the supreme power every act of obedience which is or may be in fact given to any power. If such reasoning as this be regarded as merely academic and harmless, attention might be called to the recent destruction in Italy of all associations or unions not connected with Fascism, and the reasons for such measures given by Mussolini in his public speeches. Such a theory, as Jellinek says, would reduce us all to the condition of mere "slaves of the state", and when it is put in practice the actual result is little better than slavery.

It is no wonder that such a theory should provoke a reaction, and the reaction has come in the form of a theory which makes sweeping denial of the very existence or the possibility of Bodin's *summa potestas* in any form, because the holders of this theory are afraid of the actual forces that lie behind such *potestas* and for the time being act through it. The sovereign in Bodin's sense has been used by forces in the state in ways which have worked an injury to classes or interests within it. As Rousseau would have put it, the particular will of certain powerful classes or individuals has triumphed over the *volonté générale* in securing laws or measures not for the general good, but for the good of some to the detriment of others. Hence the organs of the state through which these harmful forces have worked their will must under this theory be denied all coercive power whatever. No organs of the state really have coercive power; obedience to them is not properly enforceable by any authority, but is won only by the character of their acts, nothing more, and in competition with any other organ or association or body whether authorized by the state or not. There can be no supremacy of one such organ or association over the others, whether the latter be public or private, not even a superiority, except in the uncontrolled preferences and choice of the individual citizens themselves. If a clash occurs among the admonitions of these various organs, the citizen simply obeys whichever he pleases.

Thus, in their reasonable opposition to an exaggerated and dangerous theory, my friends the Pluralists, I cannot but feel, have at the outset made too many concessions to their opponents. The merits of this school of writers are very great, especially on the negative side, in their exposure of the historical weakness of Austinianism and of its dangerous practical tendency. But, as it seems to me, they have gone too far in admitting the claim of the Austinian sovereign to *Allmacht*, and in consequence have been compelled, in order to refute it, to deny *in toto* the possibility of any sovereignty whatever. In so doing they stand in some danger of failing, as their chief opponents have failed, to make the necessary distinction between law and fact, between what the sovereign organ may do *de jure* and the extra-legal force in the state which may or may not at any time be securing the enforcement of its will through the constituted framework of government. But neither law and force nor law and choice are quite the same thing; nor should the English Parliament and the Amalgamated Society of Railway Servants after all be put on exactly the same footing or receive precisely the same measure of obedience. "The power of the ultimate imponent of law", says T. H. Green, "cannot be derived or limited by law",[1] and it is undoubtedly true; but *authority* may come from the law, and must do so if there is to be any sanction beyond mere force. "The ultimate imponent of law", the forces that lie behind government, the powers that set it going, are not *de jure* but *de facto*. A people may set up a good government or a bad one, and in the long run it will be good or bad in about the same proportion as they themselves are good or bad, as Aristotle fully recognized;[2] for it ultimately rests upon their consent. But any political association of men which we may truly call a *respublica* and not a mere *latrocinium* will be an association *legis consensu sociatum*, as Cicero said. For the truth is, as Green says, "that an interest in *common* good is the ground of political society in the sense that without it no body of people would recognize any authority as having a claim on their common obedience. It is so far as a government represents to them a common good that the subjects are conscious that they ought to obey it, i.e. that obedience to it is a means to an end desirable in itself or absolutely."[3] And this good to be really "common" can be restricted to no single individual,

---

[1] *Lectures on Political Obligation*, p. 106.

[2] αἱ μὲν γὰρ κοιναὶ ἐπιμέλειαι δῆλον ὅτι διὰ νόμων γίνονται, ἐπιεικεῖς δ' αἱ διὰ τῶν σπουδαίων (*Eth. Nic.* K, ix, 14).

[3] *Lectures on Political Obligation*, p. 109. This is well put by Jellinek: "Das Recht bezeichnet immer nur die aktuelle Zuständigkeit des Staates. Was der Staat auf dem Wege möglicher Zuständigkeitserweiterung gewinnen kann, liegt nicht in seiner Rechtssphäre. Anderenfalls käme

class, group, or association within the state: it must be the good of the whole.[1] In a good state, the rights and claims of all groups or associations whose aims are not harmful to the whole will be respected and safeguarded; but an interest in the common good as a good superior to any particular one will require an obedience to the instrument of that common good higher than that rendered to any association whose aims are more restricted or whose benefits are less widely distributed. The Pluralists in their zeal for the rights of groups within the state and for the liberty of the subject in yielding uncontrolled obedience to these have insensibly fallen into a train

man zur völligen Vernichtung aller dem Staate eingegliederten Persönlichkeiten, denn alle Staatsmacht kann nur auf Kosten der individuellen Freiheit bestehen. Würde Souveränetät bedeuten, dass alle Möglichkeiten der Kompetenzerweiterung zur aktuellen Sphäre des Staates gehören, so wären wir alle Staatssklaven, die ein Stück Rechtsfähigkeit als Prekarium von seiten des Staates geniessen. Das war in der Tat die Ansicht der Absolutisten, die daher auch vom Eigentum behaupteten, dass es dem einzelnen nur so weit und insolange zukomme, als es der Staat ihm zuteile, welche Lehre von Rousseau vom absoluten Fürsten auf den unbeschränkbaren Volkswillen übertragen wird. Allein die blosse abstrakte Möglichkeit, ein Hoheitsrecht zu besitzen, hat nicht die geringste Wirkung auf die dem Staate eingeordneten Persönlichkeiten, seien dies nun Individuen oder Verbände. Sie haben ihre eigenen Rechte, die sie nicht auf Kündigung, nicht als Gnade des souveränen Staates, nicht als dessen Delegierte besitzen, sondern sie haben ihre Rechte kraft ihrer Anerkennung als Rechtsträger, als Personen, welche Qualität ihnen zu entziehen gänzlich ausserhalb des realen Machtbereiches des Staates liegt" (*Allgemeine Staatslehre*, 2nd ed. pp. 468–9).

[1] ἐροῦμεν γάρ, ὅτι θαυμαστὸν μὲν ἂν οὐδὲν εἴη, εἰ καὶ οὗτοι [the guardians] οὕτως εὐδαιμονέστατοί εἰσιν, οὐ μὴν πρὸς τοῦτο βλέποντες τὴν πόλιν οἰκίζομεν, ὅπως ἕν τι ἡμῖν ἔθνος ἔσται διαφερόντως εὔδαιμον, ἀλλ' ὅπως ὅ τι μάλιστα ὅλη ἡ πόλις. ᾠήθημεν γὰρ ἐν τῇ τοιαύτῃ μάλιστα ἂν εὑρεῖν δικαιοσύνην καὶ αὖ ἐν τῇ κάκιστα οἰκουμένῃ ἀδικίαν, κατιδόντες δὲ κρῖναι ἄν, ὃ πάλαι ζητοῦμεν. νῦν μὲν οὖν, ὡς οἰόμεθα, τὴν εὐδαίμονα πλάττομεν οὐκ ἀπολαβόντες ὀλίγους ἐν αὐτῇ τοιούτους τινὰς τιθέντες, ἀλλ' ὅλην· αὐτίκα δὲ τὴν ἐναντίαν σκεψόμεθα.

(Plato, *Republic*, IV, 420, B–C.)

τὸ γὰρ ὀρθὸν ληπτέον ἴσως· τὸ δ' ἴσως ὀρθὸν πρὸς τὸ τῆς πόλεως ὅλης συμφέρον καὶ πρὸς τὸ κοινὸν τὸ τῶν πολιτῶν.

(Aristotle, *Politics*, III, 13, 12.)

of thought in which the people's extra-legal "right of revolution", under which they might put an end altogether to the constitution and the existing sovereign-organ, is confused with a supposed right in the individual subject at any time to defy the commands of the highest constituted authority in the State while still professing to believe that this authority continues to exist. They attempt, in other words, to legalize disobedience instead of admitting the possibility of illegal, but sometimes justifiable revolution. Locke's political right of revolution is a corollary that must and did follow Bodin's conception of sovereignty to make liberty secure, but a legalized disobedience is *in terminis* a complete contradiction.

Speaking generally, the power of the people can have no limits. It is idle to speak of it as either *de facto* or *de jure* if this implies a difference, and if we could have nothing but small and pure democracies without representation, Rousseau's views might be considered valid enough, except that his *volonté générale* would in practice turn out to be the will of all, or of the majority which the modern fiction assumes to be all. The sovereign people would make all law and would simply delegate a power to magistrates to execute it. But in all great modern states the making of law, the chief ingredient in sovereignty as Bodin said—"primum ac praecipuum caput majestatis"[1]—as well as its execution, must be in the hands of an organ of the state, in a representative assembly, not in the people directly. Such great states as we now know would be impossible without it. But there is more truth in Rousseau's contention than is sometimes admitted. Law-making cannot be merely delegated as the execution of law may. Hence for Rousseau a country that has a representative assembly has a master and is not free, or is free only in the short and infrequent intervals when it chooses its master by election. He could think of this law-making only as "sovereign", and in the legal sense he was right. But unfortunately he confused this legal sovereignty with arbitrary and uncontrolled power, and this

[1] *De Republica*, bk. 1, ch. 10, p. 153.

led him to refuse to concede sovereignty to a representative assembly, or to any organ or body except the whole body of the citizens who constituted the state. In fact the power of such an assembly is, as Rousseau thought, legally absolute, and he was right also in thinking that it ought not to be arbitrary or irresponsible. In reality it is somewhat more difficult for it to be so from the fact that though legally free of the law, it is politically controlled by the people themselves, and it is the very possibility of this control that reconciles them to its legal supremacy. It is because it is believed to serve as "an instrument of the common good" that the people suffer it to continue as an organ uncontrolled by law. Such an organ is therefore legally sovereign, but by no means practically or politically irresponsible. "Sovereignty" properly applies only to the former of these conceptions, to legal supremacy, not to practical irresponsibility. The organ is in law sovereign, the people is in fact irresponsible. No one will question the legal authority of such a supreme legislative assembly. Its word is law. So long as it remains the sovereign organ all must obey it. But if its acts should permanently cease to be for the public good as the people see it, nothing could prevent their abolishing an organ they have ceased to trust. Their power is absolute and irresponsible, and neither based on law nor subject to any. It is simply *potentia* and neither *potestas* in the legal sense, nor *auctoritas*. Their acts would, in this case, of course, be revolutionary, but they could be neither right nor wrong in any strictly legal sense. If such a state were really a free one it would be unlikely either to destroy a good governmental organ or to set up a bad one; but only its own inherent goodness could keep it from doing either. It is idle to speak of law in connection with its actions.

With the "sovereign organ" it is far otherwise. Its authority comes from the permission of the people, and if they are an advanced people that permission will be in the definite form of law; but if its authority is the highest, it will be uncontrollable *by law*, it will be *potestas legibus soluta*. It may be destroyed or limited, but by power only, not by law. Mental confusion comes when we think of the former of these powers as restrained by law, and something worse when the sovereignty of the latter is conceived as something not originating in law. Thus Filmer was from his own point of view right enough in speaking of "the anarchy of a limited or mixed monarchy",[1] and Blackwood was also in a measure warranted in arguing that the ruler was limited by no external law in the celebrated *Digna Vox*, but only by an internal and self-imposed check.[2] We may question the propriety of his applying it to a king instead of to a people, but from his own point of view his logic is unassailable.

It would require a detailed examination of the whole development of political thought in the millennium and more between Aristotle and Bodin to show how the latter's *majestas*, which is his *summa potestas*, differs from τὸ κύριον, which is Aristotle's. Bodin's sovereign power is a thing of the law, a purely juristic notion, showing the marks of Roman law and medieval development. It had thus come to differ widely from the mere ethico-political supremacy exercised by a πολίτευμα or ruling class considered in social or economic terms rather than as a legally determined person or body of persons as conceived by John Austin, a supremacy which for Aristotle so completely determined the whole complexion and character, the "constitution", of the state, in its life, activity, ideals, and form, that he could say πολίτευμα δέ ἐστιν ἡ πολιτεία.[3] He thus identified the state with what some to-day might be inclined to call its sovereign, but as his state knew no representation, he has no sovereign organ and would place the supremacy in the class as a whole which makes the state what it is, in this respect approaching the view of Rousseau, except that the latter includes in his sovereign all

[1] *Observations upon Mr Hunton's Treatise of Monarchy: or, The Anarchy of a Limited or Mixed Monarchy* (London, 1680).
[2] *Pro Regibus Apologia* (1580), ch. xxxv, *Opera Omnia*, pp. 187 ff.
[3] *Pol.* iii, 6.

instead of a single class within the state. Bodin's sovereignty, on the other hand, is the sovereignty of a legally constituted organ, an organ created theoretically even if not historically by the whole state; but not identical with the whole state as Rousseau would have it, nor necessarily identical with a ruling social or political class within the state, as with Aristotle. It is Bodin's view rather than that either of Aristotle or Rousseau which mainly determines the character of present-day thinking on the greatest of all political questions, the nature and causes of the acceptance of ideas which "subject multitudes to the rule of one". And the very limitations which Bodin imposed upon his sovereign, limitations both in the laws of God and of nature, and in the fundamental constitution of the kingdom or state, prove the juristic nature of his conception of sovereign power. These limitations themselves have been considered by many modern historians of political thought as an indication that Bodin had not grasped the true idea as fully as Hobbes did later. I submit, however, that the great succession of French politico-juristic writers of the sixteenth and seventeenth centuries such as Blackwood,[1] du Tillet, Loyseau, Coquille, Loysel, L'Hôpital, and Lebret, and the defenders of the Gallican Liberties in general, writing as they did under the influence of the idea of the fundamental laws of *la monarchie tempérée*, in the very limitations which this idea of necessity imposed upon the power of the monarch, came nearer to the true idea of sovereignty as a juristic conception than did the English layman Hobbes, who was influenced more by the actual or impending struggle for practical supremacy between King and Parliament in England than by the theories of the

[1] Adam Blackwood, though a Scot by birth, like William Barclay and others of his compatriots who studied and taught law in France in the sixteenth century, formed his legal and political theories under the influence of French ideas of government and law. Among modern historians of the development of the conception of sovereignty, his writings have scarcely received the attention to which their power and vigour entitle them.

law which he condemned so roundly in his *Dialogue of the Common Laws of England.*

Loyseau, in particular, in the second chapter of his great treatise on Seigneuries makes clear these limitations when he says,

...As there can be no crown if its circle is not complete, so there is no sovereignty if it lacks anything. Still, as it is God alone who is all-powerful and the power of men cannot be entirely absolute, there are three sorts of laws, which limit the power of the sovereign without being concerned with the sovereignty;[1] namely, the laws of God, for that the Prince is not less sovereign for being subject to God; the rules of justice natural and not positive, because, as has been said before, it is essential to the *seigneurie publique* that it be administered by justice and not at discretion; and finally the fundamental laws of the state, in that the Prince is bound to exercise his sovereignty according to its inherent nature and in the form and with the conditions under which it is established.[2]

It is such a view in general, modified in the course of time by a changed conception of the laws of God and of nature, but still recognizing the "inherent nature" or constitution of the state, with the forms and conditions that this imposes upon the sovereign organ, that must be regarded as the richest and profoundest generalization of modern political thought. And it is important to distinguish the valuable services rendered by this rationalization of political phenomena contained in the modern legalistic conception of sovereignty and the not infrequent practical benefits that have followed its recognition, without at the same time forgetting that it is a rationalization merely, like the axioms of Euclid, only in legal not mathematical terms, and without attempting to include within it the whole range of the possible activity of men or of bodies of

---

[1] Note particularly that clause: "Qui bornent la puissance du Souverain, sans interresser la Souveraineté."
[2] *Traité des Seigneuries*, ch. ii, p. 8; *Les Œuvres de Maistre Charles Loyseau* (Paris, 1678).

men. If it is remembered that it is often no more than a fiction, we may safely recognize its value and its benefits, without either making it a cloak for oppression or rejecting it utterly as an outworn, useless, false, and dangerous abstraction.

It is still true, as it was in Aristotle's day, and in Loyseau's, that the sovereign power must be administered with justice and not at discretion. In both England and France it was recognized as early as the thirteenth century that a law, to be a true one, must be for "the common profit of the realm". The king was an "absolute" law-giver, but, in Locke's phrase, "not arbitrary by being absolute". He could in England enact statutes, but it is doubtful if he could abrogate a law. *Statutum* was, in reality, not in antithesis to law: it was merely an establishment of it, *stabilimentum*, *établissement*. The king was the highest power in enacting such *statuta* or *établissements*, whether he acted in concert with his council or not. But as du Tillet declared in France as late as the sixteenth century, "Les roys abolissent les coustumes s'ils veulent quant à leurs contracts, non quant à ceux de leur subiets pour tollir leur droit. Car les coustumes sont accordees par lesdits subiets, non ordonnees par lesdits Roys."[1] More interesting still is the dispensing power in its earlier development, and the fact that when it was defined in later times in England, its operation was confined to enactments of *novel ley* merely and never extended to the ancient law itself nor to statutes in affirmance of law.[2]

It is clear enough that the royal power, in France for example, was "sovereign", and it was frequently termed "absolute"; but it was at the same time a legal power, and one established by law and as a consequence limited by the nature of law itself. It was free in the sense in which Spinoza defines all freedom—by the absence of *external* compulsion, in this case compulsion of a legal sort. This, however, is by

[1] *Recueil des Roys de France* (Paris, 1580), pp. 173–4.
[2] For a good analysis of the cases, see Herbert Broom, *Constitutional Law*, 2nd ed. (London, 1885), pp. 492 *et seq.*

no means to say that the sovereign's power is not limited *internally*. It is founded on law and its nature is the nature of law itself. But *jus a justitia*, as the Middle Ages recognized far better than our own day, and *rex a regendo*; to tyrannize is not to rule. Kings may revoke their ordinances, says du Tillet (he is careful to say *ordonnances*, and neither *lois* nor *coûtumes*), but they are responsible to God, whose ministers they are; whatever the plenitude of their power, they are bound to exercise it with equity and justice; and then follows a striking phrase—"si leur puissance absoluë n'y est reiglee, elle deuient dissoluë".[1] For him it is clear that "absolute" and "regulated" are terms not mutually exclusive. What, after all, is this, but the view put forward by Samuel Adams in the celebrated Massachusetts Circular Letter of 1768, when he says that in all free states the constitution is fixed and even the supreme legislature, deriving its power as it does only from the constitution, "cannot overleap the bounds of it without destroying its own foundation",[2] and by Camden two years earlier in "the fundamental laws" of the British constitution, which for him guaranteed the exemption of colonists from all taxation to which they had not consented?[3] And is it not true that the *summa potestas* is limited by its nature, the nature of law—so limited in fact, that even the staunchest upholders of divine right admitted it in the seventeenth century, and in the thirteenth St Thomas Aquinas applied the limitation to God himself? It was reserved for John Austin and his followers of the nineteenth and twentieth centuries to grant to a definite person or body of persons what St Thomas denied even to God.

Of course, these limitations on which I have insisted were for long more effective in theory than in fact. Responsibility of monarchs to God for justice to their subjects was often coupled with doctrines of the completest obedience of those

---

[1] *Recueil des Roys*, p. 173.
[2] MacDonald, *Documentary Source Book of American History*, p. 148.
[3] *Parliamentary History*, vol. XVI, col. 178.

subjects to their lawful king, passive at least in character, and this was entirely logical. Bodin was logical enough too, in insisting that his sovereign, though a legal one, was free of the law. "The King can do no wrong" is an entirely consistent formula if it is not linked with personal or hereditary right, and so it has survived hereditary right in the constitution of the English monarchy. What is wrong therefore is not regal. But the real question here is whether the King's act *ipso facto* makes any action legally right, or whether such an act must be legally right before it can be considered to be truly an act of the King. The latter view has prevailed in England and the monarchy has persisted. The former view tended to prevail in France as hereditary right gradually obliterated the nation's right of election, and Bodin and Loyseau, while asserting the existence of *la loy fondamentale de l'estat*, would also have agreed that the realm of France was "une monarchie royale et non seigneuriale, une souveraineté parfaite, *à laquelle les Estats n'ont aucune part*".[1]

This will be considered a contradiction only if we continue to confound law and fact. A true theory of sovereignty must fit all times, and all forms of the state. But at the same time that du Tillet was applying truly enough his conception of a legitimate sovereignty to monarchs who were in fact becoming irresponsible rulers, others were beginning to look beyond the mere sovereignty of law with its lack of adequate human sanction, and so we have the remarkable succession of sixteenth- and seventeenth-century writers to whom Barclay's inaccurate term "monarchomachs" has stuck ever since 1600, when he first applied it. They see that a king is *legibus solutus* if by *lex* is meant nothing but positive law, but at the same time they have come to believe that the French King is a tyrant. Hence they rely on the laws of God and of nature as sources of a right of resistance even to powers legitimate by the *jus civile*. But this resistance is, of course, illegal and revolutionary, and Locke finally both admits and justifies the fact.

[1] Loyseau, *Traité des Seigneuries*, ch. ii, p. 12.

We have passed from law to fact, or to utility. But we have kept much of the old phraseology, and are unfortunately sometimes in danger of talking about one thing when we really mean another. My contention is that the legal conception of sovereignty is still useful and must be kept. *La loy fondamentale* will be found at the back of every sovereign organ, whether the state's constitution be the work of ages of slow development which Burke so revered in England, or a body of rules set forth within the four corners of some official document at some time "struck off" by the mind of particular men, as Gladstone is supposed to have thought of the Constitution of the United States.

But if the old idea of a law fundamental is to be kept, and kept in its proper place, it is well to remember that we can no more divorce politics from ethics than Aristotle could. The *damnosa hereditas* of the long reign of natural rights—useful as they were in their day in the fight against absolutism—is the habit of regarding rights instead of duties as the starting-point of political thought. Behind the sovereign and his protection of legal rights must always stand the might of the people, which can be bound by no law and must be, as Aristotle said, based upon the justice inherent in the people themselves, and upon their recognition and performance of their duties.

Morality and political subjection thus have a common source, "*political* subjection" being distinguished from that of a slave, as a subjection which secures rights to the subject. That common source is the rational recognition by certain human beings...of a common well-being which is their well-being and which they conceive as their well-being whether at any moment any one of them is inclined to it or no, and the embodiment of that recognition in rules by which the inclinations of the individuals are restrained, and a corresponding freedom of action for the attainment of well-being on the whole is secured.[1]

Such freedom can be permanently secured in no other way than the old one laid down once and for all by Plato and

[1] T. H. Green, *Lectures on Political Obligation*, p. 125.

Aristotle, in the education of the citizens of a state in the ideals and methods and duties of ruling and being ruled in turn like freemen for the sake of the good life of the whole. It is still an essential of government, as Loyseau said, that it must be administered by justice and not at discretion. There is no royal road to the attainment of that justice. Its price is struggle and effort never remitted.

III

A FRAGMENT ON SOVEREIGNTY

It requires considerable courage, or presumption, as some might prefer to style it, to ask a reader's attention once more to so well-worn a topic as sovereignty. Few political conceptions have been the subject of so much discussion amongst us in the last hundred years. But this very fact is proof of its vital importance in our modern world; and the wide variety of the views held concerning its essence, as well as the conflicting conclusions to which these views still lead, may furnish sufficient excuse for another attempt to clarify some of our ideas touching this central formula under which we try to rationalize the complicated facts of our modern political life.

If sovereignty were an idea purely abstract we should be closer than we are to unanimity as to its character; but it is traditional as well as abstract, and no attempt to analyse it can have hope of success which ignores the stages and factors in its growth.

Sovereignty is no essential part of the abstract conception of a state, but to every modern man but the anarchist some kind of supremacy is essential, if his concept is to be consistent with itself; though the idea of this supremacy may at some periods of its growth have been so blurred and indistinct as to be almost undiscoverable, as during the long sway of the feudal theory of *dominion* in the Middle Ages.

Sovereignty, in fact, is a supremacy conceived in a particular way and in particular terms; but supremacy itself is a broader concept, and it may be conceived and in certain periods has been conceived in ways and in terms which are quite different. The Greeks, for example, had a very definite idea of supremacy, but for reasons which will presently appear, it would seem better to distinguish it clearly from modern sovereignty.

Supremacy is central in the political thought of Aristotle, but it is a supremacy held in a state by a ruling class, not in terms of that state's constitution as in the case of a modern sovereign: Aristotle's ruling class exercises this supremacy simply by virtue of the fact that it is able actually to maintain it and only so long as it has the power to do so. Supremacy is a control enjoyed in fact, not a lawful authority defined, as the "sovereign's" is, by a constitution. The constitution is dictated to the state by the class in power, it is not imposed by the state upon the rulers; while a modern "sovereign", on the other hand, is constituted and defined by the constitution itself. For the Greeks, the ruling class makes the constitution; for the moderns, the constitution makes the "sovereign". The Greeks were thinking of law in terms of the state; we habitually think of the state in terms of law. No word was oftener on Aristotle's lips than the word "constitution", but he meant by it the whole complex of aims, ethical, social and economic, as well as legal, toward which the common life of the citizens was guided under the dictation and direction of the rulers or class in power; we think of a constitution merely as the sum of the provisions under which the ruler is set up and his lawful authority defined, limited and regulated. For Aristotle the constitution of a state is the ideal of social and political life which its ruling class prefers and actually imposes upon the whole body of citizens because it is physically able to enforce its will over them. The ruling class, he says, determines the constitution, and the constitution *is* the state. But compare for a moment such an assertion with any modern definition of a constitution and the vast difference between them will be apparent at once. Professor Dicey, for example, in his *Law of the Constitution*, distinguishes a constitutional law from another by restricting it to those rules which are concerned with the definition or the distribution of the sovereign power in a state.

How and when did this fundamental difference arise between antique and modern thought, and what are the new elements in our modern conception of the political relation which result from this difference?

It was in the Hellenistic period apparently that "supremacy" began to take on the distinctive characteristics which mark our modern concept of sovereignty. The Stoics saw in the world of human relations a law coeval and coextensive with man himself; a law, therefore, which no state can make, nor any ruling class within a state: that law was in existence before there were any states; and no state, in the only proper sense of the term, can ever even come into being if it does not incorporate this eternal law in its framework. The state has become a *vinculum juris*; consent to a pre-existent law (*juris consensus*) is the origin and the badge of a true commonwealth; the state does not make law, law makes the state. "Modern" political thought has in fact begun, in the habit of thinking of the state in terms of law, not of law in terms of the state; and the legalistic approach, which has been the chief theoretical characteristic of politics from Roman times to our own, is already clearly apparent.

That these newer habits of thought persisted throughout the whole period of the Roman Republic and Empire is a fact which needs no proof, and in Rome we have the first actual "sovereign". We should probably have had at the same time a definite theory of sovereignty to account for this fact if the jurists of the Empire had possessed a capacity for political speculation commensurate even in slight degree with their genius in formulating the specific rules of law. But, unlike the Greeks, they show few signs of such capacity, and a clear-cut conception of political supremacy in terms of law had therefore to wait for its next great opportunity, an opportunity which, however, was not to come to the western world again for a thousand years, when actual political relations in the nation-states of western Europe had once again assumed somewhat the same form at the end of the Middle Ages which had characterized the Roman state under the *imperium* of the emperors.

In the long interval of the Middle Ages which lies between,

conditions were unfavourable for the formulation of any theory of sovereignty, largely because there was scarcely discernible among strictly political institutions a supremacy of any kind. In the earlier centuries of this period government, usually in the form of monarchy, was taken for granted and the medieval mind was not yet mature enough to take the step from tacit acceptance to self-conscious analysis of political relations. In the eleventh century political speculation was reborn in defence or denial of papal claims to a political authority over the whole of the *Respublica Christiana*, and an authority which was fast developing into a true *plenitudo potestatis*; but in the lower sphere of secular political relations specifically, the chief new doctrine stimulated by these ecclesiastical controversies was the theory of dominion, which reflected more of the decentralization of feudalism than of the strong monarchy of the canonists.

From the thirteenth century to the sixteenth *dominium* is the prevailing formula under which men habitually think about secular government. But in essence this *dominium* is a theory of superiority rather than supremacy. For Beaumanoir, writing in the thirteenth century, the king is "sovereign" in his kingdom, but so is an earl in his earldom, and even a baron in his barony. If the king's authority is greater than the earl's or the baron's, this is primarily because it is wider than theirs, not so much because it is higher in kind. The king alone has the care (*garde*) of the whole kingdom and must have an authority commensurate with his broader responsibilities. It is true, as Luchaire has remarked, that in this whole period the conception of true kingship was never lost entirely, but it was without doubt obscured greatly by conceptions of the political relation drawn from actual conditions under feudal tenure with its graduated rights and interests enjoyed by a hierarchy of lords in the same fief and over the same tenants. In the feudal monarchy every king was *dominus* as well as *rex*, and as *dominus* his rights were scarcely distinguishable in kind from those of inferior lords.

In such circumstances the development of a clear-cut theory of any single supreme political authority over all subjects is not to be looked for. *Dominium*, as a theory of government drawn in largest part from a rationalization of the feudal relation, was destined to stand in the way of any true theory of sovereignty as long as the feudal institutions which gave life to the formula retained their own vitality. It remained until modern times a barrier to sovereignty, because it was inconsistent with a complete supremacy of any sort.

At times it has been said that the chief reason for the lateness of the appearance of a theory of sovereignty was not this dominion, but rather the prevalence in the Middle Ages of the conception of natural law; but such an explanation entails a misinterpretation of the history of the theory and implies some misunderstanding of the original notion of sovereignty itself. The earliest forms of the theory, as everyone knows, freely incorporated natural law in it, and they were entirely consistent in so doing; for sovereignty is a supreme authority not deducible from might, according to this theory, but defined by law; and if so, there is nothing to prevent the inclusion in this law of provisions which men believe to be dictated by nature, as well as those arising from custom or created by enactment. The theoretical obstacle to sovereignty was not the law of nature, except in so far as it contributed to retard men's awareness of the fact of law-making. In reality the main obstacle was twofold: the prevalence in the Middle Ages of the theory of dominion and the absence of any clear notion of legislation. What characterizes a modern "sovereign" is supreme authority to make law, but in medieval Europe it was not easy to find any authority supreme in all respects, and even if found, it was an authority merely to promulgate, administer and interpret a law already in being, not to make a new one. The legal rules issued in a king's name might be *stabilimenta*, *établissements* or *statuta*—something "established", as such terms imply; but these are not the creations of a ruler legally competent to enact legislation at will.

By the sixteenth century, however, these medieval conditions had largely been replaced in some parts of western Europe by the ones we are familiar with to-day, and before the end of that century a few keener minds had begun to discard older formulae explanatory of phenomena already outworn and to reshape the theory of the state in light not merely of traditional doctrines but of newer political conditions which they were beginning to discover in existence about them. In the more centralized states the king had at length outgrown the feudal stage and had become the true head of a nation, once more a monarch ruling over subjects instead of a lord over vassals, and ruling in accordance with a law which was truly national in scope and character. Moreover, such substantial additions and changes were now being made in the law itself, and with such frequency, that it was scarcely possible longer to conceal this fact under the older medieval doctrine that a monarch can only administer or interpret a law but not make it. The world was ripe for a new theory of the state. It finally came in the recognition that a state consists essentially in a supreme legislative authority over subjects.

Apparently the first definite and comprehensive statement of the new doctrine was by Jean Bodin. In his *Methodus ad Facilem Historiarum Cognitionem*, first published in 1566, he asserted the principle that an authority truly supreme is essential to every state and when present constitutes a state, though he still retained the medieval doctrine that the chief and the typical form of this supreme authority is the judicial—control over the administration and interpretation of law. But ten years later, in his more famous *République*, he has begun to see that it is supremacy in the making of law rather than its administration which marks the sovereign. In that epoch-making book he defines a republic as "un droit gouvernement de plusieurs mesnages, & de ce qui leur est commun, AVEC PUISSANCE SOUVERAINE"; and *puissance souveraine*, or sovereignty, as "la puissance absoluë & perpetuelle d'une

République", or, as in his Latin version of 1586, "suprema in cives ac subditos legibusque soluta potestas"; a power or authority of which the first and foremost element (*primum ac praecipuum caput*), to which all others are incidental, is "la puissance de donner loy à tous en general, & à chacun en particulier". In these few statements the whole of the theory of modern sovereignty is expressed in its classical form. Bodin is no doubt entitled to his claim to be the first among philosophers and jurisconsults to formulate this theory, and Sir F. Pollock is probably justified in saying that this formulation could not have come much earlier than it did.

For an understanding of the later history of the theory a careful consideration of every important part of Bodin's statement of it is, of course, necessary; but in this paper attention will be confined practically to one part alone, and the first: "République est un DROIT gouvernement." It is a government defined by law, and though the sovereign authority in it is *legibus soluta*, "free of the laws", yet these laws can never include the fundamental rules upon which the state itself rests and by which the sovereign is constituted and his authority defined, whether these fundamental rules be thought to be drawn from the law of God or from the law of nature, or come actually from the ancient custom of the nation or from a distinct and definite expression of the nation's will. If we assume that sovereignty is not might but authority, then a definition of such authority is an absolute necessity, and the terms of that definition will fix a limit beyond which the holder of the sovereignty can never pass without negating his very existence. Bodin did so assume, and was compelled by the logic of that assumption to place beyond the sovereign's control all the essential principles which form and enter into *un droit gouvernement*, though as sovereign he is free of all laws whatsoever made or to be made in accordance with these principles.

In Bodin's day it was generally accepted that a government could never be *droit* if it violated the principles of justice founded upon the law of nature and the law of God. Every association of men is held together by some bond of law, but if such an association is to be better than a band of robbers this must be a law based on justice, and justice comes from the nature of man himself and from the mind of God. So there never could be a true republic except one founded in justice, nor any legitimate authority within such a republic.

But the *jus civile*, public as well as private, within a particular state will consist, as Gaius said, partly of laws common to all mankind and partly of laws peculiar to that state alone. And if the fundamentals of the common law of mankind must always be incorporated in the definition of any true commonwealth which man makes, so in a particular commonwealth this definition may in addition include some peculiar principles not necessarily present in every state, but fundamental in that particular one, and an integral part of the very definition of the state itself, of its government, and of the supreme authority therein. Such particular principles Bodin saw in France in the so-called Salic Law, and in the inalienability of the royal domain and authority. These principles did not have their source in man's nature or in God's law, but they were no less essential than such to the integrity of the French kingdom and in France were therefore "fundamental" in the same sense. When, then, Bodin declares that his sovereign is "free of the laws", he restricts such laws to the ordinary rules enacted in the state pursuant to these fundamental principles and never inconsistent with them. By these fundamental principles even the highest authority is always bound; it is only of all others that he is wholly free. It has been the fashion of most modern interpreters of Bodin in England and America to condemn this reservation of fundamental law as a fatal inconsistency in his theory and a sign of failure fully to grasp the essential principle of sovereignty. In reality this condemnation is proof of their own inability to understand his true meaning, resulting usually from imperfect knowledge of the historical basis, ancient and medieval, upon which Bodin's theory actually rests.

The fundamental law of a state as Bodin conceived it must therefore embody the laws of nature and of God and may also include particular rules which are no less an integral part of that state's "constitution". For him, as was natural at the time, all such particular rules actually come from immemorial custom. But there is no logical necessity for restricting them in this way, and therefore in after times, as men became more self-conscious politically and as law-making more and more tended to replace mere law-declaring, these particular "fundamental" rules were extended to comprise new provisions as well as ancient customs, and thus the foundations of the modern "written constitution" were finally laid. The bedrock upon which all such modern written constitutions rest—all at least which originate in the people—and the only one upon which they may rest consistently, is this distinction, in essence identical with Bodin's, between those laws which a government makes and may therefore change, and the ones which make the government itself. It is immaterial whether the latter rules be drawn from the law of nature or immemorial custom as in Bodin's day, or be made by definite act of the people's will, as they usually are now; in any case they must inevitably be superior to the government they create and beyond the reach even of the sovereign organ within it whose authority they define. This is a theory of law not of might, the theory of the *Rechtsstaat*; and it is this theory which has dominated continental thought to the present day, and for two generations after Bodin dominated even English thought, the theory of Hooker, Eliot, Twysden, Philip Hunton and Sir Matthew Hale.

It remains briefly to consider the changes which in England ultimately replaced this theory by a newer one, and to compare this new theory with the old on the basis of their respective merits theoretical and practical.

It was Thomas Hobbes, the keenest and shortest-sighted of modern political philosophers, who put this newer theory in clean-cut terms as Bodin had put the older. In the struggle which became concrete in England in the summer of 1642 with the issuance of the militia ordinance, behind all the ponderous arguments from ancient precedent employed on either side, Hobbes saw clearly the true nature of the issue and its inevitable outcome, and he saw them earlier and more distinctly than most of his contemporaries, and set them forth in his *Behemoth*, or history of the civil wars. Though it was the ancient constitution which both parties were still professing to defend, the struggle between King and Parliament was at bottom a struggle not for law but for mastery, and it could end only in the actual mastery of one or the other. In his more theoretical works, especially the *De Cive* and later in the more celebrated *Leviathan*, Hobbes reduced his observations of these actual conditions in England to a formula purporting to have universal application. The supreme authority in any state is the one which can compel actual obedience. Might, not law, makes right. It is authority, and not reason, which makes a law, as he tells us in his *Dialogue of the Common Laws of England*, written to refute the traditional doctrines of Sir Edward Coke.

Like Aristotle's supremacy in Athens of the fifth century B.C., and Bodin's sovereignty in France of the sixteenth A.D., this is a rationalization of actual political conditions; in this case, conditions as they existed in England in the period of political strife and civil war between 1640 and 1660. The core of such a rationalization is naturally actual might, not legitimate authority. But the disturbed conditions of civil war furnish poor material for a general theory of settled government. It is the unlaw of the English civil wars and Interregnum to which we are indebted for that particular type of supremacy, the sovereignty of Hobbes and Filmer and John Austin, which still prevails in the political thought of England, and, strange to say, of America as well; although it was rejected by James Otis, Samuel Adams and other Americans in the eighteenth century, and notwithstanding the fact that it is utterly incompatible with the fundamental conceptions upon which our

American governments were originally established and indeed with all written constitutions and bills of rights wherever and whenever they are found, those few alone excepted which proceed from the concession of a ruler.

Nothing could show more plainly the nakedness of the might which lies at the centre of Austin's theory than his well-known reformulation of Hobbes's sovereignty in *The Province of Jurisprudence Determined*. He tells us there that when in any society a determinate person (or persons) "*habitually*" receives the obedience of "the bulk" of the members of the society, such person (or persons) must be considered to be the sovereign in that society. There is no question here of law or right. It is the mere physical fact of mastery, the actual existence and continuance of obedience whether induced by consent, fear or force, which clothes those who obtain it, no matter how or why they obtain it, with the supreme authority in a state. And furthermore, the actual submission of "the bulk" of the people is, in this theory, complete justification for a supremacy with unlimited power over all, even over those who have never consented to it. Minorities look in vain for protection under such a theory, and there is no right of an individual too sacred to be overridden with the assent of "the bulk" of the people.

If anyone should doubt the practical effects of this truly slavish theory of the state, a very slight review of certain periods of English and American history would be enough to undeceive him. It was largely by an appeal to it that Lord Mansfield defended and obtained the passage in 1766 of the Declaratory Act which affirmed that Englishmen in America were completely subject to the power of a legislative body in which they had no representatives whatever, a perfect example of Austinianism in operation; it was its influence which enabled conservatives like Lord Eldon to justify and secure the retention, even in the nineteenth century and by an unreformed parliament, of such notorious abuses as Catholic disabilities and the Test and Corporation acts, and to enact class legislation of the type of the Combination acts.

It is little wonder that such a theory should in time provoke reaction among liberal minds and meet with the opposition it deserved. The most interesting and important theoretical aspect of this opposition at the present time is the recent growth and rapid extension of the theory usually known as "pluralism".

The underlying principle of pluralism is simple in the extreme. Under it, as its name implies, it is not necessary that there be in the state any supreme authority at all. There may be one person, or institution, association, or body such as a church or guild or trade union, to whose authority a citizen defers if he chooses, or there may be more than one; and if more, the citizen himself freely determines which shall receive his obedience should their claims conflict. In effect, there is and can be no "sovereign", because sovereignty itself is a wholly inadmissible concept.

It is, however, far more than sovereignty that pluralism repudiates; it denies the existence or the right to exist of a supremacy of any kind whatsoever. There is no "sovereignty" in the state because there can be no supremacy. But such a rejection of supremacy is equivalent to a repudiation of all control over the individual citizen except that which he voluntarily imposes upon himself, a flat denial of the legitimacy of any coercive power whatever; and it is more than questionable whether anyone but a professed anarchist could make such denial without incurring the just charge of inconsistency and confusion of thought. For adherents of the theory of philosophic anarchy pluralism is an eligible explanation of political relations. How it could possibly form an integral part of any other theory of the state, it is rather difficult to see, or how anyone holding any other theory could consistently espouse it. Yet many have espoused it who are apparently unwilling to subscribe to the anarchistic creed. For most persons pluralism will contain too little and too much: too little in its assumption that all sovereignty must of necessity be Austinian sovereignty, too much in the denial that sovereignty of any kind, or supremacy even, can ever be a legitimate political concept. Political ideals are one thing; actual political phenomena often quite another. Pluralism unquestionably fits in perfectly with the high ideal of the anarchist, but he would probably be the first to admit that it accounts for no actual government existent now or hitherto.

Few countries have made more significant contribution to the modern world's stock of political institutions than the United States, but to the theory underlying them all our contribution is negligible. Our theory, such as it is, has been mainly a theory of lawyers who were usually content to accept their explanation of government at second-hand from later English legal sources such as the *Commentaries* of Sir William Blackstone, himself a political theorist far from profound or consistent, as Jeremy Bentham had little trouble in showing. Modern federalism, for example, has been largely our work, but no thoroughgoing theory of it ever appeared till after the foundation of the new German Empire in 1871.

In short, we have hitherto been satisfied to borrow and to retain, with little discrimination and no adequate examination, a traditional theory inconsistent with our national origin, outworn when we took it and tenfold more outworn now; a theory originally built upon actual conditions of civil strife instead of national well-being, and itself unfailingly productive of new strife, except when fiction or fact has stood in the way of its full operation. The time seems ripe again for a new theoretical appraisal of our political institutions which will take complete account of present-day conditions and needs. If a satisfactory theory should ever be the outcome, such a theory would, of course, have to meet and furnish explanation of actual political conditions which are vastly more intricate and perplexing than those of the simple unitary national monarchy of France which gave Bodin the principal data for his rationalization in the sixteenth century. Even if we should start with Bodin, we could certainly not end with him. But it is none the less true that no theory which proves to be unsound for a simple state can ever form the basis for a valid explanation of a complex one; the essentials must be the same in both.

It is the purpose of this brief fragment merely to give a few illustrations of the importance, for a proper testing of these essentials, of a careful review of the past development and practical results of some of the theories of government which we still employ. Such review as the writer himself has been able to make has seemed to him to show that the *Rechtsstaat*, of which Jean Bodin gave us the first analysis, is after all probably a sounder foundation on which to build than either the assertions of Hobbes or the negations of the modern Pluralists. From such a survey others may and some no doubt will be led to a different conclusion, but few are likely to dissent from the general principle that in any serious attempt to reach an adequate synthesis of present-day political relations, or a sound analysis, past experience cannot safely be ignored.

IV

WHIG SOVEREIGNTY AND REAL SOVEREIGNTY[1]

Criticisms of John Austin are usually made nowadays with bated breath if they are ever made at all. Even the great Maitland in 1900 wrote from the Canaries to Leslie Stephen, "Since I was here I wrote an article 'Hist. Engl. Law' for the *Encyclopædia Britannica* and risked about Austin a couple of sentences which are not in accordance with common repute—and now I feel a little frightened." In that "couple of sentences" Maitland had said of Austin, "But, though he was at times an acute dissector of confused thought, he was too ignorant of the English, the Roman and every other system of law to make any considerable addition to the sum of knowledge."

Under the rather lurid title prefixed to this paper—"Whig Sovereignty and Real Sovereignty"—I hope to be able to show the following, among other things:

(1) That this Whig sovereignty is essentially Austin's sovereignty.

(2) That it has no basis in earlier English constitutional precedent.

(3) That our American theory of the state was formerly opposed to it, if it should not be now.

What is to be said about Whig history and Whig theory will be, I am afraid, no more "in accordance with common repute" than Maitland's estimate of Austin; for most of our modern lawyers and historians in America like those in England have usually been Whig in sympathy, and, at the same

[1] Read at a meeting of the Michigan Academy of Science, Arts and Letters, Ann Arbor, Michigan, 15 March 1934, and reprinted from the thirty-sixth and thirty-seventh Annual Reports, published by the Academy, Ann Arbor, Michigan, 1935.

time, upholders of theories as to the nature of the state, and of the history of England and America in the seventeenth and eighteenth centuries which seem to me to be hardly distinguishable from the political doctrines of Thomas Hobbes, Sir Robert Filmer, and other notorious defenders of arbitrary government in the seventeenth century. The opposing, or anti-Whig doctrine, as it might be called, which will be defended here, Professor A. F. Pollard says, "is the royalist doctrine of Charles I". This is not strictly accurate, however, though Charles I, if his professions are looked to rather than his practice, was certainly far closer to it than John Pym was. It would be nearer the truth to call it the doctrine of Sir Matthew Hale, or of Sir John Eliot. But, as a matter of fact, it was the political creed of practically every eminent English lawyer, historian or statesman who lived before 1642, excepting only a few upholders of arbitrary government, unlimited obedience, and divine right. What happened in England in 1689, or rather, what happened after 1689, was the supplanting of the Tories' arbitrary king by the Whigs' arbitrary legislature. Both king and legislature had arbitrary power. To the Tory, prerogative could override all law; for the Whig, there was nothing which Parliament could not do. Sir M. Hale and all his great predecessors would have been as much aghast at one doctrine as at the other. For both imply a revolution in English political thought. There is no precedent for either in England before the Civil Wars.

What those wars had achieved for England by force of arms, the revolution of 1689 incorporated in the English constitution; but the negative achievement of the wars and the negative element in the revolution settlement were far more valuable than their positive results. If the English revolution was truly "the glorious revolution" which Whigs have always called it, it was glorious because it scotched for ever the personal, hereditary, divine right of the King for which the Stuarts had argued or fought from James I to James II. None but a hopeless Jacobite would deny the glory of such an achievement; and if Englishmen in North America in 1690 were as enthusiastic in accepting the revolution as any Whig in England it was for this reason alone, that it gave the death blow to the divine right of kings.

But having said this, I think we are bound to add, that if the Stuarts had been content with the moderate prerogative of Bodin or Eliot or Hale, instead of the extreme doctrines of Filmer, there would have been need for neither civil war nor revolution. Before 1642 it was nothing more than the tempered constitutional monarchy of Hale or Eliot for which the parliamentary leaders were struggling. It was only after hostilities had begun that the constitution was forgotten and actual mastery not legal right became the end to be achieved at any cost, and when the wars were over it was this actual mastery and not constitutional right which actually triumphed. It was therefore actual might, not constitutional right, which the Commonwealth and the Protectorate established; it was actual might, not constitutional right, on which Hobbes, with these facts before him, based the sovereignty in any state whatever. "It is not reason but authority which makes a law", he declares, and those who have this authority are the ones actually powerful enough to seize and hold it. It was not from English precedents that he learned this new sovereignty of might; it was from the illegal, unlimited, arbitrary, and unprecedented mastery of the Rump. No wonder that John Winthrop in Massachusetts, though a Puritan, was afraid of it.

And so for Hobbes Filmer's arbitrary royal power had come to be a power vested in either an assembly or a king, but none the less arbitrary for that. Hale or Eliot would have repudiated all arbitrary government whatsoever, whether by king or parliament; Filmer had declared that any government in England must be both arbitrary and royal; for Hobbes it must be arbitrary but not necessarily royal; for many Whigs a century later it must be arbitrary and cannot be royal. Thus after 1689, and the revolution settlement which marked the final triumph of the Whigs, the arbitrary power of Hobbes and Filmer was for the first time "engrafted into the English constitution" in the place of the constitutionalism of Eliot, or Prynne, or Hale and vested in the national assembly. It is to the civil wars of the seventeenth century and not to the precedents of the original English constitution that we are indebted for the peculiar doctrine of political supremacy of Hobbes or Austin which enthrones might in place of right and can brook no limits to the arbitrary authority of the sovereign. For the Whigs the only real sovereign must be the Parliament, that is all.

The sophism by which they have always attempted to distinguish their doctrine of the omnipotence of parliament from the ideas of Filmer and justify the arbitrary power of their supreme legislature, is the fiction of "popular sovereignty". The legislature, they say, *is* the people, and the people is sovereign: *vox populi vox Dei.* But the legislature is *not* the people. The people are legally bound to obey an act of the legislature whether they like it or not. The sovereign is the Parliament; it is not the people in any modern state with representative institutions, no matter how wide the elective franchise, and it was certainly anything but wide in seventeenth- and eighteenth-century England. Rousseau, starting with his assumption that the people must always be sovereign, was entirely logical in denying that England was ever free, except at the time of a parliamentary election. His only mistake was in admitting too much.

Popular sovereignty is, in fact, possible only in a pure democracy without representative institutions. As usually employed the phrase contains a contradiction in terms. In choosing a legislature, whether we like it or not, we are choosing a master and because we choose it, it is legally no less a master than a monarch with hereditary title. This is a fact not so easy for us to forget on this day when income taxes are due.[1] Yet it is curious how persistently men have deceived

[1] In 1934 March 15 was the latest day on which income-tax returns could be filed.

themselves on this point. They confuse the people with the legislature, power with authority. Probably the most striking instance of this confusion in our own history appeared in the debates in 1788 over the ratification of the federal constitution. It is obvious that a sovereign in the Austinian sense of that term can be bound by no legal restrictions. Bills of rights are waste-paper. There is no place for or possibility of a bill of rights in the Austinian system, which is, after all, in essence, only the system of Filmer and Hobbes; and the possibility is no greater when the sovereign happens to be a parliament instead of a king. Yet there were men in the constitutional assembly of 1787 who were not Austinians, and one of them, George Mason, author of the Virginia Declaration of Rights of 1776, insisted on a similar limitation of the government of the United States. He was overruled, and the constitution went to the states for ratification, without any formal section containing a set of prohibitions to the government. Objections were made on account of this omission and Alexander Hamilton set himself to answer them in Number 84 of *The Federalist*. His answer is illuminating, and it fully illustrates the Whig-Austinian fusion or confusion of legislature and people, of power and authority. After enumerating the restrictions imposed on English kings since Magna Carta in documents which might be termed bills of rights, Hamilton adds, referring to documents of this sort:

It is evident, therefore, that, according to their primitive signi-fications, they have no application to constitutions professedly founded upon the power of the people, and executed by their immediate representatives and servants. Here, in strictness, the people surrender nothing; and as they retain every thing they have no need of particular reservations. " *We, the People* of the United States, to secure the blessings of liberty to ourselves and our posterity, do *ordain* and *establish* this Constitution of the United States of America." Here is a better recognition of popular rights, than volumes of those aphorisms which make the principal figure in several of our State bills of rights, and which would sound much better in a treatise of ethics than in a constitution of government.

Hamilton here has confused the people and the legislature, the makers of a constitution and the sovereign authority under the constitution thus made. There is actually no limit to the *people's* power, *ergo* there can be no limitation of the *sovereign's* authority. It is a non-sequitur, which did not end with Hamilton. But Hamilton's argument had been answered before it was made. Ten years before the federal constitution was presented to the states for ratification, the first constitution of Massachusetts had been laid before the town-meetings, and had been objected to on the same grounds. Unlike Virginia's constitution of 1776, it contained no bill of rights. These and other objections are given in the remarkable document known as the Essex Result, published at Ipswich, Massachusetts, in 1778 and written by young Theophilus Parsons, later Chief Justice of the Supreme Judicial Court of Massachusetts. The following statements contain the conclusions of Parsons's argument on this point:

The following principles now seem to be established. 1. That the supreme power is limited, and cannot controul the unalienable rights of mankind, nor receive the equivalent (that is, the security of person and property) which each individual receives, as a consideration for the alienable rights he parted with in entering into political society. 2. That these unalienable rights, and this equivalent, are to be clearly defined and ascertained in a *Bill* of *Rights*, previous to the ratification of any constitution.

Parsons's argument may follow the usual eighteenth-century contract theory based on Locke and Rousseau to a degree unsatisfactory to us now, and it is noteworthy that Parsons is one of the very few Americans of the time to refer expressly to Rousseau's *Social Contract*, which had appeared some sixteen years before he wrote. But the interesting part of his statement to us is his assertion that "the supreme power is limited". He never got that from Rousseau, nor from

Hobbes. He might have got it from Bodin, or Hooker, or Hale; and James Otis had said much the same in Massachusetts some fourteen years before. "The supreme power is limited." A power, then, in Parsons's view, to be supreme need not be necessarily arbitrary or unlimited. Bills of rights are possible and even necessary for the protection of individual liberty, and this is equally true when the constitution comes from the people themselves. One of the most important arguments of a practical kind, for the inclusion of a bill of rights even in a popular constitution, was made somewhat later by Joseph Story in his *Commentaries on the Constitution*, which first appeared in 1833. There he said,

A bill of rights is important, and may often be indispensable, whenever it operates, as a qualification upon powers, actually granted by the people to the government. This is the real ground of all the bills of rights in the parent country, in the colonial constitutions and laws, and in the state constitutions. In England, the bills of rights were not demanded merely of the crown, as withdrawing a power from the royal prerogative; they were equally important, as withdrawing power from parliament.... A bill of rights is an important protection against unjust and oppressive conduct on the part of the people themselves. In a government modified, like that of the United States (said a great statesman [Madison]), the great danger lies rather in the abuse of the community, than of the legislative body. The prescriptions in favor of liberty ought to be levelled against that quarter where the greatest danger lies, namely that which possesses the highest prerogative power. But this is not found in the executive or legislative departments of government; but in the body of the people, operating by a majority against the minority.

Probably the central question in the theory of the state is as to the truth or falsity of Parsons's statement that the supreme power may be limited. The American Revolution itself, so far as its causes were theoretical, had been fought on this issue. To James Otis parliament was supreme but limited, to Lord Mansfield its power must be limitless and arbitrary. One held the definition of sovereignty framed by Bodin and accepted by Hale, the other followed Hobbes in identifying the sovereignty of the parliament with the limitless power of the people who chose it. Whichever is right, the issue is as to the true nature of sovereignty. Professor Pollard declares that "it is this denial of all sovereignty which gives its profound and permanent interest to the American Revolution". Again, he says, "The American Revolution was due to the fact that the state had grown to sovereignty in Great Britain, whereas in America limitations as potent as those of the Middle Ages had prevented anything more than a rudimentary development.... The colonists wanted a medieval restoration." They did, and in their later constitutions they insisted on placing the same medieval limitations upon their own supreme assemblies in the form of bills of rights. This is indeed a medieval restoration and, to my simple, medieval mind, none the worse for being medieval. But in Professor Pollard's view these medieval limitations, whatever else they might be, were a sign of retarded political development; they were "rudimentary". Great Britain, on the other hand, had reached maturity because she had developed an arbitrary parliament. Again we see the fine hand of Austin. Arbitrariness is maturity, limitations imply an outgrown theory of the state. "The voice is Jacob's voice, but the hands are the hands of Esau." Austin's theory of sovereignty is certainly still the one "in repute". To question it made even Maitland "feel a little frightened", as late as 1900. Yet question it I think we must. Sovereignty is the central formula of our political thought, and the key to much of our constitutional history. We must at least be clear as to what we mean by it. And Professor Pollard's able and suggestive survey of American constitutional development in his *Factors in American History* includes one important assertion which seems to be demonstrably wrong. The American contention was not, as he says, "a denial of all sovereignty", unless we accept the principle, as he appears to do in common with so many others, that the only possible form of sovereignty is the one that Hobbes laid down, that the Whigs adopted, and that Austin formulated once more in the nineteenth century. These eighteenth-century Americans were not making "a denial of all sovereignty". Such a denial is virtually anarchy, and they were far from being anarchists. They were asserting *another form of sovereignty*, fundamentally different from Whig sovereignty, the sovereignty of Bodin and Loyseau, of Hooker and Hale, against the sovereignty of Mansfield, of Blackstone and of Austin. And we, as students either of history or of politics, are faced with a necessity not to be avoided, of comparing these two rival theories of the state on their respective merits, theoretical and practical, and of deciding which of the two we must adopt, not only for the interpretation of our past development, but for the decision of the tremendous practical questions of politics which confront us at this present day. Can there be, then, or can there not be, any law beyond the reach of the sovereign power in a state? This I take to be the crux of the problem of sovereignty. The answer seems almost too easy. Of course there can be none, for if there were any law a sovereign power could not override, it would not be a sovereign power. Any other answer involves a contradiction in terms. It is logically impossible. This simple solution appealed to Sir Robert Filmer, as we have seen, to John Austin, and to many other theorists and statesmen, and apparently it still appeals to most lawyers and historians, English and American. Sir William Holdsworth, probably the greatest living historian of the law of England, says that Hobbes was the only Englishman of his day who really understood sovereignty, and Sir William is himself in substantial agreement with Hobbes's political views.

There must be a sovereign power in every state and there can be no legal limits to it. So Lord Mansfield thought. That power is in parliament, he said in 1766, and there is nothing which parliament may not do. It may enact a law which will bind Englishmen in North America "in all cases whatsoever", taxation included. Whether these Englishmen in America have or have not a voice in the election of members to parliament is a point of no legal significance whatever. The parliament is sovereign, "it had, hath, and of Right ought to have, full power and authority to make laws and statutes of sufficient force and validity to bind the Colonies and people of America, subjects of the Crown of Great Britain in all cases whatsoever". In 1839 Lord John Russell denied that responsible government could possibly be conceded to Canada as Lord Durham had advised, because the governor, if he acted on the advice of his council in Canada instead of following instructions from England, would in reality be "an independent sovereign". Mansfield and Russell were in full agreement with Hobbes. Both were echoing the thoughts of Sir Robert Filmer when he declared in the reign of Charles I:

We do but flatter our selves, if we hope ever to be governed without an arbitrary power. No: We mistake, the Question is not, whether there shall be an Arbitrary power; but the only point is, who shall have that Arbitrary Power, whether one man or many? There never was, nor ever can be any People governed without a Power of making Laws, and every Power of making Laws must be Arbitrary.

The result of Filmer's theory in Lord Mansfield's hands was the American Revolution; the answer to Lord John Russell was given two years ago, in the Statute of Westminster. With consequences as vast as this, dare anyone say that the theory of sovereignty is only an academic doctrine? May there be things which a supreme king or a supreme legislature cannot legally do, or may there not? In the eighteenth century insistence upon parliament's unlimited power lost one great colonial empire to England, and half a century later insistence on it would have lost another, if the policy had been persisted in.

I have been taken to task because some years ago I ventured to intimate that there might be a false note in this Whig chorus in favour of the doctrine that the Americans were wrong, and that Mansfield was constitutionally right—which, of course, would mean that Filmer and Hobbes were also politically right. I have in the meantime found nothing which leads me to retract the opinion then expressed: that Mansfield was wrong in his interpretation of the English constitution, and Hobbes, as well as Austin after him, unsound in his definition of political supremacy. But you should not be asked to accept such disreputable views as this without proof. In support of them it is necessary for me to show two things at least: First, that the theory of Hobbes is politically bad; and second, that it is not a necessary element in the English constitution. Is the accepted political doctrine true, then, that every sovereign must have arbitrary power, and that the English parliament in the reign of George III had such arbitrary power constitutionally?

You know, of course, that some leading Americans in the eighteenth century ventured, as I am now doing, flatly to deny Mansfield's constitutional dictum and Hobbes's theory, but it is the fashion at present to call them mistaken. In 1768, Samuel Adams set forth in the *Massachusetts Circular Letter* a view borrowed perhaps from Lord Camden, but utterly inconsistent with Mansfield's law and Hobbes's politics, when he said "that it is an essential, unalterable right, in nature, engrafted into the British constitution as a fundamental law, and ever held sacred and irrevocable by the subjects within the realm, that what a man has honestly acquired is absolutely his own; which he may freely give, but cannot be taken from him without his consent". Another statement from the same document is even more significant, a recognition—to use Adams's own words—"that his Majesty's high court of Parliament is the supreme legislative power over the whole empire; that in all free states the constitution is fixed, and as the supreme legislative derives its power and authority from the constitution, it cannot overleap the bounds of it, without destroying its own foundation; that the constitution ascertains and limits both sovereignty and allegiance". You will notice that, like Jean Bodin, Samuel Adams calls his sovereign "supreme", but in the same breath says that he is limited.

But it is no solution of this important problem of sovereignty, and it is certainly no adequate refutation of the views of Hobbes and Mansfield and of their many present-day followers, merely to quote against them the words of an eighteenth-century opponent. If Adams was right—and I think he was—and they wrong, it is necessary to show that his political views are at least not unreasonable, and that his constitutional doctrine is based on earlier English precedent or received opinion. We must therefore examine the earlier growth of the ideas of sovereignty, and also attempt to test the truth of Adams's assertion that his view of sovereignty, and not Mansfield's, was "engrafted into the British constitution". This is a matter of considerable importance, theoretical, historical, and practical, and it should be treated fully and proved at every point. There is, unfortunately, not time here for either complete statement or full proof, and I must be content with an outline that may, I am afraid, seem both fragmentary and dogmatic.

We return, then, to our original questions: Is all supreme power by definition an arbitrary power, and did such an arbitrary power belong to the sovereign in England? Filmer and Hobbes assert both in the seventeenth century. Both were denied by a number of publicists and lawyers, to some of whom I should like to call your attention. For the moment the first of these to be noted is Jean Bodin. Writing in 1576, he declared that both England and France were royal but not seignorial monarchies, that both were "absolute", that neither was arbitrary. But can any government be at once absolute and not arbitrary? Is this not what Filmer called it, a "*contradictio in adjecto*"? Bodin thought not, and his explanation might be briefly summarized thus: In every royal monarchy, which to Bodin means every monarch with free men and not slaves as its subjects, and to him both England and France were such; in fact, in every association of men whatever which is truly political, what makes it a state is the existence of a government; but not *any* government. It must be a government animated by justice and founded upon law. Otherwise the association will be no better than a band of robbers, and will, in fact, be a robber band instead of a true *respublica* or commonwealth. To be a true state, it *must* be founded in law. It must therefore have a lawful framework, a form of the state, a constitution, and this must be an embodiment of right and justice. Of necessity this involves a distinction between those rules which form and enter into this constitution itself, on the one hand, and on the other, those provisions which may be made by authority delegated by the constitution. Bodin's conception of a republic and of the sovereign authority in it can only be understood in light of this fundamental distinction between constituent law and ordinary legislation. There is and there must be, in every free state, a marked difference between those laws which a government makes and may therefore change, and the ones which make the government itself. The government set up under the terms of the constitution will be supreme, and Bodin even calls it "absolute", whether it is the government of one man, of a few, or of many. It is "free of the laws", he says, but by this he means free only of the ordinary laws which the government itself has made or may make. He does not include among these laws the fundamental principles of the constitution under which the government itself comes into being, which define and set bounds to the supreme organ in the government so created. The sovereign or supreme authority established and defined by a fundamental law is bound absolutely by that law, though he is free of all other laws. He could no more change these fundamental rules than one can change the law of his being. It is as impossible to do so as it would be for one to lift himself by his own boot-straps. But after all, what is this but to assert what Samuel Adams asserts and what Hobbes denies —that the sovereign cannot overleap the bounds of the constitution which gives him being, without destroying the very foundation on which all his authority rests?

Bodin's limitations on the sovereign's power just mentioned

are often regarded as a fatal logical flaw in his theory. As Filmer put it, it is *contradictio in adjecto*. The view of Filmer and Hobbes is still frequently said to be the only consistent theory of political supremacy, and Bodin's deviation from it is attributed to a mere confusion of thought on his part. It is true that the theory of Bodin and that of Hobbes have very little in common. They are poles apart. The former is a theory of law, the latter a theory of might. One must choose which of the two he thinks the truer formulation of political relations. He cannot waver between two opinions on this. If one of these theories be true, the other is certainly false. Nor can they be combined. They are mutually exclusive. Much of the obscurity in the modern discussions of sovereignty is due to a failure to make clear distinction between supreme might and supreme authority. We too often forget that if we mean supreme authority, that authority must be defined, if defined, then limited by its definition, and by a definition outside and higher than itself. Frequently we are caught applying to a supremacy of mere might terms which are appropriate only to a supremacy resting in law, and vice versa. The result is confusion. I am more interested just now in trying to avoid this confusion than in persuading you that Bodin is right on this important matter, and Hobbes wrong. We must, however, inevitably choose between these two theories, and to me the *Rechtsstaat*, of which Bodin seems to have given us the first clear analysis in 1576, seems not only completely consistent and logical in itself, but infinitely preferable to its competitor as an analysis of actual political relations, and free also of the disastrous practical results which history shows as arising from the more arbitrary theory of Hobbes. For, as Aristotle says, "Law is reason without passion". If we deny Bodin's essential distinction between the fundamental and the ordinary laws, what justification have we for our American constitutions or bills of rights, or, for the matter of that, for any written constitutions, or for any bills of rights?

But to go back to the issue with which we started, between

Lord Mansfield and Samuel Adams; if we are to prove the case in favour of the latter, we must do more than show that Bodin's theory is not untenable, more even than demonstrate its superiority, theoretical and practical, over Hobbes's theory of the state. In addition to that we must make it clear from earlier precedents or authorities, that it was Bodin's sovereignty and not Hobbes's which was "engrafted into the British constitution", to use Samuel Adams's phrase.

Our limited time will not permit an exhaustive examination, but a few striking instances may be given. It is important, however, to note clearly at the outset, that if Hobbes was right; if Mansfield was right and John Austin a century ago, and Sir William Holdsworth to-day; if these men were right, or even Sir William Blackstone; then Richard Hooker was certainly wrong, and Sir Edward Coke, Sir John Eliot, Sir Roger Twysden, Sir Matthew Hale, and many more. If Filmer's saying is true, that "every power of making laws must be arbitrary", then John Hampden was merely wrong-headed rather than patriotic in resisting the enforcement of the ship-money writs; but if by any chance we should think Hampden's resistance legally, or, at least, politically justified—and some of us, I think, have some suspicion of it—why, then, should we deny a like justification to James Otis, or to John or Samuel Adams? Yet our modern American historians, nine out of ten of them, are doing just that! I have little enough respect for the slavish doctrines of Hobbes in themselves, but who could help admiring the sleight of hand of the magician who can pull so big a rabbit out of so small a hat? For nearly three hundred years now Thomas Hobbes has been palming off on us mere might as the highest authority in the State, in the place of right; and the trick still works!

But let us see if Hampden and Adams really had any authority for following Bodin as they did instead of submitting to a power admittedly "arbitrary". I can give only a few instances, and among the many I must omit are some important statements of Sir Edward Coke. The first I shall give comes from the great debate in Parliament in the year 1610 on the question of James I's well-known "book of rates". The book of rates would have imposed on Englishmen a whole series of taxes, and James tried to authorize it by mere royal proclamation without consent of parliament. This was resisted in the Commons in 1610, and in the course of the debate the following remarks were made by Sir James White-locke, an able and eminent lawyer, and later a justice of the Court of King's Bench. I ask you to note the close corre-spondence of his views on sovereignty with the essentials of Bodin's theory, and also the way in which he tried to fit that theory into English political conditions, by his clear recogni-tion of the necessity for co-operation between the king and the two houses of parliament in legislation, in his definition of the sovereign in England as "the King in Parliament". Speaking to the question noted above, he said, in part:

The case in terms is this. The King by his letters patents before recited hath ordained, willed and commanded, that these new impositions, contained in that book of rates, shall be for ever hereafter paid unto him, his heirs and successors, upon pain of his displeasure. Hereupon the question ariseth whether by this edict and ordinance so made by the King himself, by his letters patents of his own will and power absolute, without assent of parliament, he be so lawfully entitled to that he doth impose, as that thereby he doth alter the property of his subjects' goods, and is enabled to recover these impositions by course of law. I think he cannot; and I ground my opinion upon these four reasons.

1. It is against the natural frame and constitution of the policy of this kingdom, which is *Jus publicum regni*, and so subverteth the fundamental law of the realm, and induceth a new form of state and government.

2. It is against the municipal law of the land, which is *Jus privatum*, the law of property and of private right.

3. It is against divers statutes made to restrain our King in this point.

4. It is against the practice and action of our commonwealth.

For the first, it will be admitted for a rule and ground of state, that in every commonwealth and government there be some rights of sovereignty, *jura majestatis*, which regularly and of common right do belong to the sovereign power of that state, unless custom or the provisional ordinance of that state do otherwise dispose of them; which sovereign power is *potestas suprema*, a power that can control all other powers, and cannot be controlled but by itself.

The sovereign power is agreed to be in the King; but in the King is a twofold power; the one in Parliament, as he is assisted with the consent of the whole state; the other out of parliament, as he is sole and singular, guided merely by his own will. And if of these two powers in the King one is greater than the other, and can direct and control the other, that is *suprema potestas*, the sovereign power, and the other is *subordinata*.

It will then be easily proved that the power of the King in parliament is greater than his power out of parliament, and doth rule and control it; for if the King make a grant by his letters patents out of parliament, it bindeth him and his successors; but by his power in parliament he may defeat and avoid it, and therefore that is the greater power. If a judgment be given in the King's Bench by the King himself, as may be and by the law is intended, a writ of error to reverse this judgment may be sued before the King in parliament. So you see the appeal is from the King out of parliament, to the King in parliament. For in acts of parliament, be they laws, grounds or whatsoever else, the act and power is the King's, but with the assent of the Lords and Commons, which maketh it the most sovereign and supreme power above all and controllable by none.

It must be borne in mind that it was a king and not a parliament that Whitelocke was opposing, and there are some things in this long statement which are certainly additions to Bodin's theory, and perhaps in one respect some inconsistency; but in essence the two political doctrines are identical. In both, the sovereign power is supreme and uncontrollable, but it is nevertheless a power defined and limited by "the natural frame and constitution of the policy" of the kingdom. Even though Whitelocke's sovereign is a parliamentary sovereign, as Mansfield also made it, it is not an arbitrary sovereign, as Filmer declared every sovereign must be, or as Mansfield said the English parliament actually was in 1766.

The next illustrations I shall give come from the martyr to the principle of freedom of speech in Parliament, Sir John Eliot, and they are the more interesting because they were written in the prison in which he was soon afterward to die. Eliot's modern Whig biographer, John Forster, has made frantic efforts to prove his hero a Whig holding the political principles common to most of the Whig party long after the Revolution of 1688, but to accomplish it he has been compelled to garble some of Eliot's statements and suppress others to such an extent that his life of Eliot is one of the most striking examples of what a biography should never be. For Sir John Eliot was no Whig, and up to the time of his death there were in England no other Whigs, as Mr Forster defines a Whig. The political principles of the Petition of Right are not the principles of the Bill of Rights. The former was a constitutional protest, the latter was a revolutionary enactment. Eliot, like the founders of Massachusetts Bay, belonged to the generation of the Petition, not of the Bill. He was a monarchist, and it was absolute monarchy, nothing less, which he advocated; but, for all that, it was no arbitrary monarchy, for it was grounded in law not upon might, and was, therefore, limited by the constitutional principles which entered into its very being and definition. But this is nothing but Bodin's original theory in its purity, and Bodin is one of the authors cited oftenest in Eliot's *De Jure Majestatis*, from which the following extracts are taken. I shall give only two short ones; the first illustrating Eliot's notion of absolute authority, the second, one of the chief constitutional limits to that authority.

The greater rights of Majesty which are called mere regalia (he says) doth so cleave to the bones and person of an absolute prince, that they cannot be separated from him without destruction of him no more than can the sun beams from the sun, and so cannot be transferred to the subject. For supreme jurisdiction is of that nature that it cannot be shared. For these rights make the essential difference between subjection and sovereignty, so that confound them, you bring them in confusion.

The next extract is the last in his treatise.

We must also take heed of this extreme that we do not confound royal authority with proprietie; as if the King because he is supreme lord of our lands and goods, might therefore alienate them at his pleasure, and dispose of them as he thinks good. For it is a rule in Law that *Rei suae quisquis est moderator et arbiter.* Everyone may dispose of his own.

It ought to be added that the extracts just given come really from an English translation made by Eliot of part of a Latin work by Henning Arnisaeus of Halberstadt; but there can be no doubt that they were adopted by Eliot as his own and are an accurate expression of his political views; as may be seen on a careful comparison of this work with the *Monarchie of Man* which Eliot composed himself in English during his imprisonment in the Tower. I have taken passages from the *De Jure Majestatis* rather than the *Monarchie of Man* merely because the former contains probably the clearest and most concise statement of political views which crop out in all Eliot's writings.

Sir Roger Twysden, the next author whom I shall cite, was one of the greatest authorities on early English institutions living in the first half of the seventeenth century, an age of great antiquaries. His views on the question at issue will be clear from his *Certaine Considerations upon the Government of England*, which was first printed in 1849 by the Camden Society. The author was a sincere monarchist, and he suffered imprisonment for it at the hands of the parliamentarians, but he had also opposed ship money, and the passages following show him to be no believer in arbitrary monarchy.

That this kingdom (he says) is called a monarchy is plain to any hath read our old historians and laws. The Conqueror himself terms it so, and divers of good esteem, both before and after him; *yet it is certain till of late all writers that ever have writ,* held he was to be guided by his laws and his politic capacity, that is, his royalty, framed by the policy of man, expressed in the severall customs, laws, and constitutions of the Kingdom, he was to rule his subjects according to their direction and no otherwise, and that it neither was a disobeying of him when they were observed, . . . nor had he any power of punishing but according to the line and measure of the law in his ordinary courts of justice. I have shewed in the former chapter, wise antiquity did conceive of laws as what were found for the moderating the exorbitancies greatness aptly falls into; but this latter age hath produced some of opinion no kings can be limited, and the chiefest reason I have heard is, because he is a monarch, sovereign and supreme in his kingdom; words we find attributed to all, at least to the kings of England. . . . It is most true that if the words "monarch", or "sovereign" be taken in that sense, some now would have them of being so absolute as he is tied to no law whatsoever, there is then, as Bodin rightly noteth, no sovereign upon earth, all kings being subject to the laws of God, nature, etc., and the severall constitutions of the kingdom; as the French of the Salic law, the English that we call the law of the land, or the common law, the which are annexed and united to the crowns of England and France as conditions with which they are received.

As an indication of the earlier prevalence of such views as this I might add the case of Willion *v.* Berkley (3 and 4 Eliz., *Plowden's Reports*, 236) where it was laid down that "altho' by the Common Law the King has many prerogatives touching his Person, his Goods, his Debts and Duties, and other personal Things, yet the common law has so admeasured his Prerogatives that they shall not take away nor prejudice the inheritance of any. . . . The King's Prerogative by the Common Law cannot prevail against such a Custom as stands with the Right of Inheritance of another."

This was at the opening of Elizabeth's reign, about three-fourths of a century before Twysden wrote. A somewhat similar instance later in the same reign was the celebrated case of Cavendish in 1587, which the late Professor Thayer considered so important that he included it among his *Cases on*

American Constitutional Law. Queen Elizabeth, by letter patent, had granted to Cavendish the right of making all the writs of *supersedeas* in the Court of Common Pleas, and sent instructions to the judges to admit him to that office. As the office was already in the possession of another, the judges refused to admit Cavendish. When the Queen ordered them to appear and explain their disobedience, their explanation was that they could not even at the Queen's order deprive another of his right. As the reporter puts it, "They said that they must needs confess that they had not performed the orders; but this was no offence or contempt to her Majesty, for the orders were against the law of the land, in which case it was said, no one is bound to obey such an order.... And they said that the queen herself was sworn and took oath to keep her laws, and the judges also, as regards their willingly breaking them." This answer was reported by the Lord Chancellor to the Queen, and as Anderson, the Chief Justice, in his report of the case, says: "Nothing more was done or heard by the judges in the said Easter Terms, or in the Trinity Term then following; which moves the judges to think that no more will ever be."

But one of the most striking of the earlier opinions tending to support the views of Adams against Mansfield is found in a paper of Sir Matthew Hale's written to refute Hobbes's definition of sovereignty; and Hale, it should be remembered, survived till 1676, only a dozen years before the English Revolution itself. Of his character and deserved reputation as lawyer, judge, legal historian and man, I need say nothing. The paper in question was printed for the first time in 1924 by Sir William Holdsworth as an appendix to volume five of his *History of English Law.* There is among the manuscripts in the library of the Harvard Law School another unprinted paper of Lord Hale on the King's prerogative, in which he takes the same view of sovereignty expressed in that published by Sir William Holdsworth, the one from which I have picked out the following passages:

There is [the Chief Justice says] a threefold effect of the laws of this or any other Kingdom. 1. *Potestas Coerciva*. This extends to all the King's subjects, but doth not extend to the King, he is not under the coercive power of the laws. 2. *Potestas Directiva*, and this obliges the King and we need not go further for evidence thereof than the solemn oath which he takes at his coronation, the iterated confirmation of the great charter and those other laws and statutes that concern the liberties of his subjects. 3. *Potestas Irritans*, and thus the laws also in many cases bind the King's acts and make them void if they are against law.... No good subject that understands what he says can make any question where the sovereign power of this kingdom resides. The laws of the land and the oath of supremacy teach us, that the King is the only supreme governor of this realm, and as incident to that supreme power he hath among others these great powers of sovereignty.

He then enumerates the various powers of the king, six in number, such as the power of making war and peace, the pardoning power, etc., and closes with the king's power of making laws. "These laws", Hale declares, "are his laws enacted by him." These six powers, in the words of Lord Hale, "are the great *jura summi imperii* that *the laws of this kingdom have fixed in the Crown of England*". "But yet", he adds, "there are certain qualifications of these powers", and enumerates some, especially of the law-making power. This requires the assent of Parliament.

. . . generally the King's proclamation cannot make a law, but laws are to be made in that solemnity and with the advice of Parliament. Though these things be unquestionably true, yet there are certain speculators that take upon them to correct all the governments in the world and to govern them by certain notions and fancies of their own, and are transported with so great confidence and opinion of them that they think all states and kingdoms and governments must presently conform to them. And these are some of the notions they vent. That there can be no qualifications or modifications of the power of a sovereign prince, but that he may make, repeal, and alter what laws he pleases, impose what taxes he pleases, derogate from his subjects' property how and when he please.... Those wild propositions are 1. Utterly false. 2. Against all natural justice. 3. Pernicious to the government. 4. Destructive to the common good and safety of the government. 5. Without any shadow of law or reason to support them.

Thus far Sir Matthew Hale.

He certainly leaves little doubt as to his own views on the question at issue, or as to his opinion of the views of the "speculators" who have opposed them, Hobbes in particular. His own notion of sovereignty seems practically indistinguishable from Bodin's. In what important way, I may ask in addition, can it be distinguished from the view of Samuel Adams? No doubt both reject the "wild propositions" of Hobbes, and Hale gives his reasons, supported by many precedents, all of which I have had to omit.

Sir William Holdsworth's comments on these passages from Lord Hale seem slightly naïve. They occur in a lecture delivered a few years ago in the Law School of Northwestern University. "Even at the end of the seventeenth century", he writes, "the theory of sovereignty was either very loosely held, or even misunderstood both by statesmen and lawyers. Hobbes, the one Englishman who had really grasped the theory, failed to influence his contemporaries because his theories were defeated by statesmen like Clarendon, by lawyers like Hale, and of course by all theologians." Lord Hale, according to Holdsworth, was particularly dense in regard to these matters. "He interpreted sovereignty as meaning simply a supremacy, which was not incompatible with the supremacy of Parliament or the law in their several spheres. This sovereignty he attributed to the king; and then proceeds to show that the sovereignty, which Hobbes analysed and explained, was contrary to the rules of English law." Sir William Holdsworth's puzzled amazement at Lord Hale's strange opinions, as indicated in the sentence just quoted, is probably natural enough in a convinced Austinian. It is almost as though the great chief justice had stood on his head in his own court. That Lord Hale, of all men, should announce such a view of sovereignty seems wellnigh incredible. How could anyone as learned as Sir Matthew Hale possibly differ from "the one Englishman who had really grasped the theory"! But may it be, after all, that it is not Hale who misunderstands Hobbes, but Holdsworth who misunderstands Hale? Or do I misunderstand Holdsworth?

There is clearly a misunderstanding *somewhere*. It is even conceivable that "the one Englishman who had really grasped the theory" had failed to grasp it quite all. Perhaps, in the long run, Lord Chancellor Northington, in supporting the Declaratory Act of 1766, was wise when he said, "My Lords, I seek for the liberty and constitution of this Kingdom no farther back than the Revolution; there I make my stand." It certainly was the safer course. Although modern historians in agreement with Northington's constitutional views have not always been quite as frank as he, one suspects that their actual procedure has often been not far different from his, and their occasional excursions back beyond the Revolution have usually given further proof of the Chancellor's good judgment.

But be all this as it may, I think I have at least succeeded in placing old Samuel Adams in fairly distinguished company, and perhaps in establishing the right to put to the modern Whig historians and to the American lawyers and historians in their wake—which I fear means most of them—one simple question: How do you manage to justify the conduct of John Hampden, and at the same time to condemn the theory of Samuel Adams?

But, it may be asked, why dig up these ancient precedents and views? If Lord Chancellor Northington in 1766 was content to go back no farther than the Revolution, why should Adams do it two years later, or why should we do it now? Whether the king had an arbitrary power in Charles I's time, as Filmer says, or whether he had not, parliament, which succeeded him as sovereign, surely had. Blackstone says so!

I am afraid our American lawyers and historians have too often been content to leave it at that; but should such an easy answer satisfy us? Can one be content to leave the question there? And this is no merely academic matter. A settlement of the far-reaching issues facing us in America now, if it were to follow the lines of Filmer's and Austin's thought, might easily lead us to the arbitrary government based on popular support which lately tore up the Weimar Constitution and overrides all limitations in Germany to-day. Or shall we, instead, retain the view of Samuel Adams, that the constitution is fixed, and that the limits set in it cannot be overpassed, not even by the sovereign?

If we do, we must be ready to accept the gibe that we are "medieval", and in Professor Pollard's view, and Sir William Holdsworth's, undeveloped or "rudimentary" when compared with Hobbes or Austin; but to a mere medievalist like myself such a gibe is not after all a very terrifying one. I venture therefore still to prefer Bodin to Hobbes, Hale to Blackstone, Camden to Mansfield, and Maitland to Holdsworth; and with Maitland I cannot but agree, though probably for very different reasons, that "j.a. [John Austin] = o°". If this is distasteful to the modernist as a "medieval restoration", I must ask him to make the most of it. For if his modernism is nothing more than a revamped Austinianism, probably the best present-day representative of it is Herr Hitler.

V

DUE PROCESS OF LAW IN MAGNA CARTA[1]

The famous thirty-ninth chapter of King John's Charter of Liberties, or the twenty-ninth of Henry III's reissue of 1225, through which it was mainly known to our ancestors, "the palladium of our liberties"—"Nullus liber homo capiatur, vel imprisonetur, aut disseisiatur, aut utlagetur, aut exuletur, aut aliquo modo destruatur, nec super eum ibimus, nec super eum mittemus, nisi per legale judicium parium suorum vel per legem terre"—is now regarded by some eminent historians not as a document of popular liberty, but rather as one of feudal reaction. They consider it a concession to the demands of the barons for a return to the feudal anarchy of Stephen's time and a repeal of the great administrative measures by which Henry II and his predecessors were moulding a national judicial system, and thus preparing the way for a common law.

Mr McKechnie, for example, says: "The clause was, after all allowance has been made, a reactionary one, tending to the

[1] On the general subject, see especially Sir Edward Coke's *Second Institute*, pp. 45 *et seq.*; Sir William Blackstone, *The Great Charter and the Charter of the Forest* (also included among his Tracts); Richard Thomson, *An Historical Essay on the Magna Charta of King John* (1829); Ch. Bémont, *Chartes des Libertés Anglaises* (1892); W. S. McKechnie, *Magna Carta* (1905); L. W. Vernon Harcourt, *His Grace the Steward and Trial of Peers* (1907); George B. Adams, *The Origin of the English Constitution* (1912). Narrative accounts are found in Stubbs's *Constitutional History*, vol. 1; Kate Norgate's *John Lackland* (1902); Sir J. H. Ramsay's *Angevin Empire* (1903) and elsewhere.

Of the commentaries the four recent ones are all of great value. Bémont gives most of the texts, with a valuable introduction. McKechnie's *Magna Carta* is the fullest modern commentary on the whole Charter. Harcourt quotes and employs many authorities outside the Charter and is very suggestive. Professor Adams's account of chapter 39, though brief, is probably the most carefully considered of all. To all these the commentary here given owes very much.

restoration of feudal privileges and feudal jurisdictions, inimical alike to the Crown and to the growth of really popular liberties."[1]

M. Petit-Dutaillis agrees with this view—the political conceptions of the baronage in the struggle were "childish and anarchical". "The English nobility of that day has not the idea of law at all";[2] and it is expressed also by Pollock and Maitland in their great history of the English law:

> Even in the most famous words of the charter we may detect a feudal claim which will only cease to be dangerous when in course of time men have distorted their meaning:—a man is entitled to the judgment of his peers; the king's justices are no peers for earls or barons.... In after days it is possible for men to worship the words "*nisi per legale judicium parium suorum vel per legem terrae*"...because it was possible to misunderstand them.[3]

This is a radical and revolutionary departure from the traditional view held from the fourteenth to the nineteenth century, that in this chapter we have our classical statement of the right of the subject to a trial "by due Process of the Common law",[4] our greatest constitutional check upon arbitrary infringements of the liberty of the individual, whose ultimate effect was "to give and to guarantee full protection for property and person to every human being who breathes English air".[5]

Some centuries of decisions have thoroughly established this traditional interpretation as a matter of law, and have given it a legal validity entirely independent of its origin in 1215. Nevertheless it is rather startling, and to the legal historian interesting, to find the constitution makers in our states,

[1] *Magna Carta*, p. 449.
[2] *Studies and Notes Supplementary to Stubbs's "Constitutional History"* (English translation), p. 143.
[3] *History of English Law*, 2nd ed. I, p. 173, n. 3. See also Professor Edward Jenks, "The Myth of Magna Carta", *Independent Review*, IV, p. 260 (1904), for a more extreme statement.   [4] 2 Inst. 50.
[5] *The Rise and Progress of the English Constitution*, by Sir Edward Creasy, 13th ed. p. 151, n. Sir Edward Creasy was Chief Justice of Ceylon.

in the twentieth century, prescribing in the exact words of the barons of the thirteenth a *judicium parium* which may now turn out to have been originally merely a protection of the immunity of the great lords from national control, and nothing more than a guarantee of their "liberties" of trying their own feudal dependents in their own courts by the customs of their own fiefs.[1] A consideration of this question should hardly be regarded by an English or American lawyer a matter of antiquarian interest merely. In dealing with it, however, he is confronted with a number of historical problems of considerable difficulty. Almost every word of this famous enactment, in fact, brings up a difficulty and a controversy.

One of these appears with the first words—*nullus liber homo.*[2] To whom was this protection intended to apply in 1215?

---

[1] For example, the constitution of Virginia, in 1902, Article I, Section 8, "that no man shall be deprived of his life, or liberty, except by the law of the land, or the judgment of his peers". The Delaware constitution of 1897, I, 7, has: "He [the accused in a criminal prosecution] shall not be compelled to give evidence against himself, nor shall he be deprived of life, liberty or property, unless by the judgment of his peers or by the law of the land."

Cf. the Massachusetts constitution of 1780, Part I, Article XII: "and no subject shall be arrested, imprisoned, despoiled, or deprived of his property, immunities, or privileges, put out of the protection of the law, exiled, or deprived of his life, liberty, or estate, but by the judgment of his peers, or the law of the land."

Similar expressions occur in the Kentucky constitution of 1890 and in earlier constitutions in Maine, Missouri, North Carolina, Pennsylvania, Rhode Island, etc.

Some state constitutions have "without due process of law", or similar expressions, instead. For example, Oklahoma's constitution of 1907, South Carolina's of 1895, South Dakota's of 1889, and many others, made both before and after the Fourteenth Amendment to the Federal Constitution.

See the various constitutions in Thorpe's *Constitutions* and the note in Cooley's *Constitutional Limitations*, p. 353.

[2] In Number 29 of the Articles of the Barons, the demands on which Magna Carta was based, the expression used is "*Ne corpus liberi hominis*" (Stubbs, *Select Charters*, p. 293).

Shall we adopt the traditional view that this included "every human being who breathes English air",[1] and thus extend its guarantees to villains, as Coke did?[2] Shall we accept the more restricted application of the words preferred by McKechnie, which includes freeholders merely?[3] Or shall we accept the still narrower interpretation, including only tenants by military tenure, insisted on in the seventeenth century by old Robert Brady, "Doctor in Physick", who says "*liberi homines* most properly were those which held in *Military*, or *Knights Service*, and in this sense of the words, all the *Earls*, *Barons*, *Knights*, and *others* that held *Knights Fees*, or *part* of *Knights Fees*, were called and esteemed *Freemen*".[4]

This question, it is obvious, is a fundamental one, and our interpretation of the whole chapter will in large part depend upon what solution we adopt. If the grantees here include none but feudal lords, then we must dismiss the rest of the people as "only followers", who merely "helped to augment the noise".

If *liberi homines* include men of lower degree, we may continue to hold, as Stubbs does, that "It is the collective people who really form the other high contracting party in the great capitulation",[5] and that the Charter is therefore "the

---

[1] *Ante*, p. 87.   [2] 2 Inst. 45.
[3] *Magna Carta*, pp. 448–9.
[4] *An Introduction to the Old English History* (1684), Glossary, p. 50. This would restrict the *liber homo* to the tenant-in-chief of the King, holding by feudal tenure, or a mesne lord, holding by a similar tenure, and could extend no further down in the feudal hierarchy than the holder of a knight's fee. "These were the *Freemen*", says Brady, "which made such a *Cry* for their *Liberties*, (as appears by *Magna Charta*, most of which is only an *Abatement* of the *Rigour*, and a *Relaxation* of the *Feudal Tenures*) the rest were but only *Followers*, and helped to *augment* the *Noise*; they were no *Law-Makers*,...for 'tis not probable, that those Men that had the Force of the Nation, would permit Men of *small Reputation* to share with them in *Law-Making*. Those that had the Power of this, and other Nations *de facto*, always did give Laws, and Tax the People" (*ibid.* p. 51). Brady was physician-in-ordinary to Charles II and James II.
[5] *Constitutional History*, I, 6th ed. p. 570.

first great public act of the nation, after it has realized its own identity".[1]

The verbs *ibimus* and *mittemus* have also given rise to widely varying interpretations. The prevailing construction has been Sir Edward Coke's, that

No man shall be condemned at the king's suite, either before the king in his bench, where the pleas are *coram rege* (and so are the words, *nec super eum ibimus*, to be understood) nor before any other commissioner, or judge whatsoever, and so are the words, *nec super eum mittemus*, to be understood, but by the judgement of his peers, that is, equalls, or according to the law of the land.[2]

This view was adopted by Hallam,[3] and has apparently been accepted in more recent times by Mr Pike in his *Constitutional History of the House of Lords*.[4] This is the most generally accepted version of *ibimus* and *mittemus* and makes them refer exclusively to the form of judicial procedure admissible.

Mr McKechnie's reading of these words is altogether different:

Their object was to prevent John from substituting violence for legal process; from taking the law into his own hands and "going against them" with an army at his back, or "sending against them" in similar wise. He must never again attack *per vim et arma* men unjudged and uncondemned.... It was the use of brute force, not merely a limited form of legal process, which John in these words renounced.[5]

It was, in short, not the manner of judicial procedure, but the complete absence of it that constituted the grievance underlying this provision.

Here is a divergence of construction of the most far-reaching character in its effect upon our interpretation of chapter 39 as a whole.

[1] *Ibid.* p. 571.   [2] 2 Inst. 46.
[3] *Middle Ages*, ch. 8, pt. 2, § 10. He translates *ibimus*: "Nor will we pass upon him."
[4] P. 169. He translates *ibimus* and *mittemus*: "Nor will we proceed against him, or direct proceedings against him."
[5] *Magna Carta*, pp. 447–8.

Still another arises upon the words, "by the legal judgment of his peers" (*per legale judicium parium suorum*).

The accepted equivalent of this famous phrase has been, up to recent times, trial by jury. "I believe that the trial by peers here spoken of means trial by jury", says Sir Edward Creasy. "The words will bear this meaning; it is certainly impossible to give them any other satisfactory meaning, and it is idle to suppose that they were thus introduced into the Great Charter without being designed to be seriously significant."[1]

Curiously enough, however, Sir Edward Coke seems hardly to have accepted this view,[2] and in recent years almost all historians seem to have rejected it. "It is now generally admitted that the phrase *judicium parium* does not point to trial by jury."[3] Rather it seems to require that the new trial by jury is to give way, in cases where the rights of feudal lords are involved, to the familiar older procedure by judgment of the lords of the fief, who are the suitors and peers of the court —*pares curtis*. In the different interpretations of this expression,

[1] *The Rise and Progress of the English Constitution*, p. 221. This view was accepted in the courts at a very early date. Just at the opening of the fourteenth century there is an interesting case of a knight arraigned before the King's justices for rape, who objects that he is a knight, and therefore entitled to a trial by his peers—"Ego sum miles, et non debeo judicari nisi per meos pares." To this the justice answers, "Since you are a Knight, we are willing that you be judged by your peers"—*per vestros pares*, and, the reporter adds, "Knights were named". The accused was satisfied with this, but excepted to those jurymen who had already been on the jury, which presented him—"In pares meos consentiam, sed non in duodecim per quos sum accusatus" (Year book, 30–31 Edw. I (Rolls Series), p. 531). Here it is clear, *first*, that the *pares* are a trial jury; *second*, that such a jury is believed to comply with the requirement for a *judicium parium*; *third*, that a knight is believed to be entitled to this protection; *fourth*, that the requirements are not complied with if a knight is tried by a jury of men of lower status.

Numberless citations of this interpretation could be made from the law reports, both English and American, and from other sources. It has been the generally accepted interpretation. Barrington, in his *Observations on the Statutes*, written in the eighteenth century, tacitly assumes that no other is possible; and all our constitutions, state and federal, assume it.

[2] 2 Inst. 48, 49.   [3] Pollock and Maitland, I, p. 173, n. 3.

then, we find another divergence of view which touches the very foundations of our constitutional system.

In like manner there has been much discussion as to whether the particle *vel*, which connects *judicium parium* with the expression *per legem terrae*, really means *or*—thus making the procedure *per legem terrae* an alternative to the *judicium parium*, and therefore different and distinct from it—or *and*, which would make *judicium parium* and *per legem terrae* simply different parts of the same procedure, and complementary to each other, instead of being alternative, mutually exclusive, antithetical, or in any way incompatible one with the other. It is, of course, a question of no small importance whether judgment of peers is merely a regular procedure *per legem terrae*, or rather something exceptional, outside and beyond "due process of law".

Hallam suggested, in a rather hesitating way, that *vel* should properly be read *and*.[1] This construction is also adopted by Pollock and Maitland,[2] and Professor G. B. Adams,[3] while Mr McKechnie considers the matter "almost beyond doubt".[4] To Mr Vernon Harcourt, on the other hand, this interpretation seems the "acme of absurdity,...a violation of the most elementary principles".[5]

In our consideration of chapter 39, we have in the last place to reckon also with the widely different views now held as to the meaning of *lex terrae*, in some respects the most important phrase in the whole provision.

---

[1] "This really seems as good as any of the disjunctive interpretations, but I do not offer it with much confidence" (*Middle Ages*, ch. 8, pt. 2, n. 16). Hallam, of course, in *judicium parium* read trial by jury, which he naturally thought not inconsistent with "the law of the land".

[2] *History of English Law*, I, p. 173, n. 3.

[3] *The Origin of the English Constitution*, pp. 262 *et seq.*

[4] *Magna Carta*, pp. 442–3. Mr McKechnie, as we shall see, considers the *lex terrae* here merely as the method of proof which follows automatically on the pronouncing of the *judicium*. *And* is therefore the only possible reading of *vel*.

[5] *His Grace the Steward and Trial of Peers*, p. 244.

Just as in the interpretation of *judicium parium*, we have for *lex terrae* also a traditional reading sanctioned by some centuries of unhesitating acceptance, and inextricably woven into our fabric of existing constitutional law. This interpretation is well expressed by Coke's classical phrase, "due process of law". But this view, though so long accepted, has, like "trial by jury", recently been the object of minute examination, and some historians have rejected it altogether.

In Mr McKechnie's view, for instance, the barons of 1215 had no conception of any "law of the land" in the sense conveyed by that expression to-day. They meant by the expression *lex terrae* to include nothing more than the modes of trial then in common use. *Lex terrae*, then, means merely a form of procedure, "wager of law", for example. It has nothing to do with substantive law or national customs. "The Great Charter promised that no plea, civil or criminal, should henceforth be decided against any freeman until he had failed in the customary 'proof'—whether battle, or ordeal, or otherwise."[1]

This view of the procedural character of the ancient *lex terrae* is held, apparently, by Mr M. M. Bigelow, though he would add presentment by a grand jury to the three older methods included by Mr McKechnie.[2] The great authority of Selden is also upon this side.[3] It needs little reflection, however, to see what havoc such a reading would play with the accepted view of Magna Carta.

In attempting an explanation of these difficult and important

---

[1] *Magna Carta*, p. 441.   [2] *History of Procedure*, p. 155, n. 3.
[3] "I would *English* it thus: ...*or by trial of him by oath, or wager, and doing his law. Lex terrae* here is only as it signifies in *amittere legem terrae*. And *ley gager*, and a jury are the two trials, as I suppose, there thought on....Every one knows that at this day *vadiare legem*, is to offer the oath upon trial that way, and *facere legem* is to make the oath. All which shew that *lex* and *lex terrae*, signify in this notion only the oath of a man not disabled by law" ("Notes on Sir John Fortescue, *De laudibus legum Angliae*, ch. 26", *Works*, edited by Wilkins, III, cols. 1895–6. These Notes were first published in 1616).

expressions of chapter 39 of Magna Carta, the investigator must, so far as he can, try to rethink the thoughts of the barons at Runnymede—"Contemporanea expositio est fortissima in lege".[1] To do so, the obvious place to turn to first will be the other provisions of the Charter itself. If this fail, recourse may be had to other documents contemporaneous with the Charter, or nearly so, together with an examination of the antecedents of Magna Carta and the circumstances which led up to the grant. It is proposed here to examine briefly the most important of the problems raised by these ambiguous expressions of the Charter by recourse to these three sources of information. The application of the first two—similar expressions within and without the Charter—calls for no explanation. But to apply the third—the antecedents of the Charter and the circumstances of its granting—requires some preliminary statement of the nature and importance of these prior documents and the events which lay behind the words of 1215. The series should probably begin with the coronation charter of Henry I, section 13.[2]

---

[1] 2 Inst. 11.

[2] Liebermann, *Gesetze der Angelsachsen*, I, p. 522. The investigation might, of course, be pushed back still further, for Henry I's charter was not without precedents. But this would involve the whole controversy as to origins. The traditional view asserted in extreme form by Freeman and stated very decidedly, though more moderately, by Stubbs, assigns a national and an English origin to both the form and the substance of Henry's charter. Its form is to be traced back through some transactions of the two Williams ultimately to the coronation oath of the Anglo-Saxon kings, whose provisions are known to us as administered by Dunstan to Ethelred (Liebermann, *Gesetze*, I, pp. 214–17). The substance of Henry's charter, according to this view, is, in the main, the *Laga Edwardi*, or traditional law enjoyed by Englishmen before the Conquest. See also Mr R. L. Poole, in *English Historical Review*, XXVIII, p. 444 (July 1913).

The non-national or feudal interpretation of Henry's charter, on the other hand, finds the formal origin of the Charter in such Norman grants as the Conqueror's famous charter to London, and its substance in feudal rather than in immemorial English custom. (See the article by Mr Henry L. Cannon, "The Character and Antecedents of the Charter of Liberties

"Lagam regis Eadwardi vobis reddo cum illis emendationibus quibus pater meus eam emendauit consilio baronum
suorum" (I restore to you the law of King Edward, together
with those amendments by which my father, with the advice
of his barons, amended it).

Passing over the two charters of Stephen and the brief and

of Henry I", in *American Historical Review*, xv, p. 37.) There is much
to be said for this newer feudal view. Any consideration of the provisions
of Henry's charter will show how large the feudal abuses bulk in it; and
certainly many of these provisions are susceptible of an interpretation
other than the national one hitherto insisted upon as the only one. But
does this in itself warrant the statement that all these elements are introduced at or after the Conquest? Was there such an antithesis as this new
school implies between what was national and what was feudal? It may
be true that English institutions had taken on a far more definitely feudal
form than ever before. The language of the feudal law, if nothing else,
would prove that. England, it is certain, had become the fief of a Norman
lord, and its laws were now ordinarily the customs of that fief, "found"
in feudal fashion by the tenants-in-chief as suitors in the lords' court, the
Curia Regis.

But even though their form had greatly changed, why should not
many of these customs have had an English origin? Henry I's charter,
it is true, promises a restoration of the Law of King Edward only "together
with" the amendments made to it by William I; but still it is the *Laga
Edwardi.* And the whole provision is little more than a repetition of an
earlier one of the Conqueror himself—which is too significant to be
overlooked—"this also I ordain and desire,—that all should have and
hold the law of Edward the King, as to lands and to all things, with those
additions which I have made for the good of the people of the English"
(Liebermann, *Gesetze*, I, p. 488).

Another provision of William provides that every Norman "who in
the time of King Edward, my relative, was in England and subject to
the dues of the English which they call lot and scot, shall pay according
to the law of the English" (Liebermann, *Gesetze*, I, p. 487). Though the
additions here referred to were all in the direction of a completer feudalism,
the maker of them himself asserts that the basis of the law "in terris et in
omnibus rebus" is to remain the law of Edward, the King, his *antecessor*
and *propinquus*; and Henry I's charter merely reiterates it.

Even without the evidence of these enactments of William I, or the
well-known fact that there was many a Norman in England before 1066
"*particeps consuetudinum Anglorum*", there are other reasons for believing
that no sharp antithesis must be imagined to exist between the *lex*

colourless one issued at the coronation of Henry II—few
promises were necessary in his case, or in Richard's or John's,
where the succession was undisputed and we find no coronation charters at all—we come to the year 1213. In that year
the barons refused to follow John across the sea unless he first
received absolution of his excommunication. Thereupon the
bishops were recalled who had been exiled during the struggle
with Innocent III, and Stephen Langton absolved John at

Anglorum and feudal custom. The coronation charter of Henry I was
largely a bid for feudal support, lay and clerical.

The royal "election" so purchased, instead of being the corporate act
of a national assembly, is probably to be considered rather as the individual
adherence of a number of powerful feudal magnates sufficient to secure
for Henry control of the treasury and the machinery of government,
thus making possible what was more important than any such "election"
—the coronation.

The feudal character of Henry's charter is emphasized by the fact that
it is the first official act of the king, ratifying these previous promises by
which the kingship had been obtained. Henry's charter is significant
because it was a *coronation* charter. But it was not the last of its kind.
Stephen came to the throne under circumstances much the same. The
rules of succession to the throne were not yet definitely fixed, as now.
His accession was purchased at a higher price than Henry's, and the
obligations he then incurred, as much as anything else, made his reign
a failure. It is clear that his "election" was an affair of individual barons
rather than of "Parliament", as a national assembly. From what we
know of elections in the Church (see Esmein, *L'unanimité et la majorité
dans les élections canoniques*, Mélanges Fitting, I, p. 355), together with
other evidence, we may assume that the person so "elected" would
ordinarily be presented to the people and received by them by popular
acclamation; but it would be rash to assert that any such "ratification"
was a constitutional necessity, or that the crowd so assenting was anything
but a fortuitous local gathering. The coronation was possibly the most
important element of all, for, as Mr Round says, "Election was a matter
of opinion; coronation a matter of fact" (*Geoffrey de Mandeville*, p. 6).
Even if we had no evidence for it in the chronicles (see Round, *Geoffrey
de Mandeville*, pp. 2, 3, and notes), the importance of the coronation
would furnish a key to some of the concessions to the Church made in
the charters.

The facts just cited go far to explain the early series of coronation
charters, and they furnish a ground for the belief that these charters are
fulfilments of promises made in return for feudal support necessary to

Winchester. But not until he had exacted from the King certain important promises under oath, which are given as follows by Roger of Wendover and repeated by Matthew Paris:

Moreover, in that absolution, the King swore, touching the holy gospels, that he would cherish, defend and maintain the holy Church and its ordained against all their adversaries, so far as in him lay, and that he would restore the good laws of his ancestors,

secure the "election". These promises mainly concern feudal matters, because only the great lay and ecclesiastical barons were strong enough to be worth bidding for. All this tends to support the feudal theory. Must it follow, however, that these feudal concessions are inconsistent with the *Lex Anglorum*, which, we are told distinctly, was retained by the Conqueror?

To me the results of Mr Chadwick's *Studies* seem significant here. From a careful study of the Anglo-Saxon Chronicle and other sources, he concludes that a royal "election" in England in the eighth century was not greatly different from what we have seen in the time of Henry I or Stephen. "I suspect then," he says, "that the 'election' of a king was originally the selection or acceptance of an overlord, and that the 'electors' acted not as the representatives of the nation but as individuals, though they naturally carried their own dependents with them" (*Studies on Anglo-Saxon Institutions*, p. 365).

It is misleading, then, to place before the student of history the dilemma of rejecting a feudal interpretation of Henry I's charter or accepting the *Laga Edwardi* as ancient national custom. Feudal custom and national law did not become incompatible through the changes introduced by the Norman kings, important as those changes were. There is no need of explaining away the term *Laga Edwardi*, as used by William or Henry. There is necessarily no antagonism between it and feudal custom.

English law at this time was both national and feudal, and possibly had long been so. It was now more definitely the law of a fief, but its substance was not necessarily wholly altered for that. In order to prove the feudal character of Henry's charter, we need not disprove all connection with the old coronation oath.

The private compilation drawn up early in the twelfth century, and known as the *Leges Edwardi Confessoris*, is no authority, and in no direct way corresponds to the *Laga Edwardi* of Henry's charter. Nevertheless, the story with which it opens is thoroughly consonant with the ideas of customary law then prevailing: "In the fourth year after the accession of William as King of that land, with the counsel of his barons he caused to be summoned in all the counties of the land the English nobles, wise and especially the laws of King Edward, that he would remove abuses, and would judge all his men according to the just judgments of his court and restore to each his rights.

This last is the significant part:

juravit rex...quodque bonas leges antecessorum suorum, et praecipue leges Eadwardi regis, revocaret, et iniquas destrueret, et omnes homines suos secundum justa curiae suae judicia judicaret, quodque singulis redderet jura sua.[1]

men, and learned in their law, in order that he might hear their customs from their own lips. These being chosen from each of the counties of the whole country, first declared upon oath in his presence, that, so far as possible, in a straightforward way, they would make known the provisions of their laws and customs, passing over nothing, changing nothing through deceit" (Liebermann, *Gesetze*, I, p. 627).

Of more authority, but tending to the same result is the statement in the *Dialogus de Scaccario* (I, 16): "Cum insignis ille subactor Anglie, rex Willelmus...ulteriores insule fines suo subiugasset imperio et rebellium mentes terribilibus perdomuisset exemplis, ne libera de cetero daretur erroris facultas, decreuit subiectum sibi populum iuri scripto legibusque subicere. Propositis igitur legibus Anglicanis secundum tripartitam earum distinctionem, hoc est Merchenelage, Danelage, Westsexenlage, quasdam, reprobauit, quasdam autem approbans illis transmarinas Neustrie leges que ad regni pacem tuendam efficacissime videbantur, adiecit."

Both these statements correspond very closely with the enactments of the Conqueror and the charter of Henry I, quoted above. Whatever conception of feudalism we adopt, or whatever our belief may be regarding the feudal or non-feudal character of institutions in England before 1066, or regarding the nature of the English laws which William "approved" and the character of the *Neustrie leges* which he "added" as "emendations" of them; there is no ground for rejecting these clear statements that a certain part of the ancient native law was actually retained, and no particular reason for refusing to identify it with the *Laga Edwardi*. On the general subject see Freeman, *Reign of William Rufus*, II, pp. 356–7; *Norman Conquest*, IV, pp. 323–5, V, pp. 149–53; Round, *Feudal England*, pp. 225 *et seq.*; Pollock and Maitland, I, Bk. I, ch. 3; G. B. Adams, *American Historical Review*, VII, p. 11, "Origin of the English Constitution", ch. i, with note B. See also the charter of William I to London, Liebermann, *Gesetze*, I, p. 486; Leis Willelme, prol. *ibid.* pp. 492–3; Quadripartitus, Argumentum, *ibid.* p. 535; Prefatio, § 12, *ibid.* p. 543.

[1] Roger of Wendover (Rolls Series), II, p. 81; Matthew Paris, *Chronica Majora* (Rolls Series), II, p. 550.

Within a few weeks events happened which serve to explain the meaning of this oath and to show John's utter disregard of it. John ordered the barons to accompany him to Poitou. The northern barons refused, and John proceeded to the North with a mercenary army to bring them back to obedience. At Northampton he was overtaken by Archbishop Langton, who had followed him to protest against the expedition, "saying that it amounted to the greatest breach of his oath which he had taken on his absolution, if he made war against anyone without a judgment of his court".[1] John, in a rage, ordered Langton about his business, but the archbishop followed him with threats of excommunication for his men, "and did not leave him until he had secured for the barons a day suitable for their appearing at the court of the King, and there submitting to the law".[2]

Meanwhile, at a council at St Albans, it was proclaimed at the King's instance, "that the laws of Henry his ancestor were to be observed by all in the realm, and all evil laws were to be wholly void".[3] But there was a more direct reference made to the charter of Henry I about this time, if Roger of Wendover is to be believed. He mentions a current rumour that in August 1213, just before starting north to prevent John's

---

[1] "Dicens, plurimum in injuriam sui sacramenti, quod in absolutione sua praestiterat, redundare, si absque judicio curiae suae contra quempiam bellum faceret" (Roger of Wendover, II, p. 83). Matthew Paris has "contra quempiam, nedum suos homines geniales bellum moveret" (*Historia Anglorum* (Rolls Series), II, p. 142).

[2] "Non prius ab eo recessit donec diem competentem ad curiam regis veniendi et ibidem juri parendi baronibus impetrasset" (Matthew Paris, *Chronica Majora*, II, pp. 551–2).

[3] "Praeceptum est quatenus leges Henrici avi sui ab omnibus in regno custodiantur et omnes leges iniquae penitus enerventur" (Wendover, II, p. 82).

"What those laws were," says Stubbs, "does not seem to have been ascertained until the twenty-fifth of the same month, when the archbishop produced the charter of Henry I" (Stubbs, *Historical Introductions to the Rolls Series, Walter of Coventry*, p. 474, n. 2. He refers to the meeting at St Paul's).

attack on the northern barons, Archbishop Langton, at a council of magnates held in St Paul's, called some of them aside,

and began to address them secretly, as follows: "You have heard", said he, "how at Winchester I absolved the King and compelled him to swear that he would do away with the bad laws and would restore the good laws, to wit, the laws of Edward, and cause them to be observed in the realm by all. Now also a certain charter of Henry first, King of England, has been found, through which, if you are willing, you may restore the liberties long lost to their former condition."[1]

Then came John's disastrous campaign ending at Bouvines. At a meeting held late in the year 1214 at St Albans, the opposition of the barons came to a head. The charter of Henry was again produced, and the barons swore that if the King refused to grant the liberties they sought they would renounce their fealty to him until he confirmed their demands by a charter over his seal. They agreed to present these demands to the King after Christmas and meantime to prepare for an armed conflict if he refused them.[2]

The promised meeting for presenting their demands occurred at the Temple in London after the New Year. The account of it given by Roger of Wendover,[3] and repeated word for word by Matthew Paris,[4] is very significant:

Coming there to the King in full military array, the aforesaid magnates demanded the confirmation of certain liberties and laws of King Edward along with other liberties conceded to them and the realm of England and the English Church, as contained in writing in the charter of King Henry I and the laws aforesaid. Besides, they asserted that at the time of his absolution at Winchester he had promised those laws and ancient liberties, and had become bound to an observance of them by a personal oath.[5]

---

[1] Roger of Wendover, II, pp. 83-4.
[2] Matthew Paris, *Chronica Majora*, II, pp. 582-3.
[3] II, p. 113.   [4] *Chronica Majora*, II, p. 584.
[5] "Venientes ad regem ibidem supradicti magnates in lascivo satis apparatu militari, petierunt quasdam libertates et leges regis Eadwardi

This was the first formal statement of the barons' demands made to the King. John asked for time to consider, and it was granted. He employed the time to reissue his charter of freedom of election to the Church, directed the oath of allegiance and fealty to be taken to him throughout the realm, and took the vow of a crusader, in order to brand all attack on him as sacrilege.

The barons were also active,[1] and when the truce expired they marched in arms to Brackley in Northamptonshire, where they presented to the King's emissaries a *cedula* of their demands "made up for the most part of the ancient laws and customs of the realm".[2]

On hearing it read, John rejected it with fury and curses and

cum aliis libertatibus, sibi et regno Angliae et ecclesiae Anglicanae concessis, confirmari, prout in charta regis Henrici primi et legibus praedictis adscriptae continentur; asserebant praeterea, quod tempore suae absolutionis apud Wintoniam illas leges et libertates antiquas promiserat et ad observationem earum sit obligatus per proprium juramentum."

[1] Both parties appealed to the Pope. John's emissary, William Mauclerc, wrote back to the King that representatives of the barons were urging the Pope to compel John to grant their demands for "their ancient liberties, confirmed by charters of your ancestors and by your own personal oath" (*antiquas libertates suas, per cartas antecessorum vestrorum et proprio juramento vestro confirmatas*). Rymer's *Foedera* (ed. of 1816), I, p. 120. The oath was, no doubt, John's oath at the time of his absolution in 1213.

[2] Roger of Wendover, II, p. 115. "The items also of the laws and liberties which the magnates there demanded confirmation of were written in part in the charter of King Henry a little earlier, in part were taken from the ancient laws of King Edward, as a later history of the time declares" (Matthew Paris, *Chronica Majora*, II, p. 586). "A schedule ...in which were included the laws and liberties written in the charter of Henry First and certain pious and just laws of King Edward" (Matthew Paris, *Historia Anglorum*, II, p. 155).

Whether the *cedula* was the same as the document now generally spoken of as the "Unknown Charter of Liberties" or not is a point much disputed. See a summary of the various views in regard to it in Petit-Dutaillis, *Studies*, pp. 116 *et seq*. The part of the Unknown Charter important for us is its first provision: "Concedit rex Johannes quod non capiet hominem absque judicio."

proceeded to strengthen his strongholds. But in a few days he himself made a counter proposal which is of the greatest importance. In May, 1215, he issued letters patent in part as follows:

> Be it known that we have conceded to our barons who are against us that we will neither arrest nor disseize them or their men, and we will not go upon them by force or by arms, except according to the law of the realm or pursuant to the judgment of their peers in our court (*quod nec eos nec homines suos capiemus nec dissaisiemus nec super eos per vim vel per arma ibimus nisi per legem regni nostri vel per judicium parium suorum in curia nostra*) until consideration shall be had by four whom we shall choose from our side and by four whom they shall choose from their side and the lord Pope, who shall be superior over them, etc.[1]

This was rejected in turn by the barons, who formally renounced their fealty to John and marched on London, where they were welcomed by the richer citizens at least.[2]

After some weeks of negotiation and intrigue, John finally consented to grant the demands of the barons, and they set the meeting for 15 June, at Runnymede. The barons presented their demands probably in the document known as the Articles of the Barons, which has been preserved to our day.[3]

---

[1] *Rot. Pat.* I, p. 141, reprinted in Rymer (ed. of 1816), I, p. 128, and in Blackstone's *Charters*.

The Pope, in his bull of August 1215 annulling Magna Carta, refers to these letters patent as promising to remove "all the abuses" then existing (*promittens quod ante omnia revocaret universos abusus quicumque fuissent in Angliam suo tempore introducti*) (Bémont, *Chartes*, p. 43). It can hardly be entirely without significance that the single promise given above is referred to as covering *universos abusus*, though too much should not be made of it.

[2] The *Liber de Antiquis Legibus* says they entered the city without resistance, and entered into a compact with the Londoners on the understanding that no peace would be made with John without the assent of both parties to it (pp. 201, 202). Wendover says the richer citizens favoured the barons and that this overawed the poorer ones (II, p. 117).

[3] For an account of the document and its history, see Blackstone's *Charters* or McKechnie's *Magna Carta*, pp. 200 *et seq.*

The clause of these Articles corresponding to chapter 39 of the Charter is the twenty-ninth, "Ne corpus liberi hominis capiatur, nec imprisonetur, nec dissaisietur, nec utlagetur, nec exuletur, nec aliquo modo destruatur, nec rex eat vel mittat super eum vi, nisi per judicium parium suorum vel per legem terrae."[1]

On the basis of these demands the Charter was drawn up and duly sealed.

These perfectly well-known facts have been placed together here only because their assistance will be necessary in interpreting the phrases of Magna Carta otherwise ambiguous. In this brief history of the years 1213–15 several things are to be noted. It seems clear that an organized and quasi-"constitutional" opposition to John is indicated here. It is aimed at the removal of a few very definite abuses. The main character of these abuses, the chief ground of complaint, and the programme of procedure for redress are all evident in the very beginning, at the time of the absolution oath in 1213. This programme is consistently followed and leads directly to Magna Carta. It was a carefully organized opposition and points to an organizing mind which originated the plan of operation and pursued it from its inception in 1213 straight to Runnymede. The organizer of opposition was Stephen Langton. He had probably never met John until he saw him at Winchester. But he was an Englishman, and during his exile had apparently pondered over the situation and determined on a plan of operation before he landed. To Langton Magna Carta is principally due.

The main point in this plan, the chief grievance to be redressed, was the King's practice of attacking his barons with forces of mercenaries, seizing their persons, their families and property, and otherwise ill-treating them, without first convicting them of some offence in his *curia*. This is the last item of the oath. It is the only thing referred to in the important letter patent of May 1215, which was issued after John knew

[1] Stubbs, *Select Charters*, p. 293.

pretty definitely what the baronial demands were. It is the substance of chapter 39.

We are not assuming too much in saying, therefore, that chapter 39 was in 1215 the most important chapter in the Charter, as it is to-day; and that it is identical in aim with the absolution oath of 1213, and designed as a fulfilment of it.

If this be true, these events and documents from 1213 to 1215 are all of a piece,[1] and every one of them, from the oath of absolution on, is of the greatest value in the interpretation of all the others. In case of need, therefore, these events and documents may be and must be employed to explain any terms of chapter 39 still remaining ambiguous after an examination of identical and similar terms in other parts of the Charter and in other contemporary documents. This is the order of procedure followed in the rest of this paper.

To return, then, to the text of chapter 39, and first to *nullus liber homo*; in its first article the grant of the Charter is declared to be "to all the free men of our realm" (*omnibus liberis hominibus regni nostri*). *Taken by itself*, this expression seems rather inclusive, and might easily bear the wide interpretation given it by Stubbs. In chapter 20 an accused *liber homo* is protected against amercements out of proportion to his offence, and the expression seems narrower in its use. Chapter 27, which provides for the distribution of the chattels of an intestate *liber homo*, and chapter 30, which protects him from the royal bailiffs in matters of purveyance, are both very vague in the use of the term. Chapter 34, however, which forbids the issuance of the Writ *Praecipe*, where "a free man may lose his court" (*unde liber homo amittere possit curiam suam*), is much more definite and clearly restricts the term to such lords as possessed a *curia* of their own. The result is singularly inconclusive. The only inference possible seems that of Professor

---

[1] Note above, pp. 97–100, especially the declaration of the barons at the Temple in London, in January 1213, when the absolution oath is specifically referred to.

Adams, "that the words *liber homo* are not used in any consistent sense in the Charter".[1]

The "prior documents" are more satisfactory.

If, as we have contended, chapter 39 is the fulfilment of John's oath of 1213, and the sequence of the intervening documents is established, then *liber homo* of the Charter means no one else than *omnes homines suos* who are to be tried only by *judicia curiae suae* under the promise of John's absolution oath.[2]

It is the same *liber homo* who is included under the "baronibus nostris" to whom the letters patent of May 1215 are directed, and under "homines suos".[3] These expressions taken by themselves can here have only one meaning, and that meaning is made still clearer by the events which preceded and followed. They include no one but John's feudal tenants-in-chief and their men. They cannot include anyone below the mesne lords or *vavassores*.[4]

The prior documents seem conclusive on this point, and they enormously restrict the scope of the chapter *as intended in 1215*.

The facts and extracts given above are also particularly valuable in determining the meaning of the verbs *ibimus* and *mittemus*, of chapter 39. As these are non-technical words, it is useless to try to determine their use here by their meaning elsewhere, in our effort to decide between the varying inter-

[1] *The Origin of the English Constitution*, p. 264. The insertion of the words, "de libero tenemento suo vel libertatibus vel liberis consuetudinibus suis" in the second reissue of *Magna Carta* in 1217, between *dissaisietur* and *aut utlagetur* of John's Charter, is variously viewed as an explanation of the meaning of the provision in 1215. By some it is regarded as indicating an extension of the provisions to further classes of men; others regard it as a restriction, both thus considering it a modification. By others it is believed to be an explanation rather than a change, and an explanation tending to strengthen a rather narrow interpretation of the original provision.

[2] *Ante*, p. 98. [3] *Ante*, p. 102.

[4] This opinion, held, as we have seen, by Brady, is held also by Professor Adams, *The Origin of the English Constitution*, pp. 264, 265.

pretations already indicated.[1] The circumstances leading to chapter 39 alone avail here. Fortunately they are conclusive. I think it will be impossible for anyone to read carefully through the extracts and documents collected on pp. 95–103 and continue to translate *ibimus* and *mittemus* "nor will we proceed against him, or direct proceedings against him".[2] The barons, in their Articles, say, "and the King shall not go against him nor send upon him *by force*" (*nec rex eat vel mittat super eum vi*).[3] John's letter patent of May 1215 is more definite still: "And we will not go upon them *by force or by arms*" (*nec super eos per vim vel per arma ibimus*).[4] They all go back to the absolution oath of 1213, where John promises to judge all his men according to the just judgments of his court.[5] It is clear that all these expressions refer not to abuses of judicial process, but to the King's practice of attacking his barons by armed force without any process whatsoever. This meaning is most clearly indicated by the words of the letter of 1215. That it is also the meaning of the oath of 1213, Stephen Langton himself puts beyond all doubt when at Northampton he warns the King that it would be a violation of that oath "*if without the judgment of his court* he should make war on anyone" (*si absque judicio curiae suae contra quempiam bellum faceret*).[6]

To me these statements do not leave a shadow of doubt that the traditional reading is wrong, and that *ibimus* and *mittemus* here refer merely to the armed attack, *without trial*, which John had employed against his barons before and after his oath of 1213 not to do so.

If *ibimus* and *mittemus* are non-technical, the very opposite is true of *per legale judicium parium suorum*. John was here

[1] *Ante*, p. 90.
[2] Pike, *Constitutional History of the House of Lords*, p. 169.
[3] *Ante*, p. 103.
[4] *Ante*, p. 102. Cf. the "Unknown Charter"—"Concedit rex Johannes quod non capiet hominem absque judicio."
[5] *Ante*, p. 98.   [6] *Ante*, p. 99.

merely promising that no armed attack should be made on the lands or persons of his tenants-in-chief or of their men, except after a judgment obtained in the ordinary course, i.e. by a *judicium parium*. This procedure here promised was nothing new. It was perfectly well understood in 1215, in England and everywhere else in feudal Europe, and had been known there for generations.

It is not judgment based on the *veredictum* of an *inquisitio* or jury that is guaranteed here. It is a judgment rendered by the *pares* of the defendant, the *pares curtis*, suitors in the same court, tenants holding of the same lord and of the same fief, his *convassalli*. This is so obvious, and now so generally accepted, that it is unnecessary to set forth here in detail the proof of it.[1]

The early disappearance after 1215 of the feudal conditions which gave rise to the *judicium parium*, and the rapid growth of a consciousness of nationality and of a really national system of representation and administration in their place, rendered men incapable of understanding the real demands of the men of 1215, and gave rise at an extraordinarily early date to the view that by *judicium parium* they meant trial by jury.

[1] The expression *sine legali judicio parium suorum* occurs in chapter 52 of the Charter, and in chapters 56 and 57, which are directed to Welsh feudatories (see *post*, p. 115). In chapter 59 the King of the Scots is promised a settlement of his claims *per judicium parium suorum in curia nostra*. Chapter 21 forbids the amercement of earls or barons *nisi per pares suos*. See also Leis Willelme, § 23, Liebermann, *Gesetze*, I, p. 511; Henry I's writ concerning the holding of the shire and hundred courts, § 3, *ibid.* p. 524; Leges Henrici, 25 and 29, *ibid.* pp. 562–3; 31, 7, p. 564—"Unusquisque per pares suos judicandus est et ejusdem provincie." For some general account of judgment of peers, see Flach, *Les Origines de L'Ancienne France*, I, p. 227 *et seq.*; Luchaire, *Manuel des Institutions Françaises*, p. 201; A. Esmein, *Cours Élémentaire d'Histoire du Droit Français*, 11th ed. pp. 292 *et seq.*; L. W. Vernon Harcourt, *His Grace the Steward and Trial of Peers*, pp. 205 *et seq.*; G. B. Adams, *The Origin of the English Constitution*, ch. 5, note D; Du Cange, *Glossarium*, s.v. *Par*; Spelman, *Glossarium*, s.v. *Pares Curiae*; Sir Thomas Craig, *Jus Feudale*, Bk. III, title 7, etc. For a modern text of the *Libri Feudorum*, see *Das Langobardische Lehnrecht*, edited by Karl Lehmann (Göttingen, 1896).

Few mistakes have been more important or more beneficent than this in their practical results. But a mistake it is, and it seems strange that generation after generation of learned jurists and historians could have gone on making it with the works of Spelman, Du Cange and Sir Thomas Craig in their hands.[1]

Of all the expressions in chapter 39 *per legem terrae* is the most important and probably the most ambiguous. Does *lex terrae* mean "the law of the land" or is it merely a mode of trial? There can be no doubt that in 1215 *lex* was often employed in the latter sense. As Professor Thayer says: "In the older days the word 'law', *lex*, sometimes indicated a form of procedure; not law, in our sense of substantive law, but a mode of trial."[2]

---

[1] Tertio & hoc etiam attendendum, quoties de paribus, aut parium judicio, mentio hic inciderit, ut de eis paribus intelligatur, qui unius Domini, & ejus curtis, sive curiae sunt pares; antea exposuimus eos pares dici in jure, qui unius Domini sunt beneficiarii sive Vassalli, & ideo Lex eos Judices constituit, quia per pares hos, rei veritas melius poterit indagari (Craig, *Jus Feudale*, Bk. III, title 7, § 3).

Et ut a digniori incipiamus, si contentio fit de feudo vel feudi parte, sive pertinentiis, dependentibus, sive accessoriis, de possessione feudi, de ejus reditibus & utilitatibus, aut de delicto, quo Vassallum Dominus a feudo cecidisse dicat, sive propter non petitam investituram, Pares sive beneficiarii illius Domini, sive curtis judicabunt (*ibid.* § 4).

Craig's great book was first published early in the seventeenth century. It was reissued at London and Edinburgh during the seventeenth and eighteenth centuries. I have used the edition published at Leipsic in 1716.

The text of the *Libri Feudorum* has long been easily accessible—for example, in the excellent editions of Cujas, *De Feudis* (Lyons, 1566 and afterwards); or as an appendix to many editions of the *Corpus Juris* of Justinian. The confusion between *judicium parium* and trial by jury is, however, a very natural one, for the *rei veritas* to which a jury swore in the *inquisitio* and the *rei veritas* found by the feudal *pares* are, after all, in some ways very much alike. In both, to use Sir Thomas Craig's phrase, "habitare in vicinia omnem ignorantiae excusationem tollat". They both have, in their origin at least, the same communal basis of neighbourhood and the general knowledge of a countryside. The lawyer's distinction between law and fact was not yet made. Thayer, *Preliminary Treatise on Evidence*, pp. 183 *et seq*.

[2] *Preliminary Treatise on Evidence*, p. 199. See his remarks in general.

There is at least one instance of it in the Charter itself. Chapter 38 forbids a bailiff to "put anyone to his law" (*ponat ...aliquem ad legem*) except under certain conditions.

A like use of the term is to be found in many places outside the Charter. Only one or two are here given. For example, the Latin text of the Grand Coutumier de Normandie declares that

consuetudines are customs observed from time immemorial, approved by princes, and preserved by the people, determining whose anything is or what its nature is. Laws (*leges*), on the other hand, are institutions made by princes and preserved by the people in a province, by which particular cases are decided. For laws are, as it were, instruments of the law for making known the truth in disputes.[1]

A clear case is given by Glanvill.[2] He says the enfranchisement of a serf will not avail against anyone but his former lord—"since if any former serf thus manumitted were introduced against a third party '*ad diracionationem faciendam...in curia, vel ad aliquam legem terrae faciendam*', he could on that ground be properly rejected". Here we have a perfect example of *lex terrae*, the very phrase of chapter 39, employed by Glanvill some twenty-five years before 1215 in a way which beyond question can have reference only to the mode of trial. It cannot mean anything else. "Making his law" must be merely proving his case by one or other of the old methods. Many other instances might be given, for this use of *lex* is very common in 1215, and even *lex terrae* is certainly susceptible of the same interpretation.

If this is the meaning of *lex terrae* in chapter 39, it might be translated "unless by a medial judgment of his peers followed by ordeal, compurgation, or duel". This is the meaning accepted by Mr McKechnie, by Selden, and apparently by Mr Bigelow.

[1] Chapter XI, quoted in Thayer, *Preliminary Treatise on Evidence*, p. 199. See also Brunner, *Schwurgerichte*, p. 177.
[2] Bk. v, cap. 5.

Mr McKechnie's view is wholly consistent. He gives to *judicium* a very narrow technical meaning—the awarding of the proof under the old procedure—while the *lex terrae* follows naturally and signifies merely the kind of proofs so awarded—battle, compurgation, or ordeal.

So interpreted, chapter 39 seems to point directly back toward the feudal anarchy of Stephen and to undo the great centralizing work of Henry II. It becomes a document of reaction, and can only become the "palladium of British liberties" when men are no longer able to understand its real meaning.

Those who hold this view have certainly been able to demonstrate that such a meaning was commonly given to *lex* and even to *lex terrae* in 1215. But is this proof that such was actually the meaning of the drafters of chapter 39? Did *lex* never stand for anything but procedure in 1215? Is the traditional meaning of "the law of the land" impossible? To Mr Vernon Harcourt it is not. He thinks "the '*lex terrae*' of the Charter has the same vague popular signification which the words 'law of the land' bear at the present day". He argues for a general instead of a technical interpretation of both *judicium* and *lex* and considers Mr McKechnie's views "unsound and untenable", the result of "extraordinarily misplaced zeal".[1]

In chapter 55 of Magna Carta mention is made of fines and amercements "facta injuste et contra legem terrae". Here the meaning is not unambiguous; but in chapter 42, which grants the right of entering and leaving the realm, exception is made of prisoners and outlaws, *secundum legem regni*. This is a different expression, and the prisoners mentioned might also be assumed to be in all cases persons condemned by the regular forms of trial. The outlaws, however, could hardly have been. In most cases we know they were persons who could not be caught and brought to trial at all.

---

[1] *His Grace the Steward*, p. 229. Mr Harcourt gives a large number of instances of the general use of the term. Only a few are included here.

Lex regni here seems to indicate "the law of the land" rather than mere trial. The same may be said of chapter 45, in which the King promises to appoint no justiciar, constable, sheriff, or bailiff, except from among those *qui sciant legem regni et eam bene velint observare.* But in neither case is the meaning so definite as to be a conclusive proof.

Outside the Charter there is less uncertainty. Glanvill has been cited to prove the narrower interpretation of *lex terrae.* I shall take from the same source one example from the many in existence of a contemporary use of the phrase *lex terrae* in the wider sense of "the law of the land". In Book 14, chapter 2, Glanvill says concerning a person suspected of concealing treasure trove "non solet juxta legem terrae aliquis per legem apparentem se purgare". "It is not customary according to the law of the land that one clear himself by the *lex apparens.*" *Lex apparens* here means a mode of proof, an open trial, as contrasted with the more secret method of compurgation; but *legem terrae* in the same sentence can scarcely refer to anything but "the law of the land".[1] Examples of this meaning could be multiplied.

Lex terrae, in 1215, is demonstrably susceptible of either interpretation—as mere mode of trial, or as "the law of the land", and Magna Carta itself gives no conclusive evidence as to which was intended by the barons and the King. We are driven once more to the antecedents of chapter 39.

We have seen how the chapter grew out of the King's oath in 1213 not to proceed by force against anyone *without* a trial. It does not so much concern itself with the manner of judgment. It is rather a promise not to proceed in arms without any judgment whatever. On this basis we have interpreted *ibimus* and *mittemus* as meaning armed force and not legal process. If these two verbs meant "we will not proceed against him or direct proceedings against him", as Mr Pike reads them, then it would be very natural to assume that *lex*

---

[1] A variant reading makes it *legem regni.*

also refers merely to the manner of these "proceedings". But if *ibimus* and *mittemus* refer not to process at all, but to armed attack, as I believe and Mr McKechnie himself strongly insists, then it would seem not so necessary to confine *lex* to so narrow a meaning. It might seem that Mr McKechnie, in interpreting *lex* as merely trial, was falling into much the same error for which he criticizes Coke's reading of *ibimus* and *mittemus*, and that the classic phrase "due process of law" is, after all, not such an incorrect rendering of the barons' *lex terrae* as he thought.

Both meanings were known in 1215, and chapter 39 is in compliance with John's oath of 1213—"quod...omnes homines suos secundum justa curiae suae judicia judicaret". But there was another promise in that oath—"quodque bonas leges antecessorum suorum et praecipue leges Edwardi regis revocaret"—"and that he would restore the good laws of his ancestors and especially the laws of King Edward".

If chapter 39 is the fulfilment of those promises, why should not the *lex terrae* of the Charter be these "good laws" of the absolution oath? There is no reason for believing that it cannot be, and very good reason for thinking it is.

Unless both *judicium* and *lex* are taken in a sense somewhat wider than Mr McKechnie's it seems hard to reconcile them with the barons' demand for frequent eyres of the King's justices to hold the possessory assizes.[1] They ask that two justices should decide such cases, together with four knights "elected" from the county, and expressly stipulate that no one else be summoned except the litigants.

Clearly the *judicium parium* of chapter 39 is not in all cases to be inconsistent with the jurisdiction of the itinerant justices over every one in the county. It may be that the *legale judicium parium* is thus to be distinguished from the *judicium parium* of the *Libri Feudorum*, where no such an exception is

---

[1] In number 8 of the Articles of the Barons and chapter 18 of Magna Carta (Stubbs, *Select Charters*, pp. 291, 299).

contemplated.[1] The "legal trial of peers", at all events, was not completely subversive of the reforms of Henry II.

From the evidence in the Assize of Northampton[2] and elsewhere, we may say positively also that the procedure by inquest under the assizes asked for in chapter 18 of the Charter was not compatible with the *lex terrae* if *lex* means merely proof by the ancient battle, compurgation, or ordeal, and nothing more.[3]

But there are positive as well as negative grounds for adhering to the wider interpretation of *lex terrae* as "the law of the land" in a real sense.

At the meeting at St Paul's, in 1213, according to the chronicler, Langton employed the exact words of John's oath in referring to *bonas leges* and the law of King Edward.[4]

The barons at the Temple demanded the confirmation of "quasdam libertates et leges regis Edwardi", along with others conceded to them, to the realm, and to the English Church; and they reminded the King that he had sworn at

---

[1] For the provisions of the *Libri Feudorum* see Lehmann's *Langobardische Lehnrecht*, pp. 107, 102, 105. See also Stubbs, *Constitutional History*, I, 6th ed. p. 578 n.; Harcourt, *His Grace the Steward*, p. 206; Adams, *The Origin of the English Constitution*, ch. 5, note D; Pollock and Maitland, 2nd ed. I, pp. 409, 410.

On this point of the relation of the king's justices to the *judicium parium*, the statement of the author of the *Leges Henrici Primi* is interesting. He says (Liebermann, *Gesetze*, I, p. 563): "Regis judices sint barones comitatus, qui liberas in eis terras habent, per quos debent cause singulorum alterna prosecucione tractari." This looks like an attempt on his part to reconcile the activities of the king's judges in the counties with the feudal law requiring trial by peers of the same fief. It would be interesting if we could find out whether the king's judges about the time of this compilation were ever sent into counties where they held no lands. It is not likely that much regard was paid to such a restriction after the eyres became more regular, if it was ever observed at all.

[2] Section 4, Stubbs, *Select Charters*, p. 151. There the procedure in the assize of *novel disseisin* is prescribed. For further information see Pollock and Maitland, 2nd ed. I, pp. 145–6; II, pp. 47 *et seq.*

[3] Harcourt, *His Grace the Steward*, p. 223.

[4] *Ante*, p. 100.

Winchester to observe "illas leges et libertates antiquas".[1] Most striking also is the brief account of Magna Carta in the Annals of Waverley, where the "good laws" are referred to as the "laws of Saint Edward and the liberties and free customs of other later Kings", and John's chief offence is considered to be his abuse of his barons *absque judicio parium suorum*. "And so his tyrannical will was his only law" (*Et ita pro lege ei erat tyrannica voluntas*).[2]

Instead of *per legem terrae*, John uses the expression *per legem regni nostri* in his letters patent of May 1215.[3]

The antecedents of the Charter seem, then, to show pretty conclusively that the demand of chapter 39 was for a restoration of the "good laws" of an earlier time, and that those good laws cannot be compressed into the narrow mould of the ancient forms of judicial proof. *Lex terrae*, in 1215, means what Matthew Paris called "the pious and just laws of King Edward".[4] It is the ancient custom of the realm, "the law of the land" in a real sense.

The men of 1368 were not far wrong in calling it "l'auncien leye de la terre",[5] and the Parliament of 1351 do not depart from the ancient meaning of *per legem terrae* when they paraphrase it "par voie de la lei",[6] nor the Parliament of 1354 in making it "par due proces de lei",[7] whence it has come, no doubt, largely through the influence of Coke's writings, into our federal and state constitutions as "due process of law".[8]

---

[1] *Ante*, p. 100.

[2] *Annales Monastici* (Rolls Series), II, p. 282. The whole passage is as follows: "Hoc anno magna orta est discordia inter regem Angliae et barones: his exigentibus ab eo leges Sancti Edwardi, et aliorum subsequentium regum libertates, et liberas consuetudines. Nam tempore patris sui, et maxime suo tempore corruptae nimis et aggravatae fuerant; nam quosdam absque judicio parium suorum exhaeredebat, nonnullos morte durissima condemnabat; uxores filiasque eorum violabat; et ita pro lege ei erat tyrannica voluntas."

[3] *Ante*, p. 102.

[4] *Hist. Anglorum*, II, p. 55. *Ante*, p. 101, n. 2.   [5] 42 Edw. III, c. 3.

[6] 25 Edw. III, Stat. 5, c. 4.   [7] 28 Edw. III, c. 3.

[8] See Adams, *The Origin of the English Constitution*, p. 243.

The meaning of *vel* in chapter 39 can only be ascertained after we have considered the meaning of the expressions connected by it. If *judicium* means the judgment and *lex* the proof following, *vel* must obviously be read *and*.

But even with the wider meaning of *lex*, *and* would seem the better reading, for there is no antithesis between *judicium parium* and *per legem terrae*. The former prescribes the manner of application, the latter the law to be applied. They are complementary to each other, not alternative.

The *judicium parium* is the mode of trial promised. Under it only the fellow vassals of the accused are to find the judgment in his case. But that judgment will be based on the law of the fief. Chapter 56 of the Charter promises a Welshman wrongfully deprived of lands or liberties a "legal judgment" by his peers, *secundum legem Angliae* if the holding affected is in England, *secundum legem Walliae* for a Welsh holding, and according to the law of the March for holdings there. The judgment in all cases will be found by his fellow peers of the same court on the same fief, whether they are Welsh or English. But the rules of substantive law which they will apply will be Welsh, English, or *lex marchiae*, according to the location of the *tenementum* in question.[1]

Chapter 39 is a promise to English feudatories mainly. They also are guaranteed a *legale judicium parium*. The law by which the *pares* are to make their findings is to be the *lex Angliae*. This, in feudal language, will be the law of the fief. But the fief will be the whole realm. The judgment will be found by

---

[1] This point is well stated by Sir Thomas Craig: "Sciendum hoc primum & pro generali regula tenendum, consuetudinem loci, in quo situm est feudum, in jure dicundo, super eo feudo, semper servandam, adeo ut si Vassallus duo diversa habeat feuda, unum in Anglia, alterum in Scotia, & controversia oriatur de hoc feudo, quod quis in Anglia habet, non secundum leges & mores regni Scotiae, jus de hoc feudo dicetur, licet Dominus Scotus sit & in Scotia habitet, sed secundum consuetudines Angliae." As examples of the difference in *consuetudines*, he cites the varying rules of succession to the fief, etc. (*Jus Feudale*, Bk. III, title 7, § 1).

the feudal *pares curiae*; but in this case the court will be the *curia regis*, and the law will be the *lex terrae*.

Though this law is a feudal law, and the law of a fief, and applied in feudal manner by the peers of the fief, there is no reason why it may not also be the law of the land. The duty of the peers was to find the law, not to make it. It is entirely possible that the law so found will consist in large part of customary rules running back beyond the Conquest for their origin.

It may very well be the *Laga Edwardi* which Henry I promised to restore, *cum illis emendationibus* which his father had made in it, the same which the Conqueror himself declared should continue in force, "in terris et in omnibus rebus",[1] while these "emendations" will be the *aliae libertates* referred to along with the *leges regis Edwardi* by the barons at the Temple in 1215.[2]

There can be little doubt that these changes were in the direction of a more developed feudalism, but there is nothing in this inconsistent with the view that the *lex* so amended was in its origin in part ancient English customary law.

It was national in a real sense. But "national" may have many meanings. The sense of completeness or universality now conveyed by the word may be inapplicable to the *Laga Edwardi* of the Norman or early Angevin period. It could hardly be applied in this sense without reservation to any period which is properly styled feudal. The same is true of the political self-consciousness implied in the word "national" as used in modern times.

Above all, the identification of "national" with "popular" in this period, as made by Freeman, is totally inadmissible.

But as a customary, substantive law, as a traditional body of immemorial custom, "found" by successive generations of suitors in the courts, running back in unbroken continuity to an origin beyond the Conquest and possibly far beyond it;

---

[1] *Ante*, pp. 94–95, and note 2, p. 94.   [2] *Ante*, p. 100.

there is nothing in the *Laga Edwardi* as a real *lex terrae* which is inconsistent with a régime essentially feudal in character.[1]

If our analysis is correct, we must give up the view that the original intent of Magna Carta was to guarantee trial by jury to anyone or to guarantee anything to all Englishmen. We must accept a feudal interpretation of the document as the only one possible in 1215; but we may still hold, as our fathers did, that the law of the land is there, *lex pro tyrannica voluntate*, to invert the words of the Waverley annalist, and we shall still mean by the law of the land substantially what old Roger Twysden meant—"nothing else but those immunities the subject hath ever enjoyed as his owne right, perteyning either to his person or his goods; and the grownd that hee doth so is, that they are allowed him by the law of the land, which the king alone can not at his owne will alter, and therefore can not take them from him, they beeing as auntient as the kingdome itselfe, which the king is to protect".[2]

[1] For a further development of this point, see *ante*, p. 94, note 2.
[2] *Certaine Considerations upon the Government of England* (Camden Society), p. 82.

ADDITIONAL NOTE

One who had been studying an important historical subject for a quarter of a century and had not changed his mind about some things in it would hardly be worth a hearing. And yet to rewrite an old essay, even a brief one, is almost an impossibility.

Since January 1914, when the article above was published in the *Columbia Law Review*, a number of important studies of the same subject have appeared: the second edition of McKechnie's *Magna Carta*; two essays on this immediate subject in the *Magna Carta Commemoration Essays*, one by the late Sir Paul Vinogradoff on *Clause* 39, the other by Professor F. M. Powicke, *Per Judicium Parium vel per Legem Terrae*; Professor Powicke's life of Stephen Langton; Sir William Holdsworth's discussions in the early volumes of the third edition of his *History of English Law*; and in 1936 a new treatment by Professor Max Radin in his *Handbook of Anglo-American Legal History*; to mention no others.

Further study of chapter 39 of Magna Carta by the help of these subsequent papers has led to considerable change in the meaning that I would ascribe to the makers of its famous phrases, *lex terrae* and *legale judicium parium*; and although this paper is reprinted exactly as it appeared in 1914, I have felt that a supplementary statement should be added summarizing these modifications.

Although the interpretation in the article printed above makes the all-important particle *vel* connecting *per legale judicium parium* and *per legem terrae* of chapter 39 roughly the equivalent of "and", and although Mr Vernon Harcourt's designation of this meaning as "absurd" has always seemed to me to be unjustifiable; yet for a long time I have had an uneasy feeling that both Professor G. B. Adams and I may possibly have exaggerated somewhat the conjunctive character of this significant particle. The statement of Professor Powicke now seems more just: "However vague or weak its disjunctive quality may be, it cannot suddenly be construed as 'et etiam' or 'id est'." In 1914 I had rejected the disjunctive interpretation of *vel* altogether, because I could not see how the two phrases it connected, meaning such different kinds of things, could possibly be alternative. This conclusion was in turn based on the conviction that the first of these phrases so connected, *per legale judicium parium*, referred to a form of procedure; while the second, *per legem terrae*, contrary to McKechnie's opinion, meant the substantive law enforced by this procedure. A better solution of the difficulty seemed finally to be offered by a brief statement of Professor Radin's: "The contrast, to make sense, should be between the *pares* and some other persons who might constitute a *judicium*." If that were true, it would be neither contrasting or supplementary procedures that the *vel* connected, as McKechnie held; nor a procedure and a substantive rule, as Sir Paul Vinogradoff, Professor Adams, and I believed; as well as Sir William Holdsworth, who accepted this part of my interpretation: the two phrases would refer to two different persons or classes of persons either of whom might establish the *judicium*, and neither phrase would then directly refer either to the procedure they followed or to the law they applied. In short it was not the procedure nor the law that the barons wished above all to put beyond question here; but the men, the class of persons who alone should pronounce a judgment on them. But in following Professor Radin's suggestions further, I found it impossible to agree when he identified those persons included under the alternative phrase *per legem terrae* as *ballivi*, bailiffs royal or manorial. The hatred of John's bailiffs is so prominent all through the barons' Articles that it seems inconceivable that these barons would have assented to any alternative authorizing mere bailiffs to constitute such a *judicium* over them. But might there not be persons other than the bailiffs to whom this phrase *per legem terrae* might more properly refer? At this point some earlier suggestions of Professor Adams and Sir Paul Vinogradoff seemed to supply one clue. Another was suggested by the interesting observation, clearly made, so far as I know, for the first time by Professor Radin,[1] that while the barons in their Articles had demanded a *judicium parium*, what they got in the Charter was a LEGALE *judicium parium*; "the word *legale* appears in the Charter by what must be considered a deliberate act of clarification". The question then arises, whose act of clarification? In the opinion of Professor Radin it is the act of the barons. "Evidently when they [the barons] added *per legem terrae* to include the possibility that in some places the judges were not the peers, but the King's bailiffs, they did not at first realize that they were putting these two forms on a par. In the Charter they attempted to avoid doing so by calling attention to the fact that the *judicium parium* was the really *legale judicium*. The *vel* clause would then be put in its proper light." This, or something like it, would seem to be the only possible interpretation if we assumed as Professor Radin does that *per legem terrae* meant a judgment by royal or other bailiffs; and the whole provision would then read, in Professor Radin's paraphrase, "except by lawful judgment of their peers or of some other persons, if that is the custom in any manor or district".

But why must one assume that this "act of clarification" in the insertion of the word *legale* before *judicium parium* in the

[1] There is a hint of it, however, in my article above, at p. 112: "Clearly the *judicium parium* of chapter 39 is not in all cases to be inconsistent with the jurisdiction of the itinerant justices over every one in the county. It may be that the *legale judicium parium* is thus to be distinguished from the *judicium parium* of the *Libri Feudorum*, where no such an exception is contemplated."

Charter when it was not in the Articles, must have been the barons' act? Whether an act of clarification or of modification, its absence from the Articles and presence in the Charter might rather suggest an act of the King. Most of the other significant differences between the Articles and the Charter seem to be changes made, not in the barons' interest but in the King's, and therefore presumably at his instance. The insertion here in chapter 39 of the word *legale* seems very like the omission in chapter 12 of *taillagiis*, a "clarification" more to the advantage of the King than of the Londoners in Professor McKechnie's opinion.

If, then, the insertion of the word *legale* is the King's act, why did he do it, and what did he mean by it? An answer to this question is suggested by both Professor Adams and Sir Paul Vinogradoff, by contemporary practice in France and Normandy, and by evidence of the former practice in England itself. But before turning to these we must, if possible, find where the two phrases *judicium parium* and *per legem terrae* first appear in this struggle between John and his barons. Neither one occurs, although the former may be implied, in John's oath of absolution in 1213, which merely specifies that John must judge his men "according to the just judgments of his court" (*secundum justa curiae suae judicia judicaret*); nor is there anything of the kind in Henry I's coronation charter which Langton later proposed to the barons as a model. The phrases do not appear in the "Unknown Charter of Liberties", which would make John promise merely not to arrest a man *absque judicio*.

So far as the surviving records show, the general tenor of the phrases and many of the exact terms seem to come first from the King in the letter patent he issued on 10 May 1215, some five weeks before the meeting at Runnymede, in which the words are, "nisi per legem regni nostri, vel per judicium parium suorum in curia nostra". Next in order comes the section of the barons' Articles dealing with the matter, apparently adopting verbatim the phraseology of John's letter patent which had probably appeared shortly before, with only two "clarifications", a reversing of the order of the two phrases, and the substitution of *terrae* for *regni nostri*; and finally chapter 39 of the Charter itself, which is identical with the Articles save for the significant insertion for the first time of *legale* before *judicium parium*.

From a comparison of all the surviving documents it would appear then that the essential words and phrases of this part of section 39 were probably originally the King's. If it was he also who inserted the word *legale* we must next inquire why he did it; for if we are right in thinking it was he, his reasons could not be those which Professor Radin ascribes to the King's opponents; and even if it were the barons, their reasons may have been very different from the ones which Professor Radin gives. An important suggestion as to these reasons—whether King's or barons' —was made by Professor Adams in 1912 in pointing out that chapter 39 as a whole was directed "against the growth of courts tending to be formed exclusively of professional justices and excluding any real *judicium parium*". The barons had begun to see "that the jurisdiction of the great curia regis was being undermined, its cases purloined from it, by the growth of a court in which there was a *judicium parium* only in theory and that, too, theory of a very bad sort as they would regard it".

If we should adopt Professor Radin's view that the antithesis between *per judicium parium* and *per legem terrae* is one "between the *pares* and some other persons who might constitute a *judicium*", and should conclude that these "other persons" are not, as he insists, *ballivi* in certain *patriae, terrae*, or local districts, but rather these "professional justices" of the King sitting in the county courts; and should further conclude (though this is less important) that the addition of *legale* before *judicium parium* is a clarification originally made not by the barons but by the King, and possibly, though not necessarily, in his own interest; we should have the basis for an explanation of these disputed phrases of chapter 39 which might be briefly and somewhat dogmatically stated thus: The phrase *per legale judicium parium suorum* in chapter 39 of John's Charter refers to allegations made against the King's tenants-in-chief which under strict feudal custom could be "legally" tried only in the King's central curia and by the whole body of the peers of that court collectively. This in strictness of feudal law is the only form of a LEGALE *judicium parium* in such cases. *Per legem terrae* on the other hand is an alternative, a trial before one or more of the barons usually presiding as itinerant justice in one of the King's courts in some county. Thus the distinction between the two phrases is a distinction between the persons of the judges, as

Professor Radin suggests; it is not a distinction between forms of procedure. Feudal tenants were always entitled to some form of *judicium parium*. It was taken as a matter of course. The only question is whether, under the alternative phrase *per legem terrae* interpreted thus as a trial before an itinerant justice, there is a sufficient approximation to the strictly "legal" trial by the collective peers to justify our conclusion that the barons would and did agree to it as acceptable for certain cases in place of the "legal" trial in the central curia to which feudal custom entitled all tenants-in-chief by military tenure. In other words, was the King's contention that a single peer acting as a royal judge fulfilled sufficiently the requirements of a *judicium parium* a valid contention, and one not too revolutionary to be acquiesced in by the barons; or was it "a theory of a very bad sort", so bad in fact, that we could not believe the barons would ever have agreed to it? This is the question on which the present interpretation of this document really turns. My belief is that the barons found the King's proposal not too revolutionary for adoption, and I have been led to this conclusion in part by the following considerations:

The *liber homo* to which chapter 39 as a whole refers, in the narrowest possible interpretation of that phrase, certainly includes sub-tenants by military tenure as well as the tenants-in-chief. Now these sub-tenants were, of course, not by feudal custom ordinarily entitled to a judgment in the King's central court, and a full century before Magna Carta, Henry I's writ for the holding of the County and Hundred courts had provided that a case of unlawful disseisin between two of them who held of different lords should be tried in the county court (Liebermann, *Gesetze der Angelsachsen*, 1, p. 524). For the *arrière-vassaux* at least, then, it seems probable that in 1215 it had long been sufficient in some instances if their cases were tried in a court presided over by one royal judge or more. In section 8 of the barons' Articles there is a demand by the barons themselves for frequent eyres of these royal justices to determine cases under the possessory assizes, and such cases must frequently have been between litigants who must be included under the term *liber homo* to which chapter 39 refers, military sub-tenants at least, if not occasionally even tenants-in-chief themselves. It seems clear then that the phrase of chapter 39, *per* LEGALE *judicium parium suorum*, if it applied only to a collective judgment of the peers of the central curia, would need supplementing by a further provision to cover other cases in which a *liber homo* might be involved, such as the ones just noted. This supplementary or alternative provision to meet these other cases, would, on this interpretation, be made by the final words of the chapter, *vel per legem terrae*; and it would be most appropriate to designate such a provision as a *lex* or a *constitutio*, because it had been originally established by royal edict or writ to which the term *lex* was often applied in distinction from *consuetudo*, as in the titles of the books of Glanvill and Bracton, *Lex et Consuetudo Angliae*. Furthermore, by 1215, after the great judicial reforms of Henry II which had extended the procedure under the assizes to every corner of England, it would be equally appropriate to refer to this provision or *lex* as *lex Angliae*, or *lex regni*, or *lex terrae*.

In the beginning, the substitution by the King of this very attenuated trial by peers for the "legal" one may have met with serious objection among the barons. One statement by the author of the *Leges Henrici Primi*, a century before Magna Carta, looks very like a reference to an attempt on the King's part to meet some such objection: "The judges of the King should be barons of the county who have free lands therein", and never *viles et inopes persone* (Liebermann, *op. cit.* 1, p. 563). Such a requirement as this would ensure the judgment by a peer, though scarcely a LEGALE *judicium* PARIUM.[1] However, although there may have been objection to such a practice in Henry I's time, section 8 of the barons' Articles would indicate that familiarity with it for a generation or more had fully reconciled the barons to its use by 1215, at least in the case of the possessory assizes.

In the *Très Ancien Coutumier de Normandie*, which was written apparently about the time of John's accession, when Normandy was still attached to the crown of England, there occur one or two statements that seem to echo the provision of the *Leges*

[1] This interpretation, of course, would require a translation of the adjective *legale* of chapter 39 in the general sense of "lawful", while the noun *lex* in the following phrase, *per legem terrae*, would have to be construed in a narrower "statutory" sense. Both uses were current at the time, however, and I see no reason to think they might not occur together in one sentence.

Henrici Primi and may throw a little further light on the problem: for example, "Assisie vero tenentur per barones et legales homines. Par per parem judicari debet: barones igitur et milites, legis statuta scientes et Deum timentes, possunt judicare unus alium, et subditum eis populum; rustico enim non licet, vel alii de populo, militem vel clericum judicare" (Cap. xxvi, Tardif, *Coutumiers de Normandie*, i, p. 24). The reply in 1233 of Pierre des Roches to the baronial demand for a trial by peers also becomes very significant in the same connection—even though one must agree with Stubbs that it is "a perverse misrepresentation of the English law": "because there are no peers in England as in the realm of the French, therefore it is permissible for the King of the English, through the justices whom he has constituted, to prosecute any of his realm as culprits and by a judgment to condemn them".

For the reasons partially and imperfectly summarized above, the statement of Professor Radin therefore now seems to me to furnish the best general explanation of these important words of chapter 39: "The contrast, to make sense, should be between the *pares* and some other persons who might constitute a *judicium*." Hence I should freely paraphrase the famous chapter somewhat as follows: No free man should be arrested or imprisoned or desseised or outlawed or exiled or in any manner destroyed; nor will we go upon him, nor will we send upon him, except upon a legal judgment of his peers, or by the justices of the King in cases in which this has become the common procedure, "the law of the land" in effect everywhere and accepted as such.

In a brilliant and penetrating analysis of the ideas lying behind and incorporated in the Charter, Mr J. E. A. Jolliffe, in his *Constitutional History of Medieval England* (London, 1937), treats this difference between the *legale judicium parium* and the *lex terrae* of chapter 39 as practically identical with that existing between the assize—which is no judgment "in the archaic sense of the term"— and the true judgment of the central *curia* (p. 254). This may account in part for the precise terms employed in the two phrases, and it is in no way inconsistent with the view expressed above that the main concern of the barons was the *personnel* rather than the procedure of the courts. It should be noted, however, that in most of the existing assizes there was to all intents a real judgment even in the archaic sense; for a *judicium* followed immediately on the *veredictum* in the grand and the possessory assizes. It was only in presentments of felonies that this was not so, and an ordeal prescribed between the inquest and the final judgment. It seems probable that the barons would be interested in ensuring what they considered a proper trial as much in the grand and possessory assizes as in the cases where a free man was accused of felony.

One further word of explanation seems necessary here in justification of the retention unchanged of the original essay on chapter 39 after so many radical changes have been made in it. The main reason is this: As Professor Adams said many years ago, "The fundamental difficulty in the interpretation of c. 39 is that created by the last phrase, nisi per legale judicium parium suorum vel per legem terrae"; and therefore the modifications I have urged in this additional note relate solely to these final words of this particular chapter; they in no way affect what was originally said of the meaning of the Charter as a whole. There is evidence in plenty, part of which is summarized in the original article, that "the law of the land" was understood in 1215 *also* to mean the substantive principles of the customary law. Such a substantive law is assumed throughout the whole Charter and it is assumed in chapter 39. This is put beyond question, I think, by one of the *addenda* to their Articles, number 44, in which the barons insisted that a Welsh baron, if his *tenementum* lies in England, is entitled in a *judicium parium* to a trial *secundum legem Angliae*. What is there expressly stated as a supplement to the Charter covering the exceptional case of a Welsh baron, is everywhere assumed as a matter of course in the main body of the document for every English baron. The conclusions set forth in the original article still hold good, I think, for the interpretation of Magna Carta as a whole, for chapter 39 itself, and for all the events and documents which led up to it. What I would now add merely is, that the particular words *per legale judicium parium suorum vel per legem terrae* at the end of chapter 39 are not *in themselves* an express reference to this broader principle, but to a narrower and more specific safeguard for it in securing a judgment by proper arbiters, either by the fellow tenants of the barons themselves, or by competent royal judges from among those only "qui sciant legem terrae et eam bene velint observare",[1] as the barons demanded in section 42 of their Articles.

[1] The corresponding words of the *Très Ancien Coutumier de Normandie* are *legis statuta scientes*, and *jurati...legalem justiciam tenere*, chapters 26–7 (Tardif, pp. 24–5). These phrases, *legis statuta* and *legalem justiciam*, seem to refer to a procedure established by royal edict, such as the assizes of Henry II, rather than to the rules of the customary law they enforce. The latter would ordinarily be found by jurors or others acquainted with the custom and not by the *justitia* who presided over the court. If this were true in Normandy in John's time, it seems not unreasonable to interpret in the same way this phrase *legem terrae* in section 42 of the barons' Articles and *per legem terrae* in chapter 39 of the Charter.

VI

MAGNA CARTA AND COMMON LAW

In estimating the importance of Magna Carta what we chiefly need is a history of the document in the period after 1215.[1] One of the most significant points in that subsequent development is the famous confirmation by Edward I in 1297. This confirmation is in part as follows:

I. Know ye that we to the honour of God and of the holy Church, and to the profit of all our realm ("et a profist de tout nostre roiaume"), have granted for us and our heirs, that the Great Charter of Liberties ("le graunt chartre des fraunchises") and the Charter of the Forest, which were made by common assent of all the realm ("les queles feurent faites par commun assent de tout le roiaume"), in the time of King Henry our father, shall be kept in every point without breach ("soient tenues en toutz leur pointz, saunz nul blemisement"). And we will that these same charters shall be sent under our seal to our justices, both to those of the forest and to the rest, and to all sheriffs of shires, and to all our other officers, and to all our cities throughout the realm, together with our writs in the which it shall be contained that they cause the aforesaid charters to be published and have it declared to the people that we have granted that they shall be observed in all points, and that our justices, sheriffs, mayors, and other officials who under us and by us have to administer the law of the land ("qui la loy de la terre desoutz nous et par nous ount a guier"), shall allow the said charters in pleas before them and judgments in all their points; that is to say, the Great Charter of Liberties as common law, and the Charter of the Forest according to the Assize of the Forest, for the relief of our people ("c'est a savoir la grande chartre des franchises cume lay commune, e la chartre de la forest solom l'assise de la forest, al amendement de nostre poeple").

II. And we will that if any judgments be given from henceforth, contrary to the points of the charters aforesaid by justices

[1] *Law Quarterly Review*, XXI, p. 257.

or by any other our ministers that hold pleas before them touching the points of the charters, they shall be undone and holden for naught.

("E volums qe si nuls jugementz soient donez desoremes encontre les pointz des chartres avauntdites, par justices et par nos autres ministres qui contre les pointz des chartres tenent plez devant eus, seient defaitz e pur nient tenuz.")

III. And we will that the same charters shall be sent under our seal to cathedral churches throughout our realm, and there remain, and shall be read before the people twice in the year.

IV. And that archbishops and bishops shall pronounce sentences of greater excommunication against all those that by word, deed, or counsel shall go against the aforesaid charters, or that in any point break or go against them. And that the said curses be twice a year denounced and published by the prelates aforesaid. And if the same prelates or any of them be remiss in the denunciation of the said sentences, the Archbishops of Canterbury and York for the time being, as is fitting, shall reprove them and constrain them to make that denunciation in form aforesaid. [1]

Under the first of these sections the King's justices are directed to administer Magna Carta "as common law" ("cume lay commune").

The sense hereof (says Coke) is, that the Great Charter and the Charter of the Forest are to be holden for the Common Law, that is, the law common to all; and that both the charters are in amendment of the realm; that is to amend great mischiefs and inconveniences which oppressed the whole realm before the making of them.[2]

This paper is an attempt to explain still further "the sense hereof". But the most difficult part of the explanation as usual lies in that part of the provision whose meaning seems at first the most obvious—"lay commune". "No tolerably prepared candidate in an English or American law school will hesitate to define an estate in fee simple", says Sir Frederick

---

[1] *Statutes of the Realm*, 1, p. 123; Bémont, *Chartes des Libertés Anglaises*, p. 96; Stubbs, *Select Charters*, 9th ed. p. 490; Blackstone, *Magna Carta*, p. lxxiv.   [2] 2 Inst. 526.

Pollock. "On the other hand, the greater have been a lawyer's opportunities of knowledge, and the more time he has given to the study of legal principles, the greater will be his hesitation in face of the apparently simple question, What is Law?"[1] One's opportunities of knowledge would have to be great indeed to be even in slight degree commensurate with his hesitation in attempting to define "common law" with all that it implied in 1297, but defined it must be in some fashion before we can understand the real significance of Magna Carta in the later Middle Ages. Some examination of contemporary records has convinced me that Coke's interpretation is in the main the correct one, but one of his statements seems also to show that it is correct in a sense possibly somewhat different from the one he had in mind. This is his inclusion without comment of the Charter of the Forest with Magna Carta as the common law. What, then, is "the law common to all", what made it "common" in 1297, how did this conception of a common law and the mass of corresponding rights actually come into existence, and finally what light is thrown by an explanation of these things upon the history and character of Magna Carta itself?

For a considerable part of the period when the common law was taking form in England there may be observed in the writers on law a certain struggle between the Roman idea of *lex* and the medieval conception of law as immemorial usage. The judges of those times, who were generally in orders, were better acquainted with Roman legal conceptions than many of their brethren of a much later time. Their knowledge and reverence for these ideas, coupled with the necessity they were under of administering a law of a different origin, at a less advanced stage of development, but with roots so deep in the traditions and habits of the people that its binding force was unquestionable—these are the chief explanation of apparently incompatible statements concerning

[1] *A First Book of Jurisprudence,* p. 4.

the basis and extent of the royal authority, which even the *addiciones* in a text like Bracton's cannot wholly explain. In the field of private law somewhat the same struggle is to be seen between *lex* and *consuetudo*; the one a product of the classical period of Roman law, the other a growth of the Middle Ages out of roots that are quite different. The medieval desire for unity led the jurists of the time to make interesting attempts to reconcile these conflicting conceptions. Constantine's famous dictum, "Consuetudinis ususque longaevi non vilis auctoritas est",[1] they gladly fasten upon, but it will not fully serve their needs until it is practically inverted.[2] So the author of Glanvill feels it necessary to apologize to his learned readers for an English customary law which he never thinks of questioning.[3] Glanvill is quoted word for word by the author of *Fleta*, but without acknowledgment.[4] Bracton also begins his treatise with the usual liberal quotations from

[1] Code, 8, 52, 2: "Consuetudinis ususque longaevi non vilis auctoritas est, verum non usque adeo sui valitura momento, ut aut rationem vincat aut legem."

[2] "Legum autem Romanorum non est vilis auctoritas, sed non adeo vim suam extendunt, ut usum vincant aut mores. Strenuus autem jurisperitus, sicubi casus emerserit, qui consuetudine feudi non sit comprehensus, absque calumnia uti poterit lege scripta" (*Libri Feudorum*, lib. II, title i; Lehmann, *Das Langobardische Lehnrecht*, pp. 114–15). See the interesting commentary of Cujas on these two passages, in his edition, *De Feudis* (1566), pp. 72–4. For a modern discussion see Savigny, *System des heutigen Römischen Rechts*, vol. I, ch. III, section 25; also note II at the end of vol. I.

[3] The customary law, *consuetudo*, he also calls *jura regni*, but he will not admit a sharp distinction between it and *lex*, though it is mainly unwritten, for he is not ignorant of the popular origin of *lex* even in Rome—"Leges namque Anglicanas, licet non scriptas, Leges appellari non videtur absurdum (cum hoc ipsum lex sit, 'quod principi placet, legis habet vigorem') eas scilicet, quas super dubiis in consilio definiendis, procerum quidem consilio, et principis accedente authoritate, constat esse promulgatas" (*Tractatus de Legibus et Consuetudinibus Regni Angliae*, Prologus). Cf. Justinian, Inst. 1, 2, 3, with which Glanvill, in common with nearly all the medieval English juristic writers, prefaces his treatise.

[4] Proemium.

the "Institutes", and borrows from Glanvill the sentence identifying *consuetudo* with *lex*, but his treatment of the subject is fuller and much more valuable.[1] It is clear that these medieval writers are faced with a *consuetudo*, a *lex non scripta*, which is binding much as *lex* was binding in the later Roman Empire. In order then, to apply their favourite texts in support of the existing law, they are under the necessity of including within *lex* what was certainly not included in Justinian's time. The outstanding fact is that custom had really become "law". It was accepted by common usage *pro lege*. This is almost the central fact in early English law; but we moderns, like the Romans of the later Empire, are so prone to identify *lex* and "law" that we can hardly appreciate the difficulty in which Glanvill and Bracton found themselves. Glanvill's apology for *consuetudo* was directed at the classicists, and is easily understood by ourselves; to a twelfth-century Englishman, if unlearned in Roman law, it probably had very little meaning.

But *consuetudo* was a thing well understood. Evidence of its importance and its binding character is abundant. Glanvill

[1] "Cum autem fere in omnibus regionibus utantur legibus et jure scripto, sola Anglia usa est in suis finibus jure non scripto et consuetudine. In ea quidem ex non scripto jus venit, quod usus comprobavit. Sed absurdum non erit leges Anglicanas (licet non scriptas) leges appellare, cum legis vigorem habeat quicquid de consilio et de consensu magnatum et reipublicae communi sponsione, authoritate regis sive principis praecedente, juste fuerit definitum et approbatum. Sunt autem in Anglia consuetudines plures et diversae, secundum diversitatem locorum. Habent enim Anglici plurima ex consuetudine, quae non habent ex lege; sicut in diversis comitatibus, civitatibus, burgis et villis, ubi semper inquirendum erit quae sit illius loci consuetudo, et qualiter utantur consuetudine qui consuetudines allegant" (folio 1 A).
"Videndum est etiam quid sit lex; et sciendum, quod lex est commune praeceptum virorum prudentum consultum, delictorumque quae sponte vel ignorantia contrahuntur coertio, rei publicae sponsio communis" (folio 2 A; Digest, 1, 3, 1).
"Consuetudo vero quandoque pro lege observatur in partibus, ubi fuerit more utentium approbata, et vicem legis obtinet, longaevi enim temporis usus et consuetudinibus non est vilis authoritas" (folio 2 A).

himself, in the passage quoted above,[1] though he is para-
phrasing the Institutes, cannot say, as they do, that in England
the "law" is what the people, or what anyone, *constituebat.*
Instead, he has to say that it consists of those things "quas
super dubiis in consilio definiendis, procerum quidem consilio, et principis accedente authoritate, constat esse promulgatas". It is something already in existence, which may indeed
need defining, but can only be promulgated, not made. The
celebrated Excommunication of 1253 mentions only those
who violate the liberties of the Church, Magna Carta, the
Charter of the Forest, "vel antiquas regni consuetudines
approbatas".[2] It is not difficult to prove that these "ancient
customs of the realm" were of binding force, even of supreme
binding force. So the author of the *Mirror of Justices*, who may
certainly be trusted as an interpreter of contemporary words
and phrases, though we can no longer believe all his stories,
declares that the article in the Statute of Marlborough concerning redisseisors is reprehensible, because "no special
ordinance ought to exceed common law" (*car nul mandement
especial ne deit passer comun dreit*).[3] And we find the justices of
both benches required to take oath that in case they receive
letters from the King commanding anything "contrary to
the law", they will enforce the law notwithstanding such
letters. The Parliament Roll of the year 1330[4] contains an
interesting petition by several nobles setting forth that they
were entitled to lands escheated at the time of the suppression
of the Templars, which lands, however, had been handed
over, by a statute irregularly procured by the Despencers, to
the Hospitallers. They pray that this statute be annulled and
quote the opinions of the judges against it—

Les dites Justices disoient appertement et expressement, qe le
Roi ne ne devote ne ne le poiet faire par Ley; non pas pur ce les
ditz Hugh et Hugh, par poair q'il avoient, firent fair un Statut,

[1] P. 130, n. 3.
[2] Bémont, *Chartes*, p. 72.   [3] Selden Society, VII, p. 184.
[4] *Rot. Parl.* II, pp. 41-2, no. 52.

sicome piert par le Statut, Qe les Hospitaliers eussent les terres de Templiers. Et en lequel Estatute poet estre trowe, qe les Justices ne s'assentirent point; car ils ne poient pur lour serment par la disheritaunce du Roy et de ses gentz. Et disoient, qe ce sunt contrarie a Ley, isse qe cel Estatut se fist contre Ley et contre reson.

In 1341, during the struggle between Edward III and his Parliament, the King had been compelled to make certain important concessions in return for the parliamentary grants, but when these had to be put in the form of a statute, the chancellor, treasurer, and some of the justices protested that they would not enforce them "en cas qe meismes les Estatutz fussent contraires a les Leies et Usages du Roialme, lesqueux ils feurent serementez de garder".[1] The reasons they assign

---

[1] *Rot. Parl.* II, p. 131*a*, no. 42. For the controversy, see Stubbs, *Constitutional History*, II 4th ed. pp. 407–10. Rymer gives one of the writs for the publication of this revocation, addressed to the Sheriff of Lincoln, dated 1 October 1341 (*Foedera* (Record Commission), vol. II, pt. II, p. 1177). In it the King declares that since the provisions complained of "(quidam articuli) legibus et consuetudinibus regni nostri Angliae, ac juribus et praerogativis nostris regiis, expresse contrarii praetendantur per modum statuti per nos fuisse concessi"; therefore, "considerantes qualiter ad observationem et defensionem legum, consuetudinum, jurium et praerogativarum hujusmodi, astricti sumus vinculo juramenti", he desires that the said statute be revoked, even though "dissimulavimus sicut oportuit et dictum praetensum statutum sigillari permisimus illa vice". But he hastens to add—and this is also significant—"volentes tamen quod articuli, in dicto praetenso statuto contenti, qui per alia statuta nostra vel progenitorum nostrorum Regum Angliae sunt prius approbati, juxta formam dictorum statutorum, in omnibus, prout convenit, observentur". By his own admission the King's action seems to warrant Stubbs's characterization of it as "a piece of atrocious duplicity", but the reasons he finds necessary to assign for it are none the less instructive. This revocation was made, however, without consulting the Commons— "volentes ea...ad statum debitum revocare, super hoc cum comitibus et baronibus, ac peritis aliis, dicti regni nostri consilium habuimus et tractatum"—and therefore, as an enactment of common law, had eventually to be put in form of a new statute with the assent of the lower house. This assent was not given until the next Parliament, which met in 1343, two years later. It is an assent only in form then, for the Commons were dissatisfied. They petitioned for the observance of recent statutes, especially

are significant whether they were sincere or not. For the year 1347 there is a petition on the Parliament Roll against a judgment made in Parliament, which is declared to be "contre le Leis de Roialme et les Usages aprovez".[1] In 1397 Parliament annulled the award of Parliament convicting Hugh Despencer, and seemingly endorsed the charge that the Act of Edward III affirming this award "fuist fait contre droit, loy, et reson...quel Estatut qant a les ditz articles n'est my droiturel ne resonable, ne deust estre de force par la ley...estoit encontre droit et reson et encontre la ley de la Terre".[2] Two years later, on the accession of Henry IV, the new King declared: "Qe il n'est pas son entente ne voluntee pur tourner les Leyes, Estatutz, ne bones Usages,...mes pur garder les anciens Leyes et Estatutz, ordeignez et usez en temps de ses nobles progenitours...solonc son serment."[3] The "Pronunciatio", by which the Parliament of 1 Henry VI was opened, declares the purpose of the session to be the enjoyment by all classes of their liberties and franchises which have not been repealed "ne par la Commune leie repellables",[4] and the statutes of the next year open with a confirmation of all such franchises "bien usez et nient repellez ne par la commune ley repellablez".[5]

Some of these examples undoubtedly arise out of factional for those made in return for their grants. The only satisfaction they got was the royal response, "Il plest au Roi qe les Estatuts soient veuz et examinez, et ceux qe sont d'amender soient amendez, et les bons estoisent en lour force." In respect to the statute annulled two years before the King answered, "Le Roi nadgairs apperceivant qe le dit Estatut feust contre son Serement et en blemissement de sa Corone et de sa Roialtee, et contre la Ley de la terre en plusours pointz, si fist repeller meisme l'Estatut. Mes il voet qe les pointz du dit Estatut soient examinez, et ceux qe serront trovez honurables et profitables pur le Roi et son poeple soient ore faitz en novel Estatut, et gardez desore" (*Rot. Parl.* II, p. 140, no. 4). No corresponding enactment is to be found on the Statute Roll of that year.

[1] *Rot. Parl.* II, p. 173, no. 65.   [2] *Ibid.* III, p. 367 A.
[3] *Ibid.* III, p. 434, no. 108.   [4] *Ibid.* IV, p. 169 B.
[5] 2 Hen. VI, cap. i.

and even revolutionary struggles, but the frequent and repeated insistence upon the supremacy of the common law, as a justification, even though it may be at times an unjust action that is justified, seems to show conclusively the position occupied by the common law. It was, in a very real sense, a fundamental law.

But if this law was really supreme it becomes the more necessary to try to discover the points in which it differed from other rules or enactments; to ascertain as nearly as we can just what was common law. From the passage quoted above from Bracton[1] it appears that custom has the force of law in England, "approbata more utentium"; and that these *consuetudines* are either "plures et diversae", i.e. particular customs; or common custom, which is "consuetudo regni Angliae". Thus he speaks of the King's retaining an outlaw's lands for a year and a day, "sicut esse debet secundum consuetudinem regni nostri Angliae";[2] or of waste "contra consuetudinem regni nostri";[3] or of an inquest "secundum consuetudinem regni Angliae".[4] So he declares:

Et sicut papa ordinare potest in spiritualibus quoad ordines et dignitates, ita potest rex in temporalibus de haereditatibus dandis vel haeredibus constituendis secundum consuetudinem regni sui. Habet enim quodlibet regnum suas consuetudines et diversas, poterit enim una esse consuetudo in regno Angliae, et alia in regno Franciae quantum ad successiones.[5]

In Bracton's day the organization and powers of Parliament were still undeveloped and the terminology of legislation was not yet fixed. His favourite term for enactments is *constitutio*, in which he shows his Roman and canon law training. He refers to the Statute of Merton as "Nova constitutio",[6] and to a violation of it as "fraus Constitutioni".[7] He says also that a writ of novel disseisin will not issue where a tenant has granted so much of his estate in frankalmoign that his lord had

---

[1] *Ante*, p. 131, n. 1.   [2] Folio 129 B.   [3] *Ibid.* 316 A.   [4] *Ibid.* 307 A.
[5] *Ibid.* 417 B. He here refers to the famous "nolumus".
[6] *Ibid.* 312 B.   [7] Folios 29 A, 32 A.

lost his service, "quia hoc est contra constitutionem".[1] In another place he asserts the same rule, "propter constitutionem libertatis".[2] These *constitutiones* are in addition to *consuetudines* which are in use throughout the realm. Hence many things are controlled by the law *and* custom of the realm. It is no accident that the writs appointing the justices for an assize of novel disseisin command them to do justice "secundum legem et consuetudinem regni nostri Angliae".[3] Judges are so to conduct themselves, says Bracton, "ut constitutiones et eorum edicta, juri et consuetudinibus approbatis, et communi utilitati sint convenientia".[4] These are the rules to which Bracton refers as "lex terrae et regni consuetudines",[5] and "jus commune".[6] Whether customary or statutory, it is the law common to the realm, as distinguished from particular law. So in discussing waste Bracton says: "Et quid debeat adjudicari ad vastum, et quid non, propter magnitudinem et parvitatem, habet quaelibet patria suum modum, constitutionem et consuetudinem."[7] And *modus*, he says, following the familiar doctrine of the Roman lawyers, though in a sense probably never meant by them, and here speaking of grants, "legem dat donationi; et modus tenendus est contra jus commune, et contra legem, quia modus et conventio vincunt legem".[8] Of the law of succession he says: "Item poterit conditio impedire descensum ad proprios heredes, contra jus commune."[9]

"And because it is given to all in common it is called

---

[1] Folio 169 B. By this *constitutio* Bracton means the provision which appeared first as article 39 of the second reissue of Magna Carta and was re-enacted as article 32 in the reissue of 1225: "Nullus liber homo de cetero det amplius alicui vel vendat de terra sua quam ut de residuo terrae suae possit sufficienter fieri domino feodi servitium ei debitum quod pertinet ad feodum illud." He cites the case of Robert de Toteshall *v.* the Prior of Bricksite in 23 Hen. III. This case is given in Bracton's *Note Book*, no. 1248.　　[2] Folio 168 B.

[3] *Ibid.* 110 B. He also speaks of a woman's having a dower greater than is proper "secundum legem et consuetudinem regni" (folio 314 A).

[4] *Ibid.* 108 A.　　[5] *Ibid.* 133.　　[6] Folios 17 B, 19 B.

[7] Folio 316 B.　　[8] *Ibid.* 17 B.　　[9] *Ibid.* 19 B.

common law", says the author of the *Mirror of Justices*, of the law with which he deals.[1] References to *the* common law became more frequent as the thirteenth century closed. For example, it is said to be "encontre la commune ley" for a subject to inflict the death penalty on a criminal.[2] Later, in the reign of Richard II, the Commons complain of royal interference with "la ley de la Terre et commune Droit".[3]

It is not necessary to multiply instances further, though they are many. The general connotation of "common law" is beyond doubt. Its exact meaning becomes clearer, however, when we take note of the special law that contemporaries were wont to contrast with it. At times we find "la commune Loy" thus designated to distinguish it from enactment.[4] Or it might be the law of the Church that was contrasted with it;[5] the "lex forestae";[6] "les Loys d'armes";[7] the laws of the

[1] Selden Society, VII, p. 5.
[2] Year Book, 20 and 21 Edw. I (Rolls Series), p. 99.
[3] *Rot. Parl.* III, p. 23, no. 96 (1377).
[4] Thus a litigant was told in 1 Edw. II: "You are not aided by the common law nor by special law" ("par la commune ley ne par ley especial") (Year Book, 1 and 2 Edw. II (Selden Society), p. 31). In the next year another was informed that he must rely either on common law or on special law ("par la commune ley ou par ley especial". Variant: "par aunciene ley ou par novele ley"), and that neither the common law nor "la novelle ley" will help him (*ibid.* p. 60). In 1377 the Commons petitioned for the observance and confirmation of "la commune Loy et auxint les especialx Loys, Estatutz et Ordinances de la terre" made for the common profit and good governance of the realm in the times preceding (*Rot. Parl.* III, p. 6, no. 20.
[5] In 1350 the King responded to a petition of the Commons against the extortion of the clergy in taking fees for proving wills, "Soit la Ley sur ceo use come devant, si bien la Ley de Seinte Eglise come la Ley de la terre" (*Rot. Parl.* II, p. 230, no. 35).
[6] See Mr G. J. Turner's introduction to *Select Pleas of the Forest* (Selden Society); Petit-Dutaillis, "Études Additionnelles", in Stubbs, *Constitutional History*, French translation, vol. II.
[7] The "Pronunciatio" of the Parliament in 2 Richard II declares that "les Loys de la terre et les Loys d'armes doivent estre come relatives, l'une Loy toutdys aidant a l'autre en tous cas busoignables" (*Rot. Parl.* III, p. 33, no. 8).

Court of the Constable and Marshal;[1] the law of the staple;[2] Roman law; or the "lex Parliamenti".[3]

But the "special law" found most often in contrast with "ley commune" is the *consuetudo*, less frequently the *lex*, of some particular region or district, which differs in its provisions from the "lex et consuetudo regni".[4]

In 2 Edward II it was argued that a manor which formed a part of the King's ancient demesne was "tiel lieu qe n'est pas a la commune ley".[5] In a case in 1307 certain tenements were declared to be devisable "solom la coustume de Everwyk" (York).[6]

Cases of the law of Kent are numerous. For example it was said in the Common Pleas in 20 Edward I that certain tenements are not transferred from the common law to a special law ("changez hors de la commune ley en la Especial ley") unless the partibility of the tenement could be proved. Here the "special law" is a customary one, "le usage du pays".[7]

---

[1] Statute, 13 Rich. II, stat. I, cap. ii, confines his jurisdiction to cases not triable "par la commune ley du Roialme".

[2] The Statute of the Staple (27 Edw. III, stat. II) provides for the trial of merchants' cases "solonc la leie de lestaple et nemie a la commune ley" (cap. ii). All things touching the staple in the staple towns were to be determined "par la lei marchant...et nemie par la commune lei de la terre, ne par usages des Citees Burghs nautres villes" (cap. viii).

[3] *Rot. Parl.* III, p. 244, no. 7. In this Parliament the lords, both spiritual and temporal, claimed it as their privilege that all cases touching them "serroient demesnez, ajuggez, et discus par le cours de Parlement, et nemye par la Loy Civile, ne par la Commune Ley de la Terre, usez en autres plus bas Courtes du Roialme". See also *ibid.* III, p. 236.

[4] Much material is found in various volumes of the Selden Society Publications, such, for example, as the volumes edited by Miss Bateson on "Borough Customs". Many local peculiarities in the towns affecting tenure have been collected in Hemmeon's *Burgage Tenure in Mediaeval England* (Harvard Historical Studies, no. xx).

[5] Year Book 2 and 3 Edw. II (Selden Society), p. 60.

[6] *Ibid.* 33–35 Edw. I (Rolls Series), p. 457.

[7] *Ibid.* 20 and 21 Edw. (Rolls Series), pp. 327, 329. See also *ibid.* 33–35 Edw. I (Rolls Series), p. 351; also the so-called statute De Praerogativa Regis (*Statutes of the Realm*, I, p. 227), cap. xviii. See further, Somner, Robinson, or Sandys on Gavelkind.

Wales and the Marches naturally give us many examples in the Middle Ages, particularly before the enactment of "Statutum Walliae". For tenements in Wales and the Marches article fifty-six of the Great Charter of John guarantees to Welshmen and Marchers trial by peers "secundum legem Walliae" and "secundum legem Marchiae" respectively.[1]

In 25 Henry III a Welsh litigant pleads "quod nescit placitare secundum consuetudinem Anglie" and obtains a continuance "ad deliberandum".[2] In 1281 Edward promised Llewelyn that the laws of Wales and the Marches should not be disturbed, and informed him that the judges had been so instructed.[3] The "Statutum Walliae" itself,[4] while asserting Edward's right to declare, interpret, increase, and take away from these particular laws, especially in pleas of the crown, expressly excepts the law of succession to lands, contracts, procedure, etc., which are to remain as they were, "quia aliter usitatum est in Wallia quam in Anglia...et a tempore cujus non extitit memoria". In a case arising upon a disseisin in 19 Edward I, the defendant answers "quod tenementa non sunt in comitatu [Hereford] sed sunt in Marchia Wallie et debent in judicium deduci secundum legem Marchie et non per legem Anglie juxta statutum de Ronemede. Et quod non sunt in comitatu et ideo non deberent tractari per legem communem". The point was conceded.[5] Two years later Richard Fitz Alan declares he is a baron of Wales, "ubi est consuetudo approbata" that the barons should submit their disputes to the arbitration of a friend of both parties.[6] In 1321 a number of persons in Wales petition the Chancellor to issue a writ to the Justice of North Wales to do justice "secundum legem et consuetudinem parcium illarum".[7] The law of the

[1] Stubbs, *Select Charters*, 9th ed. p. 300.
[2] *Abbreviatio Placitorum* (Record Commission), p. 108.
[3] Rymer, *Foedera* (Record Commission), vol. i, pt. ii, p. 593.
[4] 12 Edw. I.   [5] *Plac. Abb.* p. 286.   [6] *Ibid.* p. 231.
[7] *Rot. Parl.* i, p. 397, no. 59.

Scottish March, of course, was on the same general basis. In 1249 a commission consisting of twelve English and twelve Scottish knights were sworn to the observance of the "Leges Marchiarum".[1]

It seems clear, then, that common law is the "lex et consuetudo regni Angliae, usitatae et approbatae, communi utilitati convenientes"; and that the basis of *consuetudo*, as of *lex*, is that it is approved, if not by express enactment, "more utentium". This law is "common" because it is "jus regni Angliae", enforced and observed "de consensu magnatum et reipublicae communi sponsione". Special custom is such as in like manner "observatur in partibus"—and, it might be added, by certain classes or estates of the people—"ubi fuerit more utentium approbata, et vicem legis obtinet"; and special *leges* are those expressly assented to by the particular persons so bound by them. So we return to Coke's dictum that the common law is "the law common to all".[2]

If our difficulties ended here, it would seem rather unnecessary to labour a point so apparently obvious at such length as I have done. But Magna Carta was not only common law: it was also enactment, and constantly referred to as such. In order to understand its real significance, we must first examine the larger question of the relation of enactment in general to the "ley commune"; and to make this difficult question as clear as possible it seemed necessary as a preliminary to restate much that is obvious in connection with the common law itself.

The next problem that meets us, then, is the relation of enactment to the law, particularly the common law, in medieval England, and this is a problem of great difficulty.

As indicated above, the names of enactments of law for the realm were variable until they became stereotyped by the general acceptance of Parliament's enacting power. The author of the *Leges Henrici*, speaking probably of Henry I's famous writ for the holding of the shire and hundred courts,

[1] Nicholson, *Leges Marchiarum*, pp. 1 *et seq.*   [2] *Ante*, p. 128.

says the practice, founded in ancient custom, had lately been confirmed by a *record*—"vera nuper est recordacione firmatum".[1] The Constitutions of Clarendon are spoken of in the preamble to the document as "ista recordatio vel recognitio cujusdam partis consuetudinum et libertatum et dignitatum" of the King's predecessors.[2] Similarly the Assize of Clarendon is termed "haec assisa",[3] as is also the Assize of the Forest in 1184.[4] John's Charter of Liberties itself is called "this present charter of ours".[5] Bracton speaks, as we have seen, of the Statute of Merton as "nova constitutio",[6] and elsewhere refers to a change in the law of dower made by it as brought about "nova superveniente gratia et provisione".[7] In a case in 43 Henry III one of its sections was referred to as "Provisio de Merton".[8] "The Edictum de Kenilworth" is well known, and it was so called by contemporaries.[9] The Statute of Winchester is cited by the author of the *Mirror of Justices* as "la constitucion de Wincestre".[10] In the reign of Henry III the word "statute" begins to be prominent; but at first hardly in any technical sense and alternative with other terms. For example, in 39 Henry III the statement is made that a rule in "consilio apud Merton provisum fuit et statutum", concerning the procedure on a writ of right "post illam constitucionem".[11] So in 52 Henry III mention is made of the pardon for transgressors in the time of the recent war, "occasione provisionum seu statutorum Exoniae non observatorum".[12]

By the time of Edward I, however, it is evident that "statute" is becoming a technical term, and the other names cease to be applied to the same enactments. So the author of

---

[1] Liebermann, *Gesetze der Angelsachsen*, I, p. 553.
[2] Stubbs, *Select Charters*, 9th ed. p. 163.
[3] *Ibid.* p. 173.   [4] *Ibid.* p. 186.
[5] *Ibid.* p. 292.   [6] *Ante*, p. 135.
[7] Folio 96. See also Bracton's *Note Book*, I, p. 89.
[8] *Plac. Abb.* pp. 146–7.   [9] *Ibid.* p. 187.
[10] Selden Society, VII, p. 48. See also *ibid.* p. 28; *Plac. Abb.* p. 171.
[11] *Plac. Abb.* p. 144.   [12] *Ibid.* p. 168.

the *Mirror* in the third chapter of his first book—"Des premiers constituciouns"—tells us that Alfred ordained "pur usage perpetuele" that his nobles should assemble at least twice a year "pur parlementer sur le guiement de poeple Dieu. Par cele estatut", he says, divers ordinances were made in times subsequent.[1] "The Statutum de Marleberge" is referred to in pleas of the fifth and sixth years of the reign.[2] In Michaelmas Term, 13 and 14 Edward I, judgment was given under a rule "quod constitutum fuit per Regem per secunda statuta Westmonasteriensia".[3]

It is unnecessary to continue further a list which grows rapidly longer after this date. Statute has now become the usual word for a certain kind of enactments of Parliament, and it is sometimes applied to acts, such as the one known as "De Asportatis Religiosorum", which are known to us only in forms not usual in statutes, some of them being found only in the form of writs.[4] The uncertainty of some of these so-called statutes may be due to a looseness in the application of the term which disappeared later, when the word invariably conveyed one definite and technical meaning. *Statutum* seems to be a popular rather than a technical term before the reign of Edward I, and it is possible that the non-technical employment of it may have survived longer in isolated cases to the confusion of the modern historian.

Our real difficulty arises with the question, what was the real nature of these *statuta* after the meaning of the word had been fixed, and how did they differ, if at all, from the law that preceded them, and from enactments which were not termed statutes?

The subject of the relation of enactment to the law which

[1] Selden Society, VII, p. 8.   [2] *Plac. Abb.* p. 268.
[3] *Ibid.* p. 209.
[4] "De Asportatis Religiosorum" is referred to as *statutum* in 16 Edw. II, *Plac. Abb.* p. 341. Examples in writ form are "circumspecte Agatis, De Finibus Levatis", etc. These and a number of others are in Latin, the language of royal writs, instead of French, which was becoming the usual medium of parliamentary enactment at this time.

precedes, as that relation was understood in the later Middle Ages, is a subject that has received a good deal of attention in recent years. We have passed beyond the naïve view that men of the Middle Ages *must* have understood that relation just as we understand it to-day. We are trying to discover what the men of that time really thought about it. For example, Mr Lapsley's view that the well-known declaration of Parliament in 1322, seeming to require the participation of all the estates of the realm in binding legislation, applied merely to such constitutional arrangements as had been effected by the ordinances of 1311;[1] or Professor Merriman's interpretation of Parliament's legislative functions as the repealing rather than the enacting of law.[2]

As an alternative interpretation I submit an explanation, which might be summarized as follows:

First. Enactments of substantive law in England in the later Middle Ages were made for the general purpose of affirming the law already approved or of removing abuses which hindered its due execution—"pur surement garder les Loies ove due execution et hastif remedie pur abusion de la Loye en usurpation".[3]

Such affirmance implied frequent interpretation, the supplying of additional penalties to secure proper execution, and even supplemental enactments for the same purpose. This eventually led to changes in the law itself, but such changes came gradually and in the main only incidentally, and were not the main purpose of enactment. Repeal of the laws used and approved is in the beginning not thought of. It comes very gradually, and in the guise of the removal of provisions

[1] *English Historical Review*, no. XXVIII, pp. 118 *et seq.* This view seems also to be accepted by Professor Tout, *The Place of Edward II in English History*, pp. 150–1.

[2] *Control by National Assemblies of the Repeal of Legislation in the Later Middle Ages*, Mélanges d'Histoire offerts à M. Charles Bémont (1913), pp. 437 *et seq.*

[3] "Pronunciatio" of the Parliament of 13 Hen. IV (1411), *Rot. Parl.* III, p. 647.

which have wrongfully interpreted or added to the old law and tended to the introduction of abuses rather than the removal of them. The substance of the old law itself is in theory not repealable, at least in early times. When statutes are repealed the oft-repeated reason is that they are against the law of the land or prerogative. Repeal is strictly, in the beginning, nothing more than a remedy "pur abusion de la Loye en usurpation". Occasionally, in times of disorder, whole Parliaments were repealed in the fourteenth and fifteenth centuries, but the reason alleged is usually that their summons is irregular or their acts unlawful. It is only at a comparatively late period that the repeal of statutes is openly avowed as one of the purposes of Parliament; even then such a power is hardly considered as reaching the central principles of the common law. On the contrary, an examination of parliamentary rolls of the fourteenth and fifteenth centuries will show that the first business of a Parliament is the re-enactment or affirmance of the whole body of the fundamental law, including the statutes of the King's predecessors. This is nearly always stated among the purposes of the Parliament in the "Pronunciationes", and it is almost invariably prayed for first among the petitions of the Commons. It would not be beyond the truth to say that in this period, Parliament was, in its "legislative" capacity, above anything else, an affirming body, for such affirmations *en bloc* are almost invariable.[1] It is only in the latter part of this period that the Commons in their petition for the affirmance of preceding enactments begin to add the significant phrase, "et nient repellez".[2] There is a remarkable, and possibly not accidental, similarity between these repeated affirmations at the opening of each Parliament and the earlier proclamations of the King's peace, at the beginning of each reign.

---

[1] See *Rot. Parl.* iv, p. 130, no. 10.
[2] For repeal, see *Rot. Parl.* iii, p. 352 A; *ibid.* pp. 425 A–B; 426 A, 442 A; stat. i, Hen. IV, cap. iii; stat. ii, Hen. IV, cap. xiii; *Rot. Parl.* v, p. 374 A–B; stat. 39 Hen. VI, cap. i; *Rot. Parl.* vi, p. 191 A. See also 4 Inst. p. 52.

Second. Participation in the enactment of such laws is based on the theory that the binding enactment of a law can be made only by those whom it touches. It must be a law "approbata utentium", to use Bracton's phrase.[1] If an enactment is to bind the clergy, the clergy must assent; to one binding the baronage, the barons must assent; a provision affecting merchants is only binding on account of their consent alone; and the law of particular districts is recognized as valid "more approbata utentium". But likewise, "what touches *all* should be approved by *all*".[2] And what touches all is the law common to all—the "lex communis, lex terrae, lex regni".

On this basis of consent Glanvill had tried to fit feudal conditions into Roman terms, by saying that the people had enacted a law that had been "approved" by immemorial custom; much in the same way that Roman lawyers, ages before him, had interpreted the *uti legassit* of the Twelve Tables in the development of the law of testamentary succession. If this were true, it would not be absurd to assimilate English custom with Roman *lex*. It certainly was observed *pro lege*. All this is clear enough for local and particular customs. But what of the common law? How can it really be said to be enacted, affirmed, and "approbata utentium omnium"?

---

[1] *Ante*, p. 131, n. 1.

[2] This famous sentence appeared in the writs of summons to the clergy for the Model Parliament of 1295 (*Parl. Writs*, I, p. 30). The writs begin as follows: "Sicut lex justissima, provida circumspectione sacrorum principum stabilita, hortatur et statuit ut quod omnes tangit ab omnibus approbetur, sic et nimis evidenter ut communibus periculis per remedia provisa communiter obvietur." The *lex* here referred to is probably from Justinian's Code, 5, 59, 5, where nothing of a political character is referred to, but only the common action of several *co-tutores* appointed under a will or otherwise. The original words are, "ut, quod omnes similiter tangit, ab omnibus comprobetur". It is interesting to note that in the supplementary title "De Regulis Juris" at the end of the "Sext", published three years after Edward's writs, in 1298, Boniface the Eighth includes this maxim as regula xxix, "Quod omnes tangit, debet ab omnibus approbari".

For much of the thirteenth century the baronage, lay and ecclesiastical, made good their claim that they alone were the *populus*; that "all" included none beyond themselves. *Populus* is frequently used in that sense at that time, and their assent seems to have been considered the assent of the realm. But by the fourteenth century this was changed. Other communes besides theirs were making themselves felt in the national councils, the "communitas bacheleriae Angliae"[1] and the communities of the towns, who considered themselves a part of the "communitas Angliae"[2] to which the *lex communis* applied. It is a striking fact that Edward's principle that what touches all should be approved by all was carried no further than those communities until the Reform Bills of the nineteenth century. Those had a right to participate in the enactment of common law, to whom common law applied, and by the fourteenth century the communes of the counties and the towns were able successfully to vindicate in Parliament their claim to be a part of the *populus* to which that law and all provisions affirming it were common.

It is clear that such a principle could not be enforced, and could indeed hardly arise, before the composition of Parliament was settled on the basis which it retained until the legislation of the nineteenth century. Naturally, while that composition was still unsettled this principle was doubtful. Even if a law must be "utentium approbata", how could the whole "communitas Angliae" consent in Parliament? At first, apparently, while the composition of Parliament fluctuated, there was doubt as to the validity of an enactment until it had been proclaimed locally throughout the realm. Only gradually did the theory arise that the whole of England was constructively in Parliament; that they were all assumed to be there consenting to what Parliament did. The theory of representation was complete in the fourteenth century. The fact that much of the representation was only "virtual" need

[1] *Annals of Burton*, p. 471, quoted in Stubbs, *Select Charters*, 9th ed. p. 331.   [2] *Ibid.*

give us little concern, when we remember that this remained equally true for five hundred years after, and that to a certain extent it is true to-day. This theory then did not necessarily give to the estates in Parliament alone the right to legislate for particular persons, classes, or places. That might be done by the King by charter or otherwise with the assent of those only who were affected. Neither did it require the assent of "all" the estates in Parliament unless that assent was given to some enactment which touched them all. The one thing that obviously did touch them all was an enactment affecting the *lex communis*. To that the assent of "all" was necessary.

Third. This theory of the participation of the estates in enactment, if true, will in part explain the nature of the enactments of Parliament themselves. Statutes are enactments of law "perpetuelment a durer". If this law happens to be "common", then all must assent. But the real distinction between statute and ordinance, which gave Coke so much trouble, does not arise from the difference between enactments of common law and other enactments; nor from the fact that the King, Lords, and Commons must all unite upon a statute, while this is not necessary for an ordinance, as Coke thought. The real difference is that a statute, in its original meaning, is an affirmance of law. If it is in affirmance of the common law, it shares the nature of the law it interprets, and I have tried to show that one of the characteristics of that common law is its permanence and its supremacy in the realm. Like the law it authoritatively interprets, a statute in affirmance of the common law is permanent also; it has become in a sense a part of that law. Statutes affecting law other than common are for a long time less numerous and less important, and the name statute was probably applied to them later than to acts for the whole realm and on the analogy of the latter. But the essential characteristic in all cases seems to be the purpose on the part of those enacting that their work shall endure for all future time; a characteristic that parliamentary statutes were conceived to have, because their origin was traceable to the affirmance of a law that was permanent, extending "a tempore cujus non extitit memoria". This theory is weakened somewhat in the fifteenth century, but it is safe to say that this is the general conception of parliamentary "legislation" from the thirteenth century on. Statutes are enactments "perpetuelment a durer". It is their permanence that makes them "statutes", and necessitates somewhat greater formality in their promulgation than is necessary in acts of a character less permanent and therefore less important.

Ordinances, on the other hand, are temporary provisions, which are not considered to affect the permanent law unless they are re-enacted "in form of a statute", as they often were. The essence of a statute, then, is permanence, that of an ordinance is its temporary character. Statutes in affirmance of the common law had to be assented to by all; so had ordinances if they touched all the estates represented in Parliament. Both statutes and ordinances are found that touch fewer classes. When they are, only those classes so affected need assent in order to make them binding law for them. These distinctions are, like the conception of affirmance, much clearer in the fourteenth century than in the fifteenth; when many of the older ideas of Parliament's functions are becoming blurred, and precedents are beginning to form which are later to furnish the basis for the modern theory of legislative sovereignty.

These are the three chief points which the contemporary records seem to me to indicate in regard to the nature of enactment. Before taking up their bearing on the history and nature of Magna Carta, I shall set forth a few of these records, under the three headings mentioned above; and first, under that of—

I. The Affirmance of Common Law

In this connection, nothing is more significant than the words of the preambles of Edward I's two remarkable Statutes of Westminster, which, more than anything else he did, justify the application to him of the title the English Justinian.[1] One statement in the preamble to the second statute is particularly interesting. It recites the fact that at Gloucester, in the sixth year of the reign, certain statutes had been passed, but that certain cases remained undetermined—"quidam casus in quibus lex deficiebat remanserunt non determinati, Quaedam enim ad reprimendum oppressionem populi remanserunt statuenda". Hence the present statute. Commenting on this, the author of the *Mirror* says: "What is said in the second Statute of Westminster as to the failure of law in divers cases is open to objection, because for all trespasses there is law ordained though it may be disused, forgotten, or perverted by those who know it not. And the first three articles are no statutes, but merely revoke the errors of negligent judges." The first of these three articles is the important enactment "De Donis Conditionalibus", which certainly does do nothing but restore the law as it was before judicial decision modified it. In his biting comments on this and the other important enactments of the early part of Edward's reign, the same author says, for example: one "is no statute, but the revocation of an error"; another "affirms, rather than repeals an error"; another, though it is "but common and ancient law", gives insufficient remedy; another "is merely the revocation to right law of a prevailing error"; another "is a

---

[1] The enactments of the Statute of Westminster First (3 Edw. I, 1275) are said to be made because the King desired "to redress the state of the realm in such things as required amendment, for the common profit of holy Church and of the realm; and because the state of the holy Church had been evil kept, and the prelates and religious persons of the land grieved many ways and the people otherwise intreated than they ought to be, and the peace less kept and the laws used and the offenders less punished than they ought to be, by reason whereof the people of the land feared less to offend".

The Second (13 Edw. I, stat. i, 1285) is in some respects more explicit, as is also the Statute of Gloucester (6 Edw. I, 1278), and many others of this reign, so remarkable in this respect. Edward's preambles are much more instructive than later, when parliamentary enactment had become a matter of course, prefaced by stereotyped phrases or by none at all.

novelty injurious to the lords of fees"; another "seems rather error than law"; another, "no statute, but lawless will and pleasure"; another "is founded upon no right"; another is "not founded on law"; while others "are just humbug (*truffe*) for they are not regarded". He also refers to Alfred's laws as a "statute" under which "divers ordinances were made by divers kings down to the present time, which ordinances are disused by those who are less wise and because they are not put in writing and published in definite terms".[1]

The form of the coronation oath, which remained with but few modifications until the accession of William and Mary, was probably used first at the coronation of Edward II. It was certainly used at the coronation of Henry IV.[2] In it there is one promise that was not demanded before—"Concedis justas Leges et Consuetudines esse tenendas, et promittis per te eas esse protegendas, et ad honorem Dei corroborandas quas vulgus elegerit, secundum vires tuas. Respondebit, Concedo et promitto." This is the oath so much referred to by the King and by Parliament in the fourteenth and fifteenth centuries, and its importance is very great in the history of enactment. The celebrated ordinances of 1311 provide that all the statutes made "en amendement de la lei et au profit du poeple" by the King's ancestors, "soient gardez et maintenuz si avant come estre devient par lei et reson", provided they are not contrary to the Great Charter, the Charter of the Forest, or the present ordinances; and that if any statute were made "countre la fourme susdite, soit tenuz pur nul, et tout outrement defait".[3] Two entries on the Parliament Roll for 1343 during the struggle of the King and Parliament are instructive on this point. It was agreed that the statute of two years before (15 Edward III) "soit de tut repellez et anientez et perde noun d'Estatut, come cel q'est prejudiciel et contraire

---

[1] Selden Society, VII, 189, 8.
[2] *Rot. Parl.* III, p. 417 B. See also Legge, *English Coronation Records*, pp. xxvii, 88.
[3] *Ibid.* I, p. 285 A.

a Leys et Usages du Roialme, et as Droitz et Prerogatives nostre Seigneur le Roi". But as there are certain articles embraced in the said statute which "sont resonables et acordantz a Lei et a Reson", the King and his Council agree that these articles, together with others agreed upon in the present Parliament, "soit fait Estatut de novel" on the advice of the "Justices et autres Sages, et tenuz a touz jours".[1] In the same Parliament the Commons pray that the statutes concerning grants be observed. The King replies that since he perceived that "le dit Estatut feust contre son serment et en blemissement de sa Corone et de sa Roialte, et contre la Ley de la terre en plusours pointz", it should be repealed. But he wishes that the articles of the said statute be examined and that such as are found "honurables et profitables pur le Roi et son poeple soient ore faitz en novel Estatut, et gardez desore".[2]

In 1347 the Commons petitioned that a plaintiff recovering damages on a writ of trespass should have execution on the defendant's lands, but were answered by the King that this could not be done "sanz Estatut", upon which he desires the advice of his Council, and will do what seems best "pur son poeple".[3] In 1348 the Commons prayed that the King would give no response changing their petitions as a result of any "Bill" presented in Parliament "in the name of the Commons". By advice of the Prelates and "Grantz" the King replied to these petitions "touchantes la Lei de la terre, Qe les Leis eues et usees en temps passez, ne le Process d'icelle usez cea en arere, ne se purront changer saunz ent faire novel Estatut. A queu chose faire le Roi ne poait adonques, ne unquore poet entendre par certeines causes. Mes a plust tost q'il purra entendre", he with his Council will ordain touching those articles and others "touchantz Amendement de Lei" according to reason and equity, for "all his lieges and subjects and for each of them".[4] A very important entry occurs in

---

[1] *Rot. Parl.* ii, p. 139, no. 23.   [2] *Ibid.* pp. 139–40, no. 27.
[3] *Ibid.* p. 166, no. 13.   [4] *Ibid.* p. 203, no. 30

the roll for 25 Edward III, where the Parliament interprets the law of succession.

Nostre dit Seigneur le Roi veulliant qe totes doutes et aweres fuissent oustes, et la Lei en ceo cas declare et mise en certeine, fist charger les Prelatz, Countes, Barons, et autres Sages de son Conseil, assemblez a ceo Parlement, a faire deliberation sur cel point. Lesqueux d'un assent ont dit, Qe le Lei de la Corone d'Engleterre est, et ad este touz jours tiele....Laquele Lei nostre Seignur le Roi, les ditz Prelatz, Countes, Barons, et autres Grantz, et tote la Commune, assemblez el [en] dit Parlement, approevent et afferment pur touz jours.[1]

For much of the fourteenth and fifteenth centuries the Parliaments are regularly opened by a "Pronunciatio"; such as the one which states, among the chief reasons for the summons, "qe l'Estatutz faitz cea en arer pur amendement des Leies de la terre et du poeple ne sont pas gardez ne usez en lour effect";[2] another, which urges that the good laws and customs be guarded and preserved and violators punished;[3] another asking the Commons for information "coment ses Leyes de sa Terre et l'Estatutz sont gardez et executez"[4]; or one which announces that it is the will of the King that the laws "serroient tenuz et gardez", and promises that by letters under the secret seal or privy seal or otherwise, "la Commune Loie ne serroit destourbez, ne le poeple en lour pursuyte aucunement delaiez".[5] For the same period the petitions of the Commons usually begin with a prayer, such as the one in 1379, which asks, among other things, "that the common law of the land be held as used in the time of the King's ancestors".[6]

---

[1] *Rot. Parl.* II, p. 231, no. 41. See also stat. 25 Edw. III, stat. i. In this connection the proceedings in Parliament leading up to the Statute of Provisors are also interesting. They are found in the same words, in both the Parliament Roll and the Statute Roll (*Rot. Parl.* II, pp. 232–3, stat. 25 Edw. III, stat. iv).

[2] *Ibid.* p. 237 A.
[3] 3 Rich. II, *ibid.* III, p. 71, no. 3.
[4] 13 Rich. II, *ibid.* p. 257, no. 1.
[5] 5 Hen. IV, *ibid.* p. 529 A.
[6] *Ibid.* p. 80, no. 1; p. 321, no. 44, etc.

As seen in many of the instances given above, affirmance and interpretation often go together in re-enactments of the law, as well as supplementary provisions of great importance. But Bracton was expressing the conception of his time, in distinguishing what adds to the law from what is contrary to it: "Non destruitur quod in melius commutatur".[1] So, he says, a writ is quashed if "contra jus et regni consuetudinem et maxime contra chartam libertatis.... Si autem praeter jus fuerit impetratum, dum tamen fuit rationi consonum *et non juri contrarium*, erit sustinendum, dum tamen a rege concessum et a consilio suo approbatum."[2] The general business of a Parliament was well stated in the "Pronunciatio" of the Parliament of 38 Edward III[3] to be—"les Lois, Custumes, Estatutz, et Ordinances en son temps, et en temps de ses Auncestres faites, meintenir, et si nuls soient que busoignent declaration, ajoustement, ou artement, solonc le cas, temps, et necessite, ensement de lour bon avis et conseil declarer, ajouster, retrere, et amender". The great importance of affirmance in enactment is also illustrated in the limits which were set to the King's dispensing power. The one kind of statute with which he might not dispense, was the kind passed in affirmance of the law.[4]

---

[1] Folio 1 B. Mere interpretation, in the fourteenth century, belonged to the Council. When a solemn affirmance by "novel Estatut" was necessary in matters of common law, this could only be done in a Parliament of which the Commons were a part.

[2] *Ibid.* 414 B.

[3] *Rot. Parl.* II, p. 283 A. See also, *ibid.* II, p. 341, no. 119; *ibid.* III, p. 43, no. 46; p. 97 B.

[4] On this, it is unnecessary to do more than refer to a few of the chief authorities. E.g. Broom, *Constitutional Law*, 2nd ed. pp. 492 *et seq.*; Anson, *Law and Custom of the Constitution*, I, 4th ed. pp. 326 *et seq.*; Maitland, *Constitutional History of England*, pp. 302–6; Thomas *v.* Sorrell, *Vaughan's Reports*, p. 330; Godden *v.* Hales, 11 St. Tr. 1165, with the various contemporary tracts appended to the report; W. Petyt, *Jus Parliamentarium*; Luders's *Tracts*, Tract V.

II. PARTICIPATION

It would be rash to say that the principle underlying the participation of the various classes "represented" in the English Parliament came entirely from feudalism. There are precedents in Rome, and precedents in England and on the Continent after the fall of the Roman Empire, of quite another kind. But these came to the men of the later Middle Ages through a feudal channel. To put it in another way, feudalism is the stage through which English institutions had passed and were still passing at the time when the common law was forming and the functions of Parliament developing, and the participation of the "estates" in "legislation" can no more be understood without taking this into account than can the existence of these estates themselves. Behind them all lies the *curia* of the lord in which the laws of the fief are "found" and applied by all the tenants who owe suit there and have the corresponding right to be tried only by the *pares curtis*. The Court of the King was the *Curia Regis*, and the laws "found" there by its suitors were the *lex terrae*. But while tenants-in-chief alone might "find" those laws, they had not made them. For a long time the barons were able to make good their claim that they were the *populus*, and through that fiction might alone interpret and enforce the law, but this fiction never destroyed the underlying theory that law was approved "consensu omnium utentium", and just so soon as other classes became strong enough they asserted their right to assent to enactments affecting themselves. Precedents might be found as early as the preamble to Alfred's laws and the indefinite "right" of the people to ratify the "election" of a King, as it appears in the Norman period,[1] a "right" to be traced back no doubt to much the same origin as the similar procedure in the choice of the Popes before the "constitution" of the

[1] See, for example, the brief but excellent reference to this as a precedent for later consent in legislation, in Pike, *Constitutional History of the House of Lords*, pp. 310 *et seq.*

Papacy was definitely formed; but it seems best to go back no further than the thirteenth century. A beginning might be made with the clear statement of Bracton who mentions the "leges Anglicanae et consuetudines...quae quidem cum fuerint approbatae consensu utentium, et sacramento regum confirmatae, mutari non poterunt nec destrui sine communi consensu et consilio eorum omnium, quorum consilio et consensu fuerunt promulgatae".[1] Enactment and interpretation by the King and his curia are permissible without this *consilium omnium*, since they do not destroy, but only improve the law. "In melius tamen converti possunt, etiam sine eorum consensu, quia non destruitur quod in melius commutatur." So also things "nova et inconsueta et quae prius usitata non fuerint in regno, si tamen similia evenerint, per simile judicentur....Si autem talia nunquam prius evenerint, et obscurum et difficile sit eorum judicium, tunc ponantur judicia in respectu usque ad magnam curiam, ut ibi per consilium curiae terminentur." When, however, anything is enacted, it is "communi consensu omnium", in theory, even though not in fact. We know that the barons alone enacted what Bracton calls "quaedam constitutio quae dicitur constitutio de Merton", yet he says one of its articles "provisum est et concessum *ab omnibus*".[2] The sentence of excommunication pronounced in 1253 against violators of Magna Carta, or the liberties of the Church, "vel antiquas regni consuetudines approbatas", is followed by a ratification under the seal of the King and certain magnates, concluding with a warning, that if any additions are made to the document, "dominus Rex, et predicti magnates omnes, et *communitas populi* protestantur publice...quod in ea nunquam consenserunt nec consenciunt, set de plano eis contradicunt".[3] It seems pertinent in this connection also to refer again to the form of the coronation oath, which seems to date from 1307, under which the King promised to hold, protect, and strengthen the just laws and

[1] Folio 1 B.   [2] *Ibid.* 227 A.
[3] Bémont, *Chartes*, pp. 73-4.

customs "quas vulgus elegerit".[1] The word *vulgus* was not used by accident—nor *elegerit* either. The *consensus omnium* includes theirs, in theory at least, even though it be often merely the tacit assent to immemorial custom.

Participation in grants need not detain us. The word *consuetudines*, customs, had in the Middle Ages, as it has now, a double meaning; and undoubtedly it was the desire for a larger participation in grants rather than in enactments that led to the application by Edward I to the "Magnum Concilium" in larger measure than before of the old principle that what touches all should be approved by all. The vindication of the right of consent to grants was understood and is understood now. For participation in "legislation" more proof is needed, but fortunately it exists.

For example, in 1364 the Rolls of Parliament refer to certain good purveyances and ordinances passed with assent of "Ducs, Countes, Barons, Nobles et Communes…*et touz autres qe la chose touche*". Some of these are referred to later in the roll as "Estatutz".[2]

In 1354 the Commons complain of the ordinance of the Staple lately passed *in the Council* at Westminster. They insist that such matters can be determined only in Parliament because they really concern the King *and all his people*. They declare that they have inspected these provisions

et queles lour semblerent bones et profitables pur nostre Seigneur le Roi et tut son poeple, soient affermez en cest Parlement, et tenuz pur Estatut a durer pur touz jours. A quelle priere le Roi et touz les Grantz s'acordent unement, issint totes foitz, qe si rien soit ajouster soit ajouste, ou qe rien soit a ouster soit ouste en Parlement, quele heure qe mestier en serra, et nemye en autre manere.[3]

In 1363 the Rolls say, "Et issint le Parlement continue sur tretee de divers choses, touchantz si bien les Petitions bailliez par les Communes et autres singulers persons *come les Busoignes du Roy et son Roialme*."[4]

---

[1] *Ante*, p. 150.   [2] *Rot. Parl.* II, pp. 284*b*–285, no. 9.
[3] *Ibid.* p. 257, no. 16.   [4] *Ibid.* p. 280, nos. 38–40.

In 1371 the Commons recite the statute ordering "qe nul Justise par mandement de Grant ou Prive Seal ne lessera de faire commune Ley et Droit as parties"; and pray that it be observed, and "qe par comandement du Roi, ne prier des gentz prives, n'autres, la Commune Ley ne soit delaie ne bestourne".[1]

In 51 Edward III the Commons petition not to be bound by any statute or ordinance made without their consent, and that statutes made in Parliament be annulled only there, "et ceo de commune assent du Parlement". They pray more especially that they be not bound by any statute or ordinance granted on petition of the clergy to which they have not consented. "Ne qe voz dites Communes ne soient obligez par nulles Constitutions q'ils sont pur lour avantage sanz assent de voz dites Communes, Car eux ne veullent estre obligez a null de voz Estatutz ne Ordenances faitz sanz lour assent." The response is, "Soit ceste matire declares en especial"; probably because it might be a nice question whether the matters objected to were not really things which touched only the clergy rather than "tut son poeple", and therefore such as might rightly be determined without the Commons' assent.[2]

In the midst of the troubles of the year 1381 an interesting entry is found in the Rolls of Parliament. The Chancellor "en plein Parlement" asks the opinion "de toutz illeoques" on the repeal of the manumission recently granted to the serfs. To which the lords spiritual and temporal, the knights, citizens, and burghers, responded with one voice in favour of the repeal—"Adjoustant, qe tiele Manumission ou Franchise des Neifs ne ne poast estre fait sanz lour Assent q'ont le greindre interesse."[3]

Eight years later the Commons petition that neither the Chancellor nor the Council, after the dissolution of Parliament, should make any ordinance "encontre la commune Ley, ne les aunciens Custumes de la Terre, et Estatutz devant

[1] *Rot. Parl.* II, p. 308, no. 41.   [2] *Ibid.* p. 368, nos. 44–6.
[3] *Ibid.* III, p. 100, no. 13.

ces hures ordeinez, ou a ordeigner en cest present Parlement: *einz courge la commune Ley a tout le poeple universel*".[1]

The proclamations for the publication of statutes or of Magna Carta, and the "Pronunciationes" and petitions in Parliament also furnish considerable general evidence on this point. In all these the matters upon which the whole Parliament has acted are expressly stated to be articles "pur le commun profit du peuple e du reaume", as in the royal proclamation of the confirmation of Magna Carta in 1297;[2] or a grant "a soen poeple pur le pru de soen roiaume", in the "Articuli super Cartas" of 1300.[3] So a mandate to the Justice of Chester, of 1275, orders him to publish in Chester certain provisions and statutes enacted by the magnates "for the good of the realm and for the relief of the people".[4] Such expressions are common later in the "pronunciations du Parlement", but they are not found after Edward II's reign in cases where the Commons have not assented. For example, in 1351 there is mention made of "l'Estatutz faitz. . . pur amendement des Leies de la terre et du poeple";[5] in 1378, of the good laws and customs of the realm;[6] in 1397, "Loyes justes et honestes universelment, par queux si bien les grantes come les petitz deussent estre governez". The King wishes to know if any of his subjects have been hindered in obtaining remedies "par la commune Ley, et sur ce estre conseillez par toutz les Estatz du Parlement, et ent faire bone et due remede en cest present Parlement".[7] In 1414 the King desires the preservation of "les bones Leies de sa Terre"; and also asks Parliament "pur faire autres Leies de novell, a l'aise et profit de ses lieges".[8] The language is somewhat different from what would have been thought of a century earlier, but the principle is the same.

---

[1] *Rot. Parl.* III, p. 266, no. 30.　　　[2] Bémont, *Chartes*, p. 82.
[3] *Ibid.* p. 99.
[4] *Calendar of Patent Rolls*, 1272–81, p. 104.
[5] *Rot. Parl.* II, p. 237 A.　　　[6] *Ibid.* III, p. 32 A.
[7] *Ibid.* p. 347 A–B.　　　[8] *Ibid.* IV, p. 15 B.

The petitions of the Commons, like the "Pronunciationes" in the King's name, seem to make this distinction also. In 1341 the Commons pray for the observance of Magna Carta and "des autres Ordinances e Statutz, faitz pur profit du commune poeple entendant les pointz de la dite Chartre, ensemblement od les autres perpetuelment a durer".[1] Again in 1368 they petition for the maintenance of the charters "e touz les Estatuz faitz devant ces hures *pur profit de la Commune*".[2] The next year they ask that the statutes be maintained, "si bien l'Estatut de la Foreste, come touz autres Estatutz, lesqueux deivent suffire a bon Governement s'ils soient bien gardez".[3]

Very important is the careful answer of the Archbishop of Canterbury in 1399 to the prayer of the Commons to be excused from taking part in the judgments of Parliament.[4] It is true, he says, as the Commons have set forth, that they need not take part in Parliament's actions—"Sauve q'en Estatutz a faires, ou en Grantes e Subsides, *ou tiels choses a faires pur commune profit du Roialme*, le Roy voet avoir especialment leur advis e assent".

This evidence of the necessity for the advice of the Commons on matters "pur commune profit" is supplemented by proof of the converse—that matters which were clearly not of this character, which affected particular classes only—needed no ratification by the Commons to make them binding law for those whom they did affect.

So we find a regulation of the Exception of Neifty by "le Conseil en Parlement" in 1347;[5] and an "Accord" in 1331 by which the lords agree, "qe nul Grant de terre" will aid any robber, but give aid to the justices in punishing them.[6]

---

[1] *Rot. Parl.* II, p. 128, no. 9.   [2] *Ibid.* p. 295, no. 10.
[3] *Ibid.* p. 300, no. 14.
[4] *Ibid.* III, p. 427, no. 79. See also *ibid.* p. 243 A; also the King's answer to the famous petition of 1414 in which he promises that no enactment shall bind the Commons without their assent (*Rot. Parl.* IV, p. 22, no. 22).
[5] *Ibid.* II, p. 180 A–B.   [6] *Ibid.* p. 62, no. 9.

In 51 Edward III to a request of the Commons for an ordinance regarding foreign merchants, the King answers that he and the magnates will consider and ordain what is best.[1]

Matters specially affecting the clergy are among the most valuable on this point. In 1389 the two archbishops made a protestation in full Parliament that they do not assent to any statute of that Parliament "nunc noviter edito, nec antiquo pretenso innovato", which is in restriction of "Potestas Apostolica" or the liberties of the Church.[2]

In 1397 the prelates protest that they cannot assent to any enactment of the King or the temporal lords touching the rights of the Pope. There is no mention of the Commons.[3] The Commons had in fact petitioned that the King would, with the advice of such sages and worthies as he pleased, at the next Parliament ordain such changes in the Statute of Provisors as seemed reasonable and profitable in their discretion.[4] In the same year a committee of Parliament, consisting of lords and knights, but commissioned "par vertue e auctorite du Parlement, de l'assent des Seigneurs Espirituels e Temporels", annulled the Duke of Hereford's patent.[5]

In 1433 the Commons prayed for a modification of the Statute of the Staple of Calais, and were answered that it should be done as they desired, "Savant toutz foitz au Roy, poair et auctoritee de modifier mesme l'Estatut quant luy plerra, par advys de son Counseil solonc ceo qe meulx luy semblera pur le profit du Roy, e du Roialme".[6]

III. Varieties of Parliamentary Enactment

Enactments of Parliament are referred to in contemporary official records under various names: provisiones, etablissements (stabilimenta), constitutiones, accords, awards, ordinationes, statuta, and a number of others. Most of the

---

[1] *Rot. Parl.* II, p. 367, no. 35.   [2] *Ibid.* III, p. 264, no. 24.
[3] *Ibid.* p. 41, no. 22.
[4] *Ibid.* p. 340, no. 21.   [5] *Ibid.* p. 372, no. 87.
[6] *Ibid.* IV, p. 454, no. 63. See also *ibid.* p. 490, no. 19.

treatment of the points vital to this paper may be included, however, under the last two of these, and that treatment need not be very long, after the many excellent discussions of this subject from the seventeenth century to the present.[1]

The treatises referred to above quote or cite most of the important precedents in the Rolls of Parliament,[2] and it would therefore be useless to give here more than a few of these.

In 1324 was passed the statute concerning the lands of the Templars, which was afterwards objected to as against law. The statute was made by the King and Magnates only, but it was declared to be "concordatum...provisum et statutum pro lege in hac parte perpetuo duratura".[3]

Three years later the King replied to a petition of the Commons, that certain ordinances should be viewed and examined "et les bones soient mis en Estatut, et les autres soient oustez".[4]

The Statute of Purveyors,[5] passed by the King, Lords, and Commons, is followed by five additional articles which are to be in force without change until the next Parliament. Just following these articles there is a note on the Statute Roll— "Et memorandum quod in parliamento predicto concordatum fuit quod articuli predicti non tenerentur pro Statuto."

---

[1] See, among others, 4 Inst. 25; Prynne, *Irenarches Redivivus*; *Animadversions on Coke's Fourth Institute*, p. 13; Whitelocke, *Notes upon the King's Writt*, chs. xc, xcviii, xcix; Ruffhead's Preface to his edition of the statutes; Introduction by the Commissioners to the *Statutes of the Realm*, section v (also reprinted in Cooper's *Public Records*, i, pp. 163 *et seq.*); Hargrave and Butler's notes to *Coke on Littleton*, p. 159 B, n. 292; Amos's notes to Fortescue's *De Laudibus Legum Angliae*, pp. 59–61; Gneist, *English Constitutional History* (English translation), ii, pp. 22 *et seq.*; Maitland, *Constitutional History*, pp. 256–8; Hatschek, *Englisches Staatsrecht*, i, p. 114; Anson, *Law and Custom of the Constitution*, 4th ed. i, pp. 243–9.

[2] See the treatises above mentioned, among which the Introduction to the *Statutes of the Realm* is the most important. It cites and analyses most of the entries in the Rolls of Parliament important for this subject.

[3] 17 Edw. II, stat. 3.

[4] 1 Edw. III, *Rot. Parl.* ii, p. 11, no. 3.   [5] 10 Edw. III, stat. 2.

Probably the most conclusive entry in the Rolls of Parliament occurs in 1340, where a committee is chosen consisting of knights and burgesses as well as lords, who are instructed to look over the records of that Parliament from day to day and cause

mettre en Estatut les pointz et les articles *qe sont perpetuels.* Lequel Estatut nostre Seignur le Roi, par assent des touz en dit Parlement esteantz, comanda de engrosser et ensealer et ferment garder par tut le Roialme d'Engleterre.... Et sur les pointz et articles *qe ne sont mye perpetuels, einz pur un temps,* si ad nostre Seignur le Roi, par assent des Grantz *et Communes,* fait faire et ensealer ses Lettres Patentes.... [1]

In 15 Edward III an interesting case occurs. Apparently the previous petitions of Parliament had been assented to, but not authenticated as statutes by the Great Seal. Now, as a condition of the payment of an instalment of a previous grant, the demand is made that these be affirmed as conceded by the King —"C'est assavoir, *les pointz a durer par estatut et les autres par Chartre ou Patent,* et liverez as Chivalers des Counteez sanz rien paier." [2] The word ordinance does not occur.

In 1344 the Commons pray that the "Provisions, Ordinances, and Accords" made in a previous Parliament "soient affermez par Estatut perpetuelment a durer". [3]

In 1347 they petition that a provision already agreed on in Council without delay be made "selonc la fourme de l'Estatut", and the King promises that that article and the points contained in it "soient tenuz et gardez en touz pointz, solonc la fourme d'Estatut ent fait". [4]

The Statute of Provisors of 1351 [5] cites Edward I's Statute of Carlisle—"le quel Estatut tient touz jours sa force".

A perfectly clear instance is found in 1354. William de Shareshull, the Chief Justice, announces among the causes of the summons, the permanent fixing of the Staple. The

---

[1] *Rot. Parl.* II, p. 113, nos. 7, 8.   [2] *Ibid.* p. 133, no. 61.
[3] *Ibid.* p. 153, no. 33.   [4] *Ibid.* p. 167, no. 22.
[5] 25 Edw. III, stat. 4.

Council had made certain provisions or "ordinances" which had been published throughout the realm, and that Council had included prelates, lords, justices, serjeants, "and others of the Commune". But now

pur ceo qe nostre Seignur le Roi, et les autres, si bien Grantz come Communes qi lors estoient au dit Conseil, verroient qe la dite Estaple se tendroit et durroit perpetuelment es Roialme et terres avant ditz, si ad mesme nostre Seignur fait somondre son Parlement a ce jour de Lunedy, aufyn qe les Ordinances de la dite Estaple soient recites en meisme le Parlement, et si rien soit a adjouster q'il soit ajouste, et soit a durer perpetuelment come Estatut en Parlement.[1]

Another case, equally important, is found in 1 Richard II.[2] The Commons in that year prayed the King that the "petitions" of the recent Parliament which were "pur profit de son poeple" (no doubt to distinguish them from the "bills" presented by individuals)[3] should be now shown to the Commons, and that such as had been assented to in the form "*Le Roi le voet*" "soit afferme pur Estatut; ce q'est dit as Communes touchant partie des dites Petitions qe ce ne fuist qe Ordenance et nemie Estatut, qe ceo puisse estre viewe et rehercee as Communes, et ceo qe resonable est qe y soit ordene pur Estatut."

The next year the Commons pray that "bills" of private persons receive no response, but that their own petitions be

---

[1] *Rot. Parl.* II, p. 254 A.
[2] *Ibid.* III, p. 17, no. 56.
[3] "Bill" is the term generally used on the rolls for petitions urged by others than the Commons as a whole—"par diverses persones; Bille especialle de singuler persone"—and not "pur le commun profit du poeple e du reaume". The Commons frequently show hostility to these. For references to such "billes", see *Rot. Parl.* III, p. 61, no. 28; *ibid.* pp. 105–6; II, folio 360 A–B; III, pp. 60–1; *ibid.* II, p. 203, no. 30; p. 368, no. 46; III, p. 321, no. 44. See also the Introduction to the *Statutes of the Realm* (reprinted in Cooper's *Public Records*, I, pp. 171–2, note, with references there quoted). These are the origin of private bills. See further, Clifford, *History of Private Bill Legislation*, vol. I, ch. iii.

answered, a remedy ordained before the dissolution of the Parliament, and upon that—"et sur ce—due Estatut soit fait en ce present Parlement, *et enseale a demurrer en tout temps a venir*".[1]

In the third year of the same reign the Commons petition that an existing ordinance "soit mys en Estatut, en affirmance d'icelle"; and the King replied, "soit mesme l'Ordeinance... tenuz et gardez pur Estatut".[2]

In 1399 mention is made of certain statutes "que semper ligarent donec auctoritate alicujus alterius Parliamenti fuerint specialiter revocata".[3]

Many instances might be given to show that this distinction between statute and ordinance, apparently perfectly clear, as to form at least, in the time of Edward III, was becoming much less so in the fifteenth century.[4]

These illustrations seem to show that there was a double difference between a statute and an ordinance—a difference in subject matter, and one of form and effect. Statutes were, in the beginning, affirmances of the ancient law; other kinds of enactment were employed for temporary administrative measures.

At the opening of Parliament, the whole body of the ancient customary law, together with the two charters and all previous statutes, was affirmed or confirmed. This was on the analogy of the earlier declarations of the King's peace at the opening of a reign, and it is the nearest approach medieval

[1] *Rot. Parl.* III, p. 61, no. 28.
[2] *Ibid.* p. 86, no. 46.
[3] *Ibid.* p. 419, no. 34. See also generally, stat. 14 Edw. III, stats. 1 and 4; 11 Rich. II, cap. 11; 4 Hen. VI, cap. 2; *Rot. Parl.* III, p. 87, no. 50; *ibid.* p. 115, no. 74; *ibid.* p. 138, no. 34; *ibid.* p. 354, no. 32; *ibid.* IV, p. 128 A–B; *ibid.* p. 35, no. 12; stat. 21 Rich. II, cap. 12; stat. 1 Hen. VI, cap. 6; 18 Hen. VI, cap. 4, 13; 27 Hen. VI, cap. 5; 29 Hen. VI, cap. 2; *Rot. Parl.* IV, pp. 327–8; *ibid.* p. 328, no. 29; *ibid.* III, p. 580, no. 60.
[4] For example, stat. 4 Hen. IV, cap. 35; 13 Hen. IV, cap. 2; 9 Hen. V, stat. 2; 8 Hen. VI, preamble; 20 Hen. VI, cap. 6; 29 Hen. VI, cap. 2; *Rot. Parl.* IV, p. 352, no. 48; *ibid.* p. 354 A; *ibid.* III, p. 661, no. 34.

England shows toward a fundamental law. Before the days of modern written constitutions this was the most authoritative way in which a fundamental law could be promulgated.

After the affirmance, came, as indicated in the "Pronunciationes", the removal of abuses, or of enactments contrary to or impeding the execution of this fundamental law, and the enactment of legislation supplemental to it which might be of sufficient importance to be classed with that law itself and therefore put into a statute or statutes. As we have seen, one of the chief characteristics of the law so affirmed, interpreted, cleared, or improved, is its permanence. And the instances given above show clearly enough that the test of a statute is the question whether the enactment made by it is really incorporated into this law, along with it "perpetuelment a durer" and to be affirmed along with it in all subsequent Parliaments. The inference is clear, then, that *in the beginning*, probably all statutes were of this kind. But composed as they were of such subject matter, it is evident that their enactment is more important than other "acts" of a Parliament. As such, they required a different mode of authentication than less important acts. They were sealed with the Great Seal and engrossed upon the Statute Roll as a part of the permanent law, after which they were sent to the Chancery and the courts of the two benches, and also to Ireland and elsewhere in cases where this was necessary. Copies were also sent to the sheriffs of the counties, ordering their proclamation, preservation, and enforcement, within the counties.

This authentication was in the hands of the Council, consisting largely of the judges, or in special cases of a committee; who went over the Parliament Roll, during or after the Parliament; which led to many omissions and some changes and additions, sometimes complained of by the Commons. Ordinances, originally, as temporary law, were not affirmed generally at the opening of Parliament as the charters, ancient law, and previous statutes were. They also required a less formal mode of authentication than statutes. Without a formal engrossment they could be taken by the Council as the basis for royal writs, charters, or letters patent, by which they were published and their enforcement secured.

As time went on, the distinction between the subject matter of statutes and of ordinances became less marked. The difference came to be regarded more as a difference of form, though the real distinction did not disappear until the fifteenth century. Thus, in case of an enactment such as the ordinance concerning apparel in 37 Edward III, where the subject was new, there might be a question whether this was fundamental or not, and the Parliament was asked whether it preferred *the form* of a statute or of an ordinance—"s'ils voleient avoir les choses issint acordez *mys par voie* de Ordinance ou de Statuyt". They answered that they preferred the form of an ordinance, in order that it might be changed if necessary at the next Parliament.[1] In the fifteenth century the distinction seems to be largely disregarded, as temporary acts are termed indifferently statutes or ordinances. In the half century embraced by the reign of Edward III, however, when the original distinction is still clearly preserved, there seems no doubt that a perfectly well understood difference existed between a statute "perpetuelment a durer" and an ordinance "pur en temps".

It would hardly have been necessary to enlarge so much on this point but for the evident confusion existing even in the minds of the latest writers on this important subject. Thus Sir William Anson says: The ordinance "is an act of the King or of the King in Council: it is temporary, and is revocable by the King or the King in Council. The *Statute* is the act of the Crown, Lords, and Commons; it is engrossed on the Statute Roll; it is meant to be a permanent addition to the law of the land; it can only be revoked by the same body that made it and in the same form."[2]

He proceeds to prove this by an entry from the roll of 1340

---

[1] *Rot. Parl.* II, p. 280, nos. 38–40.
[2] *Law and Custom of the Constitution*, 4th ed. I, pp. 241–3.

which is certainly the clearest statement of the real difference to be found in the Rolls of Parliament.[1] But an examination of it shows—and this is corroborated by dozens of other instances—that the ordinances in this case, as well as the statutes, were assented to by King, Lords, and Commons. It proves his statement that the statutes were permanent law and the ordinances temporary provisions; it expressly contradicts his other assertion that an ordinance is necessarily "an act of the King or of the King in Council" in distinction from a statute, to which the Commons' assent must be added.

It is said in the excellent preface to Ruffhead's edition of the statutes,[2] that the real difference between the subject matter proper to a statute and to an ordinance lies in the distinction between ancient law and "novel ley"; which is undoubtedly true, but I think hardly in the sense in which Ruffhead meant it. He says many acts were not entered upon the Statute Roll, "For if the Bill did not demand 'Novel Ley', that is, if the Provision required would stand with the Laws in Force, and did not tend to change or alter any Statute then in being, in such Case the Law was compleat by the Royal Assent on the Parliament Roll, without any Entry on the Statute Roll: and Such Bills were usually termed Ordinances." But the term "novel ley", as used in the Rolls themselves and in the Year Books of the time, does not seem to mean new law so much as new enactment. Acts in affirmance are continually spoken of as "novel ley" in distinction to the ancient law lying behind it. And while the rest of his statement seems to be completely supported by the Rolls themselves, this assertion and his inference based upon it seem to go too far.

One more point in regard to enactment seems in need of explanation before we are in position to form a true estimate of Magna Carta at this time, and that is the legal necessity, and the legal effect, of the publication of statutes.

[1] It is given above, p. 162.
[2] Pp. xii–xiii.

The sealing,[1] engrossing,[2] and publication,[3] are the outward marks of an early statute. The procedure is so fully described in the introduction to the *Statutes of the Realm*,[4] that it need not be repeated here. Their publication, however, was so important a part of the authentication of statutes in early times that a statute is usually referred to before the middle of the fourteenth century as *statutum editum* in a certain Parliament or year.[5]

The theory of "representation" is found surprisingly early in England, but so long as the composition of Parliament was uncertain, publication in the counties must have been of even greater importance than it was afterward. It is probable that some doubt existed in this period as to the reality of the assent *omnium utentium* unless a statute had been actually proclaimed locally throughout the realm.

This probability is strengthened by the cases where the King, who alone could give effect to an enactment, saw fit temporarily to suspend its operation. In the later Middle Ages there is considerable evidence of the existence of a suspending

---

[1] Sealing seemed to be necessary. See Year Book (Hilary Term), 8 Edw. II, pp. 264–5 (edition of 1678); *Rot. Parl.* II, p. 113, nos. 7, 8.

[2] *Ibid.*

[3] For publication, see introduction to *Statutes of the Realm*; 2 Inst. 526; 3 Inst. 41; 4 Inst. 26; 12 Rep. p. 56. Instances are very frequent in contemporary records. The writs for publication are frequently found with the statutes in the modern printed collections, and a few of the early statutes are known only from these writs. See also, for example, *Calendar of Close Rolls*, 1234–7, p. 353; *ibid.* 1302–7, p. 396; *Calendar of Patent Rolls*, 1272–81, p. 335; Rymer, *Foedera* (Record Commission), vol. II, pt. I, p. 275; pt. II, pp. 745, 753, 828, 937; vol. III, pt. I, p. 272; *Placitorum Abbreviatio*, pp. 332, 339, 340–1, 348; stat. 23 Edw. III, cap. 7; stat. 34 Edw. III, preamble; stat. 7 Rich. II, cap. 6; *Rot. Parl.* II, p. 10; p. 62, no. 10; p. 113, nos. 7, 8; folio 254 A; III, folio 370 A–B; p. 478, no. 114.

[4] Section V, II, 2.

[5] For example, "Istud statutum [De Quo Warranto] fuit editum in Parliamento Regis…anno regni sui decimo octavo" (*Plac. Abb.* p. 225 (Hilary Term, 19 Edw. I)). See also *ibid.* pp. 226, 321, 334; *Liber Albus* (Rolls Series), p. 441; Rymer, *Foedera* (Record Commission), vol. III, pt. I, p. 217.

power on the part of the King, notwithstanding the summary dismissal of it as "pretended" by the Parliament in 1689.[1]

It seems certain, however, that when the composition of Parliament settled down into its final form, such doubts, if they existed, were swept away by the full acceptance of the theory that the whole body of the people were constructively in Parliament and therefore were bound by all its statutes on their mere enactment without publication, though the publication was actually continued until the invention of printing made it no longer necessary. This view was stated with vigour and clearness in 39 Edward III, in the case of Rex *v*. The Bishop of Chichester.[2] The prosecution was under the Statute of Provisors, and Serjeant Cavendish, counsel for the bishop, set up as a part of his defence that this enactment was not binding because it had not been published in the counties. He was answered by Sir Robert Thorpe, the Chief Justice:

Granting that proclamation was not made in the county, nevertheless every one is considered to know what is done in Parliament; for so soon as Parliament has concluded anything, the law presumes that every person has notice of it; for the Parliament represents the body of all the Realm; wherefore it is not necessary to have proclamation where the statute took effect before.

It now remains to apply these deductions to Magna Carta and to Edward I's mandate requiring its enforcement by his judges, as common law.

John's Charter was in form a royal grant guaranteeing rights almost all of which had already existed by feudal custom or otherwise. It was granted primarily to his tenants-in-chief and their *homines*. It was a feudal rather than a national document, and the grantees were probably then conceived to include none lower than *vavassores*.[3] But the reign of Henry III

[1] For example, *Rot. Parl.* I, p. 217 B (1306); stat. 43 Edw. III, cap. 2; stat. 9 Rich. II, cap. 1.

[2] Year Book, Pasch. 39 Edw. III, p. 7. See also Coke's commentary, 4 Inst. p. 26.

[3] I have treated this point more fully elsewhere. See "Due Process of Law in Magna Carta", *ante*, pp. 86–126.

was, from the point of view of the development of institutions, almost a revolutionary epoch. The loss of Normandy and other influences brought about in this period a remarkable development of the idea of nationality, which is reflected in the growth of the National Assembly and in other respects.[1] This influence can be seen in Magna Carta. In addition to the extension of John's articles on the forest into a new, separate, and more detailed charter, Magna Carta itself was reissued three times, with new clauses, defining, interpreting, and enlarging some of the original articles of a permanent nature and omitting the parts obviously temporary. In addition, it was solemnly confirmed by an excommunication against all who should break or change it, and it was confirmed by the Statute of Marlborough. An examination of these documents and incidental inferences in other writings of this reign, official and non-official, leads to the conclusion that contemporary ideas of the nature of Magna Carta greatly changed during this period. It was now seen that this was more than a *carta libertatum*: it was a *carta libertatis*. Though originally granted only to feudal *homines*, it was now applied to all *liberi homines*; though "conceded" at first as by royal favour, in this period it comes to be regarded as a solemn affirmance of fundamental rights, guaranteed to all, and approved by all. For the year 1225 the Annals of Dunstable, in speaking of the reissue of Magna Carta in that year, say, that in the "colloquium generale" in London, "Post multas vero sententiarum revolutiones, communiter placuit quod rex *tam populo quam plebi* libertates, prius ab eo puero concessas, jam major factus indulsit".[2]

[1] Powicke, *The Loss of Normandy*, particularly ch. x.

[2] P. 93 (*Annales Monastici*, Rolls Series), quoted in Stubbs, *Select Charters*, 9th ed. pp. 322–3. With this compare the ratification of the sentence of excommunication in 1253, containing a protest against any additions to or changes in it, by the King, all the magnates, "et communitas populi" (Bémont, *Chartes*, p. 74); also the writ of Edward I in 1297 ordering the publication of the Charter there declared to be made in "relevacionem omnium incolarum et populi regni nostri" (*ibid.* p. 92).

The sentence of excommunication in 1253 condemns all
who shall violate, infringe, diminish, or change the rights of
the Church, the ancient and approved customs of the realm,
"et praecipue libertates et liberas consuetudines que in *cartis
communium libertatum* et de foresta continentur".¹ Bracton
calls the third reissue of Magna Carta *constitutio libertatis*² or
constitutio merely,³ and, as we have seen, Magna Carta is
referred to in 19 Edward I as "statutum de Ronemede".⁴
The author of the *Mirror of Justices* mentions it as "la
constitution de la chartre des franchises".⁵ By 1297 it has
become "la graunt chartre des fraunchises d'Engleterre",
proclaimed "pur le commun profit du peuple e de reaume";⁶
or Magna Carta "domini Henrici quondam regis Anglie...
de libertatibus Anglie";⁷ though to Pope Clement V it is only
"concessiones variae et iniquae".⁸ By the time the word
statute has come to have a definite meaning, we begin to find
that term also applied to Magna Carta.⁹ In 15 Edward III the
Commons strengthen one of their petitions by a reference to

les pointz de la Grande Chartre faitz par les nobles Rois et ses
Progenitours, et les Grantz du Roialme sages et nobles adonques
Pieres de la terre, et puis sovent confirmez de divers Rois; Et puis
molt des autres Ordinances, e Statutz, faitz pur profit du commune poeple entendant les pointz de la dite Chartre, ensemblement od les autres perpetuelment a durer, sanz estre enfreintz
sinoun par acorde et assent des Pieres de la terre, et ce en pleyn
Parlement.¹⁰

¹ Bémont, *Chartes*, p. 72.   ² Folio 168 B.
³ *Ibid.* 169 B.   ⁴ *Ante*, p. 139.
⁵ P. 151 (Selden Society).
⁶ Bémont, *Chartes*, pp. 82, 83. See also p. 99.
⁷ *Ibid.* pp. 90, 92; in the "inspeximus" of the same year.
⁸ Bull annulling the Charter in 1305, Bémont, *Chartes*, p. 110.
⁹ E.g. Year Book, 11 and 12 Edw. III, p. 63 (Rolls Series); *Rot. Parl.*
II, p. 265, no. 12, where Magna Carta and the Charter of the Forest are
spoken of as "ditz Estatutz"; stat. 38 Edw. III, stat. i mentions the two
charters et "les autres Estatutz" faitz in past times. This expression is very
common. See, for example, *Rot. Parl.* II, p. 269; III, p. 647 B; IV,
p. 403, no. 36.   ¹⁰ *Rot. Parl.* II, p. 128, no. 9.

In 1432 the Commons appeal to "ye Statut of the Grete Chartre, confermed by diverse oder Statutes".[1]

Thus it is clear that Magna Carta had come to be considered an enactment much in the original sense of a statute: in affirmance of ancient law. The quotation above from the roll of 15 Edward III brings this out clearly.[2] It also shows that Magna Carta was regarded as common law, with its interpretations.

It is such statements as this that enable us to put Magna Carta in its true setting in the fourteenth century. While much the same in character as other statutes, in binding force it is classed above them. While it is said they may be changed in Parliament, this statement does not include Magna Carta itself. We shall see later that this distinction was constantly made. Magna Carta had, in fact, from the time of Henry III, been recognized as in some sense a law fundamental. Henry III's reissue of 1225 was the form considered final. We have evidence of this as early as Bracton's time. In a quotation given above, Bracton says a writ is to be quashed "si impetratum fuerit contra jus et regni consuetudinem et *maxime* contra chartam libertatis".[3]

The author of the *Mirror*, in his fifth book, "De Abusions", begins with Magna Carta, "cum la lei de ceste reaume *fondee sur xl pointz de la grande chartre des fraunchises* soit desusé dampnablement par les guiours de la lei e par estatuz pus fetez contraianz a ascuns de ces poinz".[4] He then proceeds to enumerate the "defautes" of the various articles of the Charter, implying that they are in affirmance of the law (*fondie sur dreit*), though in some cases incomplete (*defectif*);[5] but he has no doubt that they render invalid (*destrut*) any subsequent statute inconsistent with them.[6] "And", he declares, "what is said of this statute [Merton] is to be understood of all statutes made after the first making of the Great Charter in the time of Henry III, for it is not law that anyone should be punished

---

[1] *Rot. Parl.* IV, p. 403, no. 36. [2] *Ante*, p. 171.
[3] *Ante*, p. 153. [4] P. 175 (Selden Society).
[5] *Rot. Parl.* IV, p. 176. [6] *Ibid.* pp. 179, 180, 181, 199–200.

for a single deed by imprisonment or any other corporal
punishment, and in addition by a pecuniary punishment or
ransom."[1]

In 14 Edward I the sheriffs of London had been violating
the article of Magna Carta guaranteeing judgment by peers.
"Et justiciarii dicunt, quod Dominus Rex hoc nullo modo
concedere, secundum Magnam Chartam Angliae, sed est
ultra regiam potestatem et contra omnem justitiam", etc.[2]

The so-called statute "De Tallagio non Concedendo"
provides that if, against the ancient laws and liberties or against
any article of Magna Carta, any statute had been published by
the King or his predecessors, or any customs introduced, such
statutes and customs "vacua et nulla sint in perpetuum".[3]
We have seen that the confirmation which was actually
enacted at that time declared null, not previous acts, but
"jugementz donez desoremes".[4]

The terms of the letters patent of confirmation in 1301 are
very interesting. There it is declared that "si que statuta
fuerint contraria dictis cartis vel alicui articulo in eisdem cartis
contento, ea de communi consilio regni nostri modo debito
emendentur vel eciam adnullentur".[5]

The difference between this provision and that of the
confirmation of 1297, as well as the possible relation of both
to the provision in the so-called statute "De Tallagio non
Concedendo", is very significant.

By 1301 the normal way of obtaining the common counsel
of the realm on the amendment or annulling of any law—the
modus debitus—had certainly become an enactment by Parliament. An accord or judgment of Parliament was "le plus
haute le plus solempne juggement de ceste terre"; an award
"fait en la plus haute place en le Roialme".[6] Whether, in

---

[1] *Rot. Parl.* IV, p. 182.
[2] *Liber Custumarum*, p. 410 (Rolls Series).
[3] Bémont, *Chartes*, pp. 88–9.   [4] *Ante*, pp. 127–128.
[5] Bémont, *Chartes*, p. 109.
[6] *Rot. Parl.* II, p. 24 A–B (1328).

dealing with Magna Carta, Parliament should act in its judicial capacity or in a legislative way by statute, no more effective sanction could be devised in those days. The confirmation of 1301 must be considered as an honest attempt to secure enforcement, in the most effective manner known, of the provisions of Magna Carta.

It would seem fair to say, then, that Magna Carta was considered a really "fundamental law"; and that the confirmation of 1301 first authorized the manner of confirming it which was regularly followed until all confirmations ceased.

After this confirmation no additions were made to the Charter, and it became the custom to confirm it as a matter of course at the beginning of each Parliament. This is as near to a fundamental law as the conceptions of medieval Englishmen could reach. We should not expect to find more.

Parliament was not content in the years following merely to confirm Magna Carta: it occasionally declared in general terms that all inconsistent acts should be void. The famous ordinances of 1311 declared that any such act "soit tenuz pur nul, et tout outrement defait".[1] In 1368, in response to the Commons' petition, the King promised that the charters should be observed and that any statute passed "a contrarie soit tenu pur nul".[2] The statutes of that year add these words to the usual confirmation.[3]

In 1376 the Commons complain of infringements of Magna Carta "par sinistrers interpretations d'ascuns gentz de Loi", and pray that it be observed, notwithstanding any statute, ordinance, or charter to the contrary.[4] The same request was made in another Parliament in the same year.[5] A similar one is found in 1379.[6]

In 1 Henry IV the Commons petition for the repeal of a statute of the King's grandfather which they allege to be

---

[1] *Rot. Parl.* I, p. 285, no. 31.
[3] Stat. 42 Edw. III, cap. 1.
[5] *Ibid.* 364.

[2] *Ibid.* II, p. 295, no. 10.
[4] *Rot. Parl.* II, p. 331 A.
[6] *Ibid.* III, p. 61, no. 27.

"expressement fait encontre la tenure et effect de la Grande Chartre".[1]

In 1397 Parliament declared the "award" of Parliament against the Despencers void as against law, right, and reason, and against Magna Carta.[2]

In 1341 the Peers prayed that infringements of Magna Carta should be declared in Parliament, and "par les Pieres de la terre duement redrescez".[3]

During the fourteenth and fifteenth centuries the practice continued of confirming Magna Carta, as is proved by both the Parliament and the Statute Roll; but it would serve no purpose to refer to any of these numerous confirmations, which are usually brief and stereotyped in form. The regularity of the practice was recognized in 1381 in a petition of the Commons praying, since by the Great Charter it was ordained and affirmed "communement *en touz autres Parlementz*", that law be not denied or sold to anyone, that therefore fees be no longer taken by the Chancellor for writs.[4]

The confirmations of these years vary in the comprehensiveness of their statements, but they almost invariably include Magna Carta, the Charter of the Forest, and former statutes. In the fifteenth century the reference to these statutes (but not to the charters) is usually limited by the phrase "et nient repellez".

Sometimes the Commons try to go further than a mere confirmation. In 1341 they petitioned that all the great officers of the realm be sworn to observe Magna Carta and the other laws and statutes,[5] that Magna Carta be publicly read and affirmed by oath, and that penalties be inflicted on sheriffs or other ministers of the King who failed to enforce its observance.[6] In 1354 they petitioned for the reading of Magna Carta.[7] In 1377, at the opening of the new reign, the

---

[1] *Rot. Parl.* III, 443 A.
[3] *Ibid.* II, folio 127 B to 131.
[5] *Ibid.* II, p. 128, no. 10.
[7] *Ibid.* p. 259, no. 28.

[2] *Ibid.* 365 A.
[4] *Ibid.* III, p. 116, no. 88.
[6] *Ibid.* p. 129, no. 20.

Commons again asked that it be read in Parliament; and this was done.[1] It was read again in the Parliament of 1380.[2]

Occasionally there is a demand that the Charter be not merely read, but officially interpreted.[3] In 1377 this demand goes further. The Charter was not only to be read, but it was to be declared point by point by the members of the Continual Council with the advice of the judges and serjeants or others if necessary. The "pointz" so declared and amended were to be submitted to the Lords and Commons at the next Parliament, and then "estre encresceez e affermez pur Estatut s'il semble a eux q'il soit a faire; eiant regarde coment le Roi est chargee a son Coronement de tenir e garder la dite Chartre en touz ses pointz". The King, in general terms, promised that it be read and observed, but ignored the request for interpretation.[4]

If space permitted, many instances might also be given of Parliament's solicitude, not merely for general confirmations of the Charter, but also for the observance of its specific provisions by the courts.

Magna Carta, in the later Middle Ages, is looked upon and treated as an enactment in affirmance of fundamental common law, to be confirmed and observed as a part of that law; but undoubtedly all other enactments of such law are regarded as less important.

The evolution of a "constitutional law" in America has generally been considered by British writers as without precedent in earlier English institutions. Such a view is hardly supported by a study of those institutions in the Middle Ages, before the modern doctrine of the legislative sovereignty of Parliament had taken definite form.

But it seems hardly possible completely to identify the "fundamental law" of medieval England with the usual modern forms of such a law. In fact the content of that law,

[1] Stat. 1 Rich. II, cap. 1.   [2] *Rot. Parl.* III, p. 88 A.
[3] *Ibid.* I, p. 286, no. 38. See also *ibid.* II, p. 7, nos. 1, 3.
[4] *Ibid.* III, p. 15, nos. 44–5.

of which Magna Carta is the best example, was not entirely nor mainly "constitutional". "Rigid" constitutions are a development of modern times. To us it seems natural to place the framework of government in a class by itself. We think of it alone as the fundamental law. We go so far as to make of "fundamental" and "constitutional" practically equivalent terms. This was not done in medieval England.

For the Englishmen of that day the "fundamental law" did indeed include the law of the Crown, but it included also the law of the realm, and the second bulked larger than the first. Even what we might be tempted to call "the law of the constitution" was in those days what it still remains, in England and even in great measure in the United States, notwithstanding our written constitutions: "little else than a generalization of the rights which the Courts secure to individuals".[1]

Though this be true, an added interest is undoubtedly given to a study of the earlier manifestations of the idea of a law fundamental by the growing tendency in certain quarters in England, arising out of the recent and almost revolutionary constitutional changes, to demand that the structure of the State be placed above and beyond the possibility of change by the ordinary law-making organ.

[1] Dicey, *Law of the Constitution*, 7th ed. p. 196.

VII

WHO WAS "ROSSAEUS"?

In recent years historical research in the field of the French wars of religion in the sixteenth century has given considerable attention to the question of the authorship of the more important books and pamphlets which played so significant a part in that struggle, writings, which, for obvious reasons, were anonymous in the majority of cases.

Thus recently Professor Ernest Barker has effectively reopened the old question of the authorship of the famous *Vindiciae contra Tyrannos* and reinforced the view of Bayle in favour of Hubert Languet, which had been pretty generally rejected for a quarter of a century or more on the basis of a statement in the memoirs of Madame Mornay which seemed to point to her husband as the true author. Some, like Professor J. W. Allen, seem still to be in doubt as to the authorship of another important book of the time, the *De Jure Magistratuum in Subditos*, though the authorship of Theodore Beza seems to be conclusively proved by the researches of Elkan and others, if not by those of Thomas McCrie more than a century ago.

A similar dispute has been carried on concerning the authorship of one of the most important and most extreme of the books which emanated from the Catholic League, the *Liber de Justa Reipublicae Christianae in Reges Impios et Haereticos Authoritate*. This book was published at Paris in 1590 with a dedicatory letter addressed to the Duke of Mayenne and signed "G. G. R. A. Peregrin. Roman." It was attributed to one "Rossaeus", and Rossaeus has generally been identified with Guillaume Rose, Bishop of Senlis, whom Bayle with some justification calls the most furious of all the *Ligueurs* in France.

This view still prevails and the book is assigned to Rose without question by Professor Barker in the bibliography to his recent translation from Gierke and Troeltsch.[1] But why should a Bishop of Senlis call himself *peregrinus*? Charles Labitte in his important book, *De la démocratie chez les prédicateurs de la Ligue*, first published in 1841, seems to have doubts of Rose's authorship. Considering the great ability and importance of the book, he gives it very scant attention compared with Boucher's *De Justa Abdicatione Henrici Tertii*, which is, on the whole, inferior to it, though he devotes much space to Rose himself. The most Labitte will say is that the book of this anonymous writer, rival of Boucher, has long been attributed to Guillaume Rose.[2] Professor Allen is equally cautious.[3] He considers Rose incapable of writing such a book, and thinks "there are grave objections to the authorship" of William Reynolds, an English Catholic exile and member of the League, to whom it is sometimes attributed. Who then is the *peregrinus Romanus* who signs himself G. G. R. A.? If the G and R do not indicate Gulielmus Rose, possibly G. R. A. may stand for Gulielmus Raynoldus (or Reginaldus) Anglicanus, as I think they do.

That William Reynolds was the author of the *De Justa Authoritate* seems to be established by external evidence which is explicit, contemporary, and as nearly authoritative as could be expected. In *An Exact Discoverie of Romish Doctrine in the Case of Conspiracie and Rebellion*, written by Thomas Morton, later bishop, and published at London in 1605, on pp. 8–9, a quotation is given from p. 8 of the *De Justa Authoritate*, which is mentioned by name and attributed without question to "Reinaldus".

Two years afterwards, in 1607, Robert Parsons the famous

---

[1] *Natural Law and the Theory of Society from 1500 to 1800* (Cambridge, 1934).

[2] *De la démocratie*, 2nd ed. p. 172, n. 1.

[3] J. W. Allen, *A History of Political Thought in the Sixteenth Century* (London, 1928), p. 351, n. 2.

Jesuit answered Morton's book in *A Treatise Tending to Mitigation towardes Catholicke Subiectes in England*, and on p. 58 referred to "M. Reynoldes" and "his booke De iusta Reipublicae potestate & C." Again on pp. 68–9 of the same work Parsons declares that one of Morton's arguments "is out of M. William Reinoldes in his book De iusta Reip. auctoritate & c." In 1609 Parsons makes similar statements in regard to the authorship of Reynolds in another book, *A Quiet and Sober Reckoning with M. Thomas Morton* (pp. 326–32).

In 1612 William Warmington published his *Moderate Defence of the Oath of Allegiance*. Warmington, an Oxonian, converted to the Catholic Faith, had been a student at Douai, and later chaplain to Cardinal Allen. After the enactment of the law prescribing the new oath of allegiance he became convinced that English Catholics could and should take this oath. The *Moderate Defence* contains a justification of this position. In the course of his argument, Warmington refers to the sermon of Pope Sixtus V after the murder of King Henry III of France in 1589, which, in his opinion, contains an implied approval of the assassination. In proof of this he adds:

Besides, this likewise is true, that M. *William Reynolds*, then being in the Low Countries (to whom as to my speciall friend I sent a copie of the Oration) esteemed it (so did many others) as an approving of the Friars act. For, returning me an answer to my letter, he gave me heartie thankes for it, saying, that I could not have gratified him with any thing more, then by sending him the approbation of the Sea Apostolicke, which came in very good season, he being at that time writing his *Rossaeus Peregrinus*, a booke of such a like subject (p. 147).

By this meanes the Oration was set forth, and published among divers particular friends, and so I reserved to my self a copie, which I sent (as I have said) soon after to my beloved friend M. *William Reynolds* (p. 148).

In 1613 John Pits finished his *Tomus Primus Relationum Historicarum de Rebus Anglicis*, or *De Illustribus Britanniae*

Scriptoribus, and it was published at Paris in 1619. Like Reynolds, Pits had been a member of New College, Oxford; like Reynolds he was an English Catholic refugee, residing at times at Douai, Rheims, Rome, and elsewhere on the Continent; and in 1580–81 it seems that both men were in residence together in the college at Douai. In Pits's *De Scriptoribus*, in the section "De Guilhelmo Reginaldo" (pp. 790–92), which is very laudatory, occurs the following statement, which, in all the circumstances, is, in my opinion, conclusive in favour of the authorship of William Reynolds:

Ad instantiam Principum Galliae scripsit de iusta reipublicae auctoritate in principes haereticos. De quo Cardinalis Sega Placentinus Episcopus, & Papae Clementis octavi apud Galliae principes legatus Remis in honoratissimorum virorum conventu pronunciavit, in illo libro strictim contineri, quicquid sparsim apud omnes alios scriptores in negotio quod tunc apud Gallos agebatur, inveniri posset.

Pits also includes the *De Justa Authoritate* without remark in his list of Reynolds's works, and at the end he quotes the following words of the epitaph on Reynolds's tomb at Antwerp: "Honorabili Domino D. Guilhelmo Reginaldo, *alias Rossaeo*."

The case seems complete; and it is of added interest to remember that this author, who proves in one chapter of his book that "modern Protestantism is worse than ancient heresy" and in another "that Calvinism is far more detestable than paganism, or the faith of the Turks", is an elder brother of the celebrated John Reynolds, the Calvinistic leader and spokesman of the Puritan party at the Hampton Court conference in 1604, author of *Libri Duo de Romanae Ecclesiae Idolatria* (Oxford, 1596), and the man from whom apparently came the first suggestion which resulted in the King James version of the English Bible. So far as I have been able to check the writings of the two brothers, each seems always discreetly to omit the other's name from the list of opponents whose views he is attacking. A quaint story is told

of these two brothers; how in earlier life William, the Protestant, had set out to convert his Catholic brother John, and
John in turn to convert William to Catholicism; and how
each had completely succeeded in accomplishing his purpose.

This story "seems apocryphal" to the Reverend Thomas
Fowler, John Reynolds's biographer and successor as president
of Corpus Christi College,[1] but apparently it was widely
current in the seventeenth century. William Alabaster, or
Alablaster, once famous as the author of *Roxana*, "a most rare
poet as any our age or nation hath produced",[2] wrote a Latin
poem of twelve lines on the subject, *In duos Reginaldos inter se
de religione certantes*, preserved among the Ashmolean manuscripts in the Bodleian Library.[3] Alabaster himself had been
converted to Catholicism about 1596, but returned after some
years to the Church of England. Presumably he had access
to reliable sources of information concerning the two brothers,
and his poem affords some indication of his belief in the story
of their conversion. Peter Heylin, in his *Cosmographie*,[4] translated Alabaster's poem into English and added some details
drawn either from other sources or from his imagination.
Henry Foulis, in his *History of Romish Treasons and Usurpa-
tions*,[5] repeats what Heylin had written but avoids any
commitment as to the truth of the story. Fuller, on the other
hand, who briefly recounts the matter in his *Church History
of Britain*, gives it as a matter of fact.[6] In his *Letters on
Toleration* John Locke makes considerable use of this story in
support of his argument.

[1] Rainolds, John, in the *Dictionary of National Biography*.
[2] Thomas Fuller, *The Worthies of England*, Nuttall's edition, III, p. 185.
[3] *Catalogue of the Ashmole MSS*, by W. H. Black, pp. 38, 87. This short
Latin poem is referred to inaccurately as "an unpublished tract" in the
article on William Alabaster in the *Dictionary of National Biography*.
[4] London, 1657, p. 303.
[5] 1666, 2nd ed. London, 1681, p. 421.
[6] London, 1655, Book x, section III, p. 47.

VIII

THE HOUSE OF COMMONS IN 1621[1]

The value of a contribution to history should never be judged exclusively by its "timeliness", but there are times when certain parts of the past have peculiar analogies with the present, and there never has been a place or a time where a careful study of the English constitutional struggles between 1603 and 1642 was more pertinent or more necessary than in America at this day.

These seven magnificent volumes, which bring together for the first time all the hitherto unprinted journals thus far discovered of James's third parliament, furnish the necessary basis for all future studies of one important stage in that remarkable constitutional development. They form one part of a much greater project undertaken some twenty years ago by Professor Notestein, to prepare the way "for a new study of parliament and of the constitutional significance of the period". The considerable portion of this great plan already accomplished—*Commons debates for 1629*, edited by Professors

[1] *Commons debates*, 1621. Edited by Wallace Notestein, Yale University; Frances Helen Relf, Wells College; Hartley Simpson, Yale University. Vol. I, *Introduction and index*; Vol. II, *The anonymous journal*; Vol. III, *The notes by Sir Thomas Barrington of the house of commons in 1621*; Vol. IV, *All the remarkable passages of the things done in the lower house of parliament*, a diary by John Pym; Vol. V, *The Belasyse diary*; *Observations at the parliament*, by John Smyth of Nibley; *Some observations and collections*, made by Sir Thomas Wentworth; *Parliament notes*, by Sir Nathaniel Rich; Vol. VI, *The parliamentary notes of Sir Thomas Holland*; *Z diary*, some notes by an unknown writer; *Book of Committees*; *Notes of debate and procedure at the parliament*, by Sir Charles Howard; *Selection from the historical collection of Robert Horn*; *The Minnesota manuscript*; *Excerpt from the Egerton MS. 2651*; *Book of orders*; Vol. VII, Appendix A: *Bills*, Appendix B, Part 1: *Schedules of grants*; Part 2: *Papers relating to grants*; Appendix C: *Miscellany*. ("Yale historical publications. Manuscripts and edited texts", Vol. XIV.) New Haven: Yale University Press, 1935; seven volumes.

Notestein and Relf;[1] *The journal of Sir Simonds D'Ewes from the beginning of the Long parliament to the opening of the trial of the Earl of Strafford* in March 1641, edited by Professor Notestein;[2] these seven volumes of Commons journals for the Parliament of 1621; and Miss Relf's volume of Lords' debates 1621–28, published by the Royal Historical Society[3]— justifies a student of English constitutional history in the belief that this series, when complete, will be the most important contribution to any part of that history made in our time. If historical work may ever be spoken of as "definitive", these precious journals (if all are edited as those already published have been) will fully merit that term. Future discoveries may, and probably will, make additions to this work; but they can only supplement—they are not likely to supersede it.

In 1923 Professor Notestein indicated that the series would end at the year 1642, when the English parliament "lost much of its character as an institution rooted in the past". This would be an adequate reason for continuing the publication of D'Ewes's *Journal* no farther than that year, if it were not pretty clear that parliament's own realization of the loss of its traditional character did not come quite as soon or as suddenly as the loss itself. From 1642 to about 1645 the debates still continue to throw a diminishing light backward on earlier parliamentary history. I should therefore hope the *terminus ad quem* might be put about 1645 instead of 1642.

The parliament of 1621 covered by the present volumes is one of the most important of the stages in "the winning of the initiative by the House of Commons". Questions of monopolies, monopolists, and corruptionists, with which it dealt, and the great matter of consent to taxations had, for the most part, come up before; but in this parliament of 1621 the Commons, shocked and alarmed at the possible effect on their country and the Protestant religion of the Spanish match and the fatuous foreign policy of James, for the first time ventured to debate the great question of England's foreign relations.

[1] Minneapolis, 1921.   [2] New Haven, 1923.   [3] London, 1929.

In rebuking them for it, James, *more suo*, declared that their freedom of debate was no more than a royal concession, not their inheritance, and thus brought on one of the most momentous struggles in the whole history of modern constitutionalism. Every scrap of information concerning these vital debates is therefore precious; every word uttered is important; and the diaries here first printed add much to our previous knowledge.

If we consider the parliament of 1621 from the point of view of general history, possibly the most important thing in it is the final scene when the famous declaration of the freedom of debate was adopted, the declaration which King James later in full council tore from the journal book. The notes of the debates preceding this famous resolution now made available here for the first time, do not essentially alter the admirable account in Gardiner; but they do supply additional details of the greatest importance, and frequently give us the very words of the speakers, which otherwise we should not have known. The *Old parliamentary history* gives no reports of these debates. Cobbett's *Parliamentary history* reports them, but usually from a single source. In this collection five diaries are printed which cover the period of these debates. Unfortunately, both Pym's and Wentworth's notes break off before this period. But in the Belasyse diary, in Smyth's, and in one anonymous one, we have independent accounts in which important variations are noted. These notes serve to heighten the impression obtained from the sources available before of the great reluctance on the part of the parliamentary leaders to oppose the King or trench on his prerogative. They are further evidence of the correctness of Gardiner's contention that the inevitable constitutional changes of the seventeenth century might well have been obtained by peaceful means from kings less headstrong than James or Charles. What impresses one in these important speeches on the freedom of debate is the great moderation of the speakers. In reading them over, one is conscious all the while that the words of the speakers fall far short of their thoughts, that they are constantly imposing a restraint on themselves under very great provocation. These diaries strengthen the belief that the chief blame for the violence of the constitutional conflict lies not on those "fiery and popular spirits" in the House against whom James inveighed, but on the King himself.

The King's attitude toward the House's right of debate was probably never better expressed than in the words of Weston, chancellor of the exchequer, reported in one of the anonymous diaries for December 3, when he said: "It's good when the king adviseth with his parliament of war but for the parliament to advise the king of war is presumptuous. It's not enough to know what we ought to speak but we must also know what is fit for him to hear." The reply of Sir Thomas Wentworth, though studiously moderate, shows how wide the gulf had become between this view and the one held by the House of Commons:

> Remembering who gave me a tongue I cannot but afford it him when his cause is in hand. We may take great care not to displease his Majesty and yet (so far as we may) do that which shall be for the good of religion and the commonwealth.... We are they that represent the great bulk of the commonwealth.

"The king", he adds, no doubt with Ferrer's case of Henry VIII's reign in mind, "is never greater than in parliament." He closes with words of which the King's favourite might have taken notice: "There are some among us who act the devil's part by making dissension between his Majesty and this House and laugh at it when it is done."

When the King's answer to the Commons' petition for their liberty of debate was reported to the House, the Belasyse diary reports Sir Edward Coke's speech of December 15 in words to be found nowhere else:

> The libertie of everie Court is the Lawe of the Court. Magna Charta is called *Charta libertatis quia liberos facit*. I will not dispute with my Maister for his words, but when the kinge sayes he can

not allowe our liberties of right, this strikes at the roote. Wee serve here for thousands and tenn thousands.

This looks like a report more nearly verbatim than any we have known hitherto. The great influence of Coke over the House is made even more evident in these newly discovered diaries than it was known to be before.

Although it involved no quarrel with the King, the attack on monopolies in the earlier part of the session is of great importance, as well as the investigation of judicial abuses. On both these matters the new diaries give us considerable new evidence. On the most important of these matters, however, the charges of corruption against Sir Francis Bacon, the Lord Chancellor, the Commons wisely decided to let the decisive action be taken by the Lords; therefore the diaries throw less new light on it than on some other matters.

Probably the point on which they contribute most is the debate on Floyd's case, in which the Commons took the initiative. Floyd, apparently, was an inoffensive old man, a Catholic, in no way connected with the parliament, who had merely let fall some contemptuous remarks about the King's daughter and her husband.

The impression one gets in reading over these amazing debates is that the members of the House, unable to attack the King for his utterly fatuous policy in defence of his son-in-law, are here venting all their wrath on the head of this unfortunate and obscure victim. However that may be, the Commons' claim to jurisdiction over outsiders, made in this case under the pretext of privilege, is the most extensive and the least justifiable, perhaps, in all parliamentary history; and the far-fetched arguments brought forward in the debates in support of the claim are of great interest. One of the fullest and most valuable accounts of these debates is in Barrington's diary, which has been hitherto unknown. On 28 April the House issued an order for the appearance of the Warden of the Fleet and "one Floud that Doctor Willet accuses to have sayed,

Now goodman Palsegrave and goodwife Pallsegrave runn away, and that he ever lookt for that day".[1] "He is a dangerous fellow", Coke declared. "Lett us labor to punish all such offendors and to suppress such insolency as farr as we can find it in any who soever."[2] Sir Robert Philips cried out:

Lett him be carried from Westminster Hall with his face to the horses breich, with a paper to signify A popish wretch punished for depraveing his Majesty's children. And if we doe not punish such, in time we may crye Oh Lord it is to late.

SIR THOMAS ROE. To whipp him and to complain first to the Lords because else *illicitum quia* ther prisoner.

SIR DUDLEY DIGGS.... Lett him be whipt through the streetes and that to testyfye to all the world our affection to her and hers, and this to signify to the Lords that theay may have part of this honor.

SIR FRANCIS KINISTON. This house is an Idea of the Celestiall court of Judgment. Applyes that Regimen to him *aqua et panis afflictionis sic Turri Londoniensi hic.*

SIR GEORGE MORE. We may enlarge and make presidents. Lett us make this incomparably wicked man an example to all others. Lett us whipp him first, and then leave him to the Lords for greater punishment.

MR. WHITTSON *pro Pinguare hispanensi*, vzt. hott Bacon dropt on him at every 6 lashes.

MR. RAINSFORD. No corporall punishment of the whipp, but to lett him pay 1000*li.* to the warrs of the Palatinate.

MR. NEALE. The Tower first, and then the Lords to have him to prosecute.

SIR FRANCIS SEAMOUR. To have him goe from Westminster with his dublett of, and to have as many lashes as beades.

MR. SALTER. To be whippt, lye in little ease, and then leave him to the Lords with him.

SIR EDWARD GILES. The pillery with a paper, then stript, and to have the beades and the Fryars girdle, and as many stripes as beades, first at Westminster then at the Court, then *tot* at Temple. And not to take him from the Fleete till the Lords please....

SIR JAMES PARRET. For banishment....

[1] *Commons debates*, 1621, III, p. 109.   [2] *Ibid.* p. 117.

SIR FRANCIS DARCY. To bore him through the toung, and the pillery....

SIR GEORGE GOREING. At the Massacre at Valteline one sett on an Ass with his tayle in his hand, with his chapps cutt of and his eares; so this man, but insteade of theis a halter and hange him.

MR. SALISBURY. This man hath sayd he would no more care to sware on a bible then on a doggs tayle, *ergo* to punish him for blasphemy and allso for offending against the Lords anointed....

SIR THOMAS WAYMAN. To have him whipt, and then shew his papers, and doubts not but we may find cause to hang him.

SIR JOHN STRANGWAYS. Ill words merritt blowes, *ergo* stripes, pillery; and after consider the further desert; and lett us create a president if none be present.

SIR EDWARD WARDER. To retourne him to the dungeon in the fleete. Then whipt with as many stripes as the Lady is old.

SIR GYE PALMS. Whipt with his beades with him. Eliz. 13, he might forfeite all his estate upon a premunire for his beades.

MR. ANGELL. Whipping, paper on his forhead. Gagg in his mouth that he may not crye to have any man pitty him....

SIR RICHARD WYMAN. Barefoote and barelegged, and the rest *ut ante*....

SIR HENRY ANDERSON. Only paper, and brand of a popish King, ride backward, naked above the waste, and the beads and trumpery aboute him, and the apprentices whoope at him if theay will.[1]

It requires such touches as these, many of which are to be found in no other diary than this, to appreciate the extraordinary state of mind existing in the Commons in 1621, and no doubt among the people as well. Such fantastic, cruel, and absurd proposals as many of these, totally unwarranted in law and beyond the competence of the House, furnish concrete proof of the deadly fear of the counter-reformation which was sweeping over England at this time. I know of nothing quite like it in English history except the hysteria at the time of the Popish Plot. Nothing less than this, coupled with a feeling of complete frustration arising out of the King's flabby

[1] *Commons debates*, 1621, III, pp. 123–6.

foreign policy and his truckling to Spain, could have led able men and trained lawyers to propose measures so flagrantly illegal against Floyd, a person of no consequence and no danger whatever to the state. Reports like these of Barrington's, unusually vivid, hurried, and disjointed as they are, may in no way change the accepted view of the historical development of the time, but they do supply new and invaluable evidence of the emotions which alone make that development explicable. It is fully as important for the historian to understand why things happen as to know how they happen. For the former, nothing brought to light in recent years serves so well as these diaries, hitherto unpublished and, in some cases, unused.

Among the members of the House in 1621, there were some who did not lose their heads, and there were others whose remarks show that they knew their proposals for Floyd's punishment had no warrant in law. Barrington's notes bring out both of these points clearly. From the beginning Sir Edwin Sandys had been opposed to this madness. On 1 May he said:

See the authority of punishing, our owne or the Lords. We should not trouble them too much, *quia* theay may dispatch that we have allready preferred to them. 2ly, The cause of his punishment, and in considering of it lett us not touch on religion *quia tum Martirum aut Confessorem facimus*. 3ly, The manner of his punishment, it must be proportionable to his fault. He is a gentleman, lett him not be whipt till degraded. *Corpus liberi hominis flagris ne caedatur*. And torturing is unlawfull on the rack for a knight and so a Lord. As good cause hath bredd a badd president. Lett us not be so overcaryed with affection as that we punish illegally and irregulerly.

The next day he added,

I am sorry that we have so many unhappy diversions; dayly, we are diverted by motions rather springing from passion then iudgment. All the world never will call a man to answer as a delinquent unless he be charged with somm crime worthy of it.

Lett us looke if either in Patent or execution he be faulty; and then proceed impartyally if he deserve censure, and if otherwise lett us leave theis fruitless Questions.

There are few more interesting cases than this of a parliament swept away by the passion of a moment into an indefensible position. When the members came to their senses, the House could only retreat, saving what dignity it could. "I will never give my voyce to acknowledg an error to be in this iudicature", cried Sir George Moore; but Wentworth's words, as reported by Barrington, probably better represented the view of the majority:

We see 13 E. 3 that the whole parliament may err; and Moyses in zeale when he brake the Tables of Stone went farr. If the King thinke it not iust that is donn, the suite is not so fitt. Therefor the course of a lawe for his punishment is the best way, for that Confirms owr sentence and is a very iust way, and tis better to acknowledg that we have trod awrye then obstinately to persist.

Floyd's case may not be the most important of the transactions of this parliament, but it is very important; and there is no better index of contemporary feeling. I have used it, therefore, as one concrete example of the general importance of these journals as a historical source. For this, Pym's diary or Wentworth's might have been chosen instead of Barrington's. No future biographer of Pym or Wentworth can neglect these, but for the purpose in hand the rougher running notes of Barrington seemed better.

There are about a dozen of these diaries, some of them carefully rewritten afterward, as Pym's was; others hastily scribbled on bits of paper held on the knees of the diarists, and differing widely in historical value and the length of time covered, from the brief fragment of a page or two, taken from the Egerton manuscripts, to the notes of Sir Thomas Barrington, which fill an entire volume, or the anonymous work of another diarist, which fills a second. Among them is a set of notes for part of the parliament, attributed by the editors to Sir Thomas Wentworth, which display in a most interesting way the well-known characteristics of that remarkable man. There are notes by Sir Thomas Belasyse extending to about two hundred and fifty pages, of John Smyth of Nibley only a little shorter, of Sir Thomas Holland, Sir Nathaniel Rich, and other note-takers known and unknown. None of these diaries has been printed before, and in the introductory volume the editors have collected everything known about the manuscripts and much about their authors. Treatment of the general historical significance of the debates disclosed in these notes they have properly decided to postpone, to be included in the introduction to the diaries of James's last parliament, because of the similarity of the constitutional questions debated in both parliaments.

In some ways the most valuable of these diaries—and in many ways the most interesting—is the one written by John Pym, printed here for the first time, which fills one entire volume of four hundred and fifty pages. This diary, even if anonymous, would be of the greatest importance; but its importance is heightened if Pym wrote it. The editors, from internal evidence, seem to me to have established Pym's authorship beyond a reasonable doubt; and they have done much more than that—for they have shown, not merely that this diary is his, but that another important one for James's last parliament, to be published later, was also written by him. Nor is this all. By the same kind of evidence they have proved conclusively that the manuscript edited by Gardiner in 1873 for the Camden Society as *Debates in the house of commons in 1625*, on which so much of our knowledge of Charles's first parliament is based, must have been by the same author as the other two, and is therefore Pym's likewise. Gardiner was aware of the fact that the writer of his manuscript had also written a diary of the parliament of 1624 now in the British Museum, but he hazards no guess as to who the author was, and says nothing of this 1621 diary.

Hardly secondary in importance to the added information afforded in these diaries of 1621 concerning the struggle for

freedom of debate is their value for the history of the growth
of parliamentary procedure in its most critical period. The
effectiveness, for example, of that remarkable expedient, the
committee of the whole, is illustrated nowhere better in its
earlier development than in this parliament of 1621. These
accounts of the doings of the House day by day, often in the
very words used, are valuable supplements to the treatises of
Hakewill and Elsynge and every here and there supply facts
not known before. An amusing instance occurs in Pym's
diary, which seldom mentions matters of this kind. Two
members had risen to speak at the same time, and

Mr. Speaker, instead of Decydinge the precedence, said That
he hoped the wisest would sitt downe first. Against this Mr. Noy
tooke exceptions, as a Jeast unfitt the gravitye of this Assemblye
And desired the Speaker might be punisht, which was likely to
come to Question if Mr. Glanvile [one of the two who had risen
together] had not diverted it by a very modest and discreet
speeche.

Since no single diary of this parliament of 1621 dwarfs the
rest as the *Journal* of D'Ewes does all others for the Long
Parliament, and since some of them cover only a part of the
time parliament was in session, the editors were here unable
to follow the simple and admirable method employed in
editing the *Journal* of D'Ewes, of taking a single diary as the
text for the whole and placing all important variants or
additions in footnotes. Here it was necessary to use several
diaries in succession as text; and it was desirable, in addition,
to print some others in full even where they covered the same
period. It is, therefore, somewhat more difficult to follow a
day's debate in these volumes than in D'Ewes's *Journal*; but
it is hard to see how materials of this peculiar kind could have
been made more easy of access than they are, and the difficulty
is reduced to a minimum by cross-references, and particularly
by a detailed and elaborate index which is a model of its kind.

But it is not merely these excellences in method of arrange-
ment or accuracy of detail that distinguish this work among

others of its kind. Its value is due in large part to the trained skill of the editors in the handling of a type of manuscript far more difficult to decipher than most of those with which either the medieval or the modern historian has to deal.

No one without historical imagination could have conceived or executed the plan of this great series; no one, I believe, but Professor Notestein would have ferreted out so many unpublished diaries as have been printed in it, or gone so far in determining their provenance; and few have the unusual equipment of its editors for the preparation of an edition of such supreme excellence as this. Its importance is by no means confined to the Stuart period, which it covers. It extends forward to affect the whole subsequent development of parliament and parliamentary institutions. As an illustration of the light it tends to throw backward over the Tudor period and even as far as the Lancastrian constitution, one might cite the recent publication of the *Fane fragment of the 1461 Lords' journal*[1] from a manuscript discovered during the editors' search for these parliamentary materials of the seventeenth century. And there is a relation far more fundamental than this between the constitutional struggles of the seventeenth century and the medieval precedents the antagonists were so fond of citing. As Professors Notestein and Relf said in 1921,

The Stuart period must be re-examined in the light of earlier English history, particularly in the light of the fourteenth and fifteenth centuries. The many precedents of which Coke, Cotton, and the parliamentary lawyers and the antiquarians made elaborate use must be looked up and evaluated. How far were those men right in their struggle with the King? Were they reclaiming ground that had been lost or pushing forward to new ground? Was the Lancastrian period that glorious epoch of parliamentary rule that we have supposed? Had the constitution been won by 1485? We suspect that such a study will prove that Coke, Eliot and Digges, Pym, St John, Whitelocke and the rest were really

[1] New Haven, 1935.

driving parliament forward to new positions, that they were over-valuing much of Lancastrian precedent honestly enough no doubt.

This early suspicion of the editors has been more than verified by the results of recent important studies in the Lancastrian period, and the revival of historical interest in that period which has resulted in these studies is itself due in very large part to this suspicion of the correctness of the citations made from it in the constitutional struggles of the seventeenth century. History, as Maitland said, is a seamless web.

IX

A FORGOTTEN WORTHY, PHILIP HUNTON, AND THE SOVEREIGNTY OF KING IN PARLIAMENT

In the spring and summer months of the year 1642 England was at the parting of the ways. The crisis of those weeks is one of the most momentous in English history, and in the development of English political thought probably the most momentous of all. The militia ordinance issued by the two Houses of Parliament without the King, which Charles denounced as void and illegal, and the defence of their action by the Houses, these constitute the first formal break in the ancient constitution which was so soon to lead to war and revolution,[1] and they mark the point from which the paths sharply diverge which lead on the one hand straight to the royal absolutism of Filmer and on the other to the anti-monarchical republicanism of Milton, each without precedent in the older law. All moderate men were filled with foreboding during that summer of 1642 and the months following, whichever turning their convictions were finally to force them reluctantly to take, and one can understand how a patriot like Sir Edmund Verney, in defence of a monarch like Charles, should choose death on the field rather than the destruction of the ancient constitution and the prospect of proscription for friends of a lifetime who felt in conscience bound to choose a path diverging from his own.

"I have eaten his bread, and served him near thirty years, and will not do so base a thing as to forsake him," he declared to Clarendon in speaking of the King, "and choose rather to lose

[1] The Statute of Monopolies of 1624 might be considered the first, but the King's assent obscured the fundamental issue involved in it. The constitutional question was not yet quite ripe.

my life (which I am sure I shall do) to preserve and defend those things which are against my conscience to preserve and defend." "He was as good as his word, and was killed in the battle of Edgehill within two months after this discourse."[1]

It was in like agony of spirit that another "earnest desirer of his countrie's peace" turned to the pen rather than the sword in the vain hope of offering some basis of compromise, "wishing it were worthy to be scanned by those in whose hands it is to heale our divisions". His *Treatise of Monarchie* was published in 1643.[2] Later in the same year Henry Ferne, the King's chaplain, published a moderate and well-reasoned *Reply unto Severall Treatises Pleading for the Armes now taken up by Subjects in the Pretended Defence of Religion and Liberty.* In it he devotes most attention to the author of the *Treatise of Monarchie,* who, he says, seems to be "a man of reason", and he even finds much in the *Treatise* itself which refutes the more radical views expressed in the other books written in defence of the Houses. In 1644 the author of the *Treatise* answered Ferne's *Reply* in *A Vindication of the Treatise of Monarchie.* The importance of the *Treatise* in the constitutional struggle of 1689 is evidenced by the fact that it was reissued twice in that year, the first reissue omitting the last chapter, the second reprinting the whole *Treatise,* as well as the *Vindication* in somewhat abridged form. The first of these reissues was included in the *Harleian Miscellany* (edition of 1745, VI, p. 296). In 1648 Sir Robert Filmer issued an answer to Hunton's *Treatise, The Anarchy of a Limited or Mixed Monarchy.* This was reprinted at London in 1679 and issued along with several other works of Filmer's under the title of *The Free-holders Grand Inquest,* from the name of the first tract in the volume which is there attributed to Filmer.[3] Filmer's

---

[1] *The Life of Edward, Earl of Clarendon,* Part II.
[2] George Thomason's copy is dated 24 May. *Catalogue of the Thomason Tracts,* I, p. 262.
[3] The full title of the 1679 reprint is *Observations upon Mr Hunton's Treatise of Monarchy: or, the Anarchy of a Limited or Mixed Monarchy.*

answer is less moderate and more discourteous than Ferne's *Reply*, though Filmer does pay Hunton the compliment of saying that "The Author of the Treatise of Monarchy hath copiously handled the nature and manner of *Limited* and *Mixed* Monarchy, and is the first and only man (that I know) hath undertaken the task of describing it; others only mention it as taking it for granted." It is chiefly from such books as these that an estimate may be formed of Philip Hunton's theory of the state.

About his life we know comparatively little.[1] Apparently it was a rather uneventful one except for the effect on him of the inevitable ecclesiastical changes which came at the beginning and the end of the Interregnum. The man himself is more important than the events of his life, and the man is disclosed in the short but eloquent preface to the first edition of the *Treatise*, which I reprint entire since it was omitted in all later editions. Its modest and simple directness, in such contrast to the usual artificial preface of the time, larded with classical allusions; its transparent sincerity; and even after three centuries the pathos of its moving appeal to all lovers of their country, cannot but stir in the reader something of the emotion which the writer felt so deeply.

I write not this Discourse [he begins] to foment or heighten the wofull dissention of the Kingdome; but if possible to cure, or at least to allay it: That former too many have done already, this latter, much too few. When a Patient lies sicke under the destroying paroxismes of a Fever, every stander-by will be telling his Medicine, though he be no Physitian: O then let no Sonne of this State account it presumption in me, for putting in my judgement, and speaking that which I conceive might, if not remove, yet mitigate this fatall distemperature of our common Mother: at another time perhaps it might be censurable, but in this exigence laudable.

Something I was full of, which I conceited might doe good; here I have produced it. And now if any man can finde a better

[1] See the article on Philip Hunton by W. A. J. Archbold, in the *Dictionary of National Biography*.

way to appeasement, for the sake of peace let him speedily declare it.

I intend not these ensuing Disputes to any high-flowne judgements, who looke down on all mens, but their owne, to censure, not to be informed; nor to any which hath designes of his owne, which on the opportunity of this Division hee meanes to follow; nor to any who is already possessed by an opinion, which hee resolves to make good: But to the calme and impartiall spirit of every judicious, peacefull man; Let him weigh my Assertions by my grounds on which I build them, and if he find them any where unsound, let him shew mee in what, and I will gladly and thankfully reforme my errour: For as I love not obstinacy in groundlesse opinions in others, so I would avoid it in my selfe.

I have not annexed my *Name*, not that I am ashamed to owne what I conceive to be the truth; but because I know who I am, and that my Name could adde no estimation to the Treatise: Nor do I desire it should: They who search for Truth must regard *Things*, not *Persons*: Give me therefore the now *common Liberty* to goe namelesse; many have taken it for worse ends. If any condemn me for any thing here, it must be for endevouring a thanklesse Moderation 'twixt two Extremes. But I will detaine you no longer at the doore.

Our interest to-day in the body of the *Treatise* which follows is in the author's theory of mixed monarchy, criticized by Dr Ferne, condemned by Sir Robert Filmer, and usually dismissed by modern historians as unimportant or confused; but Hunton's own purpose was an intensely practical one, "to cure, or at least to allay" "the wofull dissention of the Kingdome", and his specific proposals to this end come at the close of his treatise. The very conservatism and moderation of these proposals, coming after the clash of arms, was enough to ensure their certain failure, as we can easily see now, and a fact which at the time did not escape the keen eye of Hobbes, who was one of the first to perceive that this struggle over the militia was no mere difference between conflicting views of the Constitution, but had become a duel which must go on till force and not law should determine which of the two antagonists was to have the mastery. But the ineffectiveness of Hunton's solution of the issues of war should not make us blind to the merits of his conception of monarchy or to its real importance as an interpretation of the English constitution, and as a formulation of political relations which might be valid once more after peace was finally restored.

The *Treatise* is short and preferable to any inadequate summary, but in lieu of the text I shall have to include here an analysis of its essentials as concise as possible. Hunton's treatment of monarchy is divided into two main parts, "Of Monarchy in generall" and "Of this particular Monarchy". Monarchy in general may be either absolute or limited. "Absolute monarchy is when the sovereignty is so fully in one that it hath no limits or bounds under God but his own will." Hunton concedes that this is not necessarily a tyranny, and that it is legitimate where men have "put themselves into this utmost degree of subjection by oath and contract". A limited monarch, on the other hand, "must have his bounds of power *ab externo*, not from the free determination of his own will"; he is a limited monarch, "who hath a law beside his own will for the measure of his power", but it must be "a limitation of the power itself, not barely of the exercise". The author is careful to add, and with the greatest emphasis, that such a limitation in the "fundamental constitution" implies no legal control by his subjects over the monarch's acts within the legitimate sphere thus marked out and defined. Such monarchs are no "tenants at will from their people". "It were unreasonable to say" that subjects who have voluntarily "constituted a monarchy", "that is, invested one man with the sovereignty of power", "yet have it in themselves; or have a power of recalling that supremacy which by oath and contract they themselves transferred on another". It is not true, he holds, that the *populus universus* is above the King, for "if he be a monarch he hath the *apex* or *culmen potestatis*, and all his subjects *divisim* and *conjunctim* are below him: They have divested themselves of all superiority, and no power left for a positive opposition of the person of him whom they have invested."[1] This is a logical deduction which won the commendation even of his adversary, Dr Ferne, who was quick to cite it in refutation of the popular sovereignty of the more radical authors of *Scripture and Reason pleaded for Defensive Armes*. But this denial of the subjects' right of "positive opposition" applies only to the monarch's legitimate acts and commands, and if the sphere of these be limited by law, there remains always the possibility of "exorbitancies" which have no warrant in law. And if these occur, as they may, who is to judge of their character, and to determine that such commands are void and should not receive the obedience due to every legitimate expression of the monarch's will? This is really the crux of Hunton's theory: "Who shall be the judge of the excesses of the sovereign lord in monarchies of this composure?" If the monarch himself were the judge, the monarchy would be truly absolute, not limited; if decision lay with the *populus*, there would be no monarchy at all; if with a foreigner, "then we lose the freedom of the state". "There can be no judge legal and constituted within that frame of government" of "the sovereigns transgressing his fundamental limits". This is a defect inherent in the very nature of limited monarchy itself "for which there can be provided no remedy"—by which Hunton means no *legal* remedy. "It is a transcendent case beyond the provision of that government, and must have an extraordinary judge and way of decision." If such an excess

be mortall and such as suffered dissolves the frame and life of the Government and publique liberty. Then the illegality and destructive nature is to be set open and redresment sought by Petition; which if failing, Prevention by resistance ought to be. But first that it is such must be made apparent, and an Appeale made *ad conscientiam generis humani*, especially of those of that Community, then the fundamentall Lawes of that Monarchy

[1] Here, and hereafter, when the word "power" occurs, it is to be understood usually, as Hunton understood it, in the sense of legal authority.

must iudge and pronounce the sentence in every mans conscience; and every man (as farre as concernes him) must follow the evidence of Truth in his owne soule, to oppose, or not oppose, according as he can in conscience acquit or condemne the act or carriage of the Governour. For I conceive, in a Case which transcends the frame and provision of the Government they are bound to, People are unbound, and in state as if they had no Government; and the superiour Law of Reason and Conscience must be Judge: wherein every one must proceed with the utmost advice and impartiality: For if hee erre in iudgement, hee either resists Gods Ordinance, or puts his hand to the subversion of the State and Policy he lives in.

And this power of judging argues not a superiority in those who Judge, over him who is Judged: for it is not Authoritative and Civill, but morall, residing in reasonable Creatures and lawfull for them to execute, because never devested and put off by any act in the constitution of a legall Government, but rather the reservation of it intended: For when they define the Superiour to a Law, and constitute no Power to Judge of his Excesses from that Law, it is evident they reserve to themselves, not a Formall Authoritative Power, but a morall Power, such as they had originally before the Constitution of the Government; which must needs remaine, being not conveyed away in the Constitution.

This was written by Philip Hunton in 1643. In his *Second Treatise of Government*, licensed on 23 August 1689, John Locke declares,

Where there is no judge on earth the appeal lies to God in Heaven. That question then cannot mean who shall judge, whether another hath put himself in a state of war with me, and whether I may, as Jephtha did, appeal to Heaven in it? Of that I myself can only be judge in my own conscience, as I will answer it at the great day to the Supreme Judge of all men.[1]

For wherever any two men are, who have no standing rule and common judge to appeal to on earth, for the determination of controversies of right betwixt them, there they are still in the state of Nature, and under all the inconveniences of it.[2]

[1] *Second Treatise of Government*, ch. 3.   [2] *Ibid.* ch. 7.

And thus the community may be said in this respect to be always the supreme power, but not as considered under any form of government, because this power of the people can never take place till the government be dissolved. In all cases whilst the government subsists, the legislative is the supreme power.[1]

The old question will be asked in this matter of prerogative, "But who shall be judge when this power is made a right use of?" I answer: Between an executive power in being, with such a prerogative, and a legislative that depends upon his will for their convening, there can be no judge on earth.... And therefore, though the people cannot be judge, so as to have, by the constitution of that society, any superior power to determine and give effective sentence in the case, yet they have reserved that ultimate determination to themselves which belongs to all mankind, where there lies no appeal on earth, by a law antecedent and paramount to all positive laws of men, whether they have just cause to make their appeal to Heaven.[2]

These are among the most important statements of Locke's famous "right of revolution". In the discussion of it Hunton's *Treatise* is nowhere mentioned, though the objections "to Mr Hunton" in Filmer's *Observations* are referred to in Locke's *First Treatise*, and among the books in his library was *A Treatise of Monarchy*, 1643.[3]

Hunton, after this discussion of the difference between absolute and limited monarchy, deals next with the distinction between elective and "successive" monarchy, which he believes makes no difference between them so far as concerns the nature and extent of the monarch's authority, or the duty of subjects to obey. In the last chapter of the first part, he takes up the important question of the possibility of a mixed

[1] *Second Treatise of Government*, ch. 13.   [2] *Ibid*. ch. 14.
[3] For this information I am indebted to Dr Benjamin Rand, who was kind enough to let me see his manuscript of Locke's list of the books in his own library, now almost ready for publication. Since the above statement was written news has come of Dr Rand's death. Whether he left any instructions for the publication of his manuscript I have not heard.

monarchy and of its true character. A simple form of government exists wherever

the Government absolute or limited is so intrusted in the hands of one, that all the rest is by deputation from him; so that there is no authority in the whole Body but his, or derived from him: And that One is either individually one person, and then it is simple Monarchy: Or one associate Body, chosen either out of the Nobility, whence the Government is called a simple Aristocracy: or out of the Community, without respect to birth or state, which is termed a simple Democracy. The supreme authority residing exclusively in one of these three, denominates the government simple which ever it be.

In cases where the government is mixed of all three, the usual and the best form is where there is "priority of order" in one of the three; but in a government of this kind, called monarchy because such priority is in the prince, this "priority of order" is of order only; it implies no subordination of the Estates to the King *in authority*. If monarchy is truly to be a mixed and not a simple one, "the sovereign power must be originally in all Three, *viz*. If the composition be of all three, so that one must not hold his power from the other, but all equally from the fundamentall Constitution."

Every mixed government therefore implies such a "fundamental Constitution". That is, every mixed government must be a "limited" one, though not every limited government needs be mixed. If such a mixed government is to be termed a monarchy, an authority must be vested by the Constitution in the prince "which is not so great as to destroy the mixture, nor so titular as to destroy the monarchy". Such an ideal form Hunton evidently thinks he finds in the English monarchy. The King has "priority" in the fact that all are his subjects and sworn to obey his commands if according to law; that while the power of the Estates comes not from him, "yet the definement and determination of it to such persons is from him, by a necessary consecution"; that the power of summoning and dissolving Parliament is his; and that his assent is necessary as the consummation of its acts. But even such "priority" as this in the King does not indicate simple monarchy if the legislative power is shared with the Estates; for Hunton, like most of his contemporaries, follows Bodin in the belief that the legislative power is *primum ac praecipuum caput majestatis*.

> If the Legislative be in one, then the Monarchy is not mixed but simple, for that is the Superiour, if that be in one, all else must needs be so too.

> For the Prince in a mixed Monarchy, were there no definement of him to a Law but only this: that his Legislative acts have no validity without the allowance and joint authority of the other: this is enough to denominate it exactly a limited Monarchy: and so much it must have, if it be mixed.

Thus to Hunton legislation is the final test. If by the constitution authority is held jointly with the Estates, the monarchy is mixed, whatever other powers the prince may legitimately exercise alone. Such a mixed monarchy is the highest and best form of government, and in England it is the form established by "the fundamental Constitution of the State".

The obvious answer, and the one actually made by all Hunton's opponents, was a reiteration of the dictum of Bodin that sovereignty cannot be divided, that mixed monarchy, and in fact any mixed government, is an absolute contradiction in terms and in actual operation can be nothing but anarchy, or the negation of all government. Hunton's brief anticipation of this objection is his principal contribution to the theory of mixed government; and, though it was not entirely original with him, it is probably the most significant part of his whole theory of the state.

These "diverse concurrent powers", "these joined persons, have they any concurring power to do those acts for which they are joyned?" If their power is not distinct from the monarch's they are sharers only in the exercise of power, not in the power itself, and are mere agents or deputies of the prince. If on the other hand they have a real share in *power*, it may be objected that "such a mixture would make several independent powers in the same state or Kingdom, which is most absurd". "I grant it is absurd," answers our author, "if you speak of several *complete* independent powers; but to affirm several incomplete independent powers concurring to make up one *Integral* mixt power, it is no absurdity at all."

In short, Hunton's sovereign, like Bodin's, must always be single and undivided, but, unlike Bodin's, it may also be *corporate*; in England the sovereign is the King *in Parliament*, and in order to function, all parts, Estates and King alike, must be in agreement; legally to obtain the obedience of the nation, an act can be nothing less than the joint act of King and Estates in which all three have freely concurred. Such a "trinal unity" is no "system of checks and balances", nor "separation of powers", nor is it "popular sovereignty". It is, in effect, Henry VIII's ideal of a commonwealth in which the King and his Parliament are "knit together", expressed in terms of Bodin's new legislative sovereignty; rather than Montesquieu's caricature of it, incorporated by the Fathers in the Constitution of the United States. It is not unlike the ideal co-operation of *regnum* and *sacerdotium*, impossible but magnificent, which constituted the true *Republica Christiana* for Engelbert of Admont in the fourteenth century. The question whether such a conception is "most absurd" or not may be left aside for the moment, or whether it is unimportant historically; but it is sufficiently clear that if co-operation of all the members of the sovereign corporation alone is government, then antagonism or conflict between them is its negation, and must result in the dissolution of the Frame of the State by which alone the legitimacy of all acts of government can be determined. For, since the distribution of power among its agents in every form of mixed government must be made by the rules of an antecedent constitution or frame of government which these agents may not alter, it follows, as Hunton says, that every mixed monarchy is a limited monarchy and subject to the same inherent defect of its merits found in every limited government; there can be no constituted judge of the "exorbitance" of the sovereign, nor—for the actual result is the same—of any of the members which may together constitute the sovereign, if such an excess should occur or be alleged; and in 1643 the King was accused of an "exorbitance" of this fatal kind by the House of Commons after the attempt on the five members, while the adherents of the King in turn alleged that it was the House which had first destroyed the ancient Constitution in the enactment of the militia ordinance. As Hunton puts the case,

One inconvenience must necessarily be in all mixed Governments, which I shewed to be in limited Governments, there can be no Constituted, Legal, Authoritative Judge of the Fundamental Controversies arising betwixt the three Estates [*sic*]. If such do arise, it is the fatal Disease of these Governments, for which no Salve can be prescribed; for the established being of such Authority, would *ipso facto* overthrow the Frame, and turn it into absoluteness: So that if one of these, or two, say their power is invaded and the Government assaulted by the other, the Accused denying it, it doth become a Controversie: Of this Question there is no Legal Judge; it is a case beyond the possible provision of such a Government. The Accusing side must make it evident to every Mans Conscience. In this case, which is beyond the Government, the Appeal must be to the Community, as if there were no Government; and as by Evidence Mens Consciences are convinced, they are bound to give their utmost assistance. For the intention of the Frame in such States, justifies the exercise of any power, conducing to the safety of the Universality and Government established.

Such a "thanklesse Moderation 'twixt two Extremes" does great credit to Hunton's fairness and shows his sympathy for those whose consciences compelled them to take the King's side. This sympathy, and his reverence for the ancient constitution, made him one of those who "dreamt of a mixed power of the King and the two Houses. That it was a divided power, in which there could be no peace, was above their understanding."[1] While Hunton thus conceded to every man the right to choose his side, in his own mind it was the King and not the Commons who had first broken the ancient frame of the state. His opinions on this point may probably be indicated best in the later words of Locke, who adds nothing to Hunton except possibly a greater facility of expression.

The constitution of the legislative is the first and fundamental act of society, whereby provision is made for the continuation of their union under the direction of persons and bonds of laws, made by persons authorised thereunto, by the consent and appointment of the people, without which no man, or number of men, amongst them can have authority of making laws that shall be binding to the rest.... Every one is at the disposure of his own will, when those who had, by the delegation of the society, the declaring of the public will, are excluded from it, and others usurp the place, who have no authority or delegation. This being usually brought about by such in the commonwealth, who misuse the power they have, it is hard to consider it aright, and know at whose door to lay it, without knowing the form of government in which it happens.

Assuming then a legislature such as the English Parliament, composed of King, Lords and Commons, it is evident, says Locke,

First, that when such a single person or prince sets up his own arbitrary will in place of the laws which are the will of the society declared by the legislative, then the legislative is changed.... Secondly, when the prince hinders the legislative from assembling in its due time, or from acting freely, pursuant to those ends for which it was constituted, the legislative is altered.... For it is not names that constitute governments, but the use and exercise of those powers that were intended to accompany them; so that he who takes away the freedom, or hinders the acting of the legislative in its due seasons, in effect takes away the legislative, *and puts an end to the government.*[2]

This interpretation of English monarchy and of monarchy

---

[1] Hobbes, *Behemoth* (Molesworth's edition), p. 319.
[2] *Second Treatise of Government*, ch. 19. The italics are mine.

in general is indeed "a thankless moderation 'twixt two extremes", and from contemporary extremists it received the treatment always given to moderate theories; but to me it seems nothing short of amazing that modern accounts of English political thought in the seventeenth century should entirely ignore, as they usually do, Philip Hunton's contribution to it, or should dismiss his *Treatise* as an evidence only of "the confusion that reigned in many minds"—"extraordinary confusions", which "naturally gave the absolutists an easy triumph".[1]

The present paper is an outcome of this amazement, and is in substance a plea for revision of this unfavourable estimate, urged on three grounds especially; first, the substantial accuracy of Hunton's analysis of the English constitution as existing in 1640; second, the merits of his general theory of the state when compared with those of contemporaries; third, the closeness of the parallel between his political formula and the actual government of England after the Revolution settlement.

It is clear enough to us now, as it was to Hobbes at the time, that by 1643 England's malady had become so serious that no salve could cure it: the knife was necessary; it was too late for law; force had already replaced it. The House of Commons had branded as an enemy of his country everyone who had joined the King, and Charles had declared all to be traitors who, like Sir John Hotham, had obeyed the mandate of the Houses instead of the King's. Hunton would have limited his proscription to those only whom he considered to be the original instigators of the first breach of the Constitution; probably few beyond Strafford, who was dead, the Primate, who was in prison, and Digby, who was or had been in exile; most of the other adherents of the King, like

---

[1] *English Democratic Ideas in the Seventeenth Century*, by G. P. Gooch, second edition by Professor H. J. Laski (Cambridge, 1927), pp. 95–6. I have cited Professor Gooch's unfavourable estimate because he is one of the few who have noticed Hunton at all, and because his book is the best account extant of English political thought in this period.

Clarendon and Falkland, had broken no law, for the Constitution was already destroyed; even in joining the King they were at most only exercising a natural right to obey the promptings of a misguided conscience. Such moderate theories usually bring fewer victories than the extremer views to which they are opposed, but they may furnish a better basis for the government of a peaceful commonwealth.

The various theories of government held in England in 1643 when Hunton wrote may be reduced roughly to four. *First*, the belief that government, whatever its origin, must in its nature always be arbitrary, especially in the making of law, which is the ultimate act of sovereignty. Filmer and Hobbes were in agreement on this, though they differed as to the source and seat of authority. There were, however, comparatively few in England as early as 1643 ready to accept a political doctrine so extreme. *Second*, the theory of popular sovereignty which followed the dictum of the *Vindiciae Contra Tyrannos* in placing the prince in a monarchical state below the *populus universus*, and thus making him the mere agent of the people, who holds from them a revocable commission no higher than that of the humblest magistrate save in title and dignity only. This theory was not new, either in England or on the Continent, but in 1643 its English adherents were probably not very numerous, though their number was growing rapidly. *Third*, a theory of monarchy similar in every important respect to that of Bodin, by whom it had been greatly influenced, a theory of limited monarchy as Hunton's is, but simple, and not mixed, as he believed the traditional government of England to be. The highest type of human government, of which England is a notable example, is under this theory a monarchy which must always be limited by law, but one in which the supreme authority can never rest in any but the prince alone. If others, such as the English Lords and Commons, have a part in acts of government, their part is limited to advice and assistance only, it never does and never can extend to a sharing of the sovereign power. Monarchy should be limited, but never can be mixed. Such was the view of Dr Ferne, one of the ablest and most moderate of Hunton's opponents, and ideas very like his were apparently held by many of the ablest jurists and most learned antiquaries of England. Many of these who seem to hold this theory of monarchy had, like Sir Roger Twysden, strongly opposed the levy of ship money and denounced forced loans, admitting perhaps, as the judges asserted, their possible legality in the event of an emergency threatening the state's existence, which "private persons could not modestly think themselves qualified to discern"; but nevertheless regarding all such exactions in a period of profound peace as "very grievous", especially when defended by a logic "that left no man anything which he might call his own".[1] For sovereignty, as many of them followed Bodin in defining it, under the constitution of a "royal" monarchy includes no authority to take the goods of subjects without their consent, except in a national emergency evident and extraordinary; otherwise the monarchy would be *seigneuriale* rather than royal, and the subject a slave and not a citizen. Subsidy is normally no part of sovereign power. But legislation unquestionably is, and therefore the consent of the Estates, while absolutely necessary in a grant, is never essential to the making of a law; the laws are the King's laws, and in their promulgation—which is the principal head of all sovereignty—the Lords and Commons are sharers only in the administration of the Realm, they have no portion of its authority; such law-making power as they actually enjoy is wholly a derived power, and not their own; all sovereign authority is in the king alone, and may be delegated but never parted with.

From this form of limited monarchy it may seem a very slight step to Hunton's conception of a limited and mixed one, the fourth and last variety of monarchical theory which men seemed to have in mind in England in 1643; but the practical differences are profound. On Dr Ferne's principles the first

[1] Clarendon, *History of the Rebellion*, Book I.

breach of the Constitution was made by the two Houses in their ordinance for the militia; Hunton believed the King had made it in the attempt on the five members.

Perhaps in 1683, when Hunton's theories were condemned in the home of lost causes, a comparison of his limited and mixed monarchy with Filmer's arbitrary one might have had some point, but it had little point in 1643 or before 1643, and in our own time it has even less, except, apparently, for American historians of the American Revolution. The two main theories with which Hunton's conception must stand comparison are the titular monarchy of the republicans and the limited monarchy of Dr Ferne.

Hunton's theory of sovereignty is in substantial agreement with Bodin's in every important respect save one, the possibility of mixture; sovereignty is primarily legislative and the sovereign is single, undivided, and *legibus solutus* with reference to every law but those fundamental rules which constitute the frame or constitution of the state itself and therefore define and set limits to every legitimate organ of government within it, high or low. And since republican objections to views like Hunton's were never based on the existence of any mixture in administration, provided the will which moves it all be conceded to be the will of the *populus*, an abstract comparison of Hunton's conception of government with republican thought becomes at bottom the contrasting of a theory which concentrates the supreme authority of the state in a single organ of administration, with another which regards sovereignty as the incommunicable power of the *populus*; it is in essence a comparison of Bodin or Loyseau with Althusius, whose respective merits have divided the world from their day to our own.

But, as has been said, the principal object of Hunton's writing was, after all, more practical than theoretical, and it was, therefore, more to the immediate purpose for him to show that his form of monarchy was a true interpretation of the English Constitution, than merely to demonstrate its logical soundness. And whatever hesitation a theorist might have in choosing between the sovereignty of Hunton and that of Henry Parker or Charles Herle, no student of history could long remain in doubt as to the respective merits of the Huntonian and the republican idea of government as an interpretation of earlier English constitutional precedent. It is only since the eighteenth century that constitutional republicanism has become effective practically in the decisive sphere of legislation, through the suppression of the royal right to refuse assent to a bill; and to this day this suppression still rests on mere convention, without any sanction in the "Law of the Constitution". An English statute must be enacted by the King as well as by Lords and Commons, if it is to be enforced by the courts or obeyed by the people. Even such a convention was far in the future in 1643, and before that date it would be hard to find any precedent after the ordinances of 1311, which the Statute of York in 1322 had declared to be illegal and void, prescribing for time to come, that

the matters which are to be established for the estate of our Lord the King and of his heirs, and for the estate of the Realm and of the people, shall be treated, accorded, and established in parliaments, by our Lord the King, and by the assent of the prelates, earls and barons and the commonalty of the Realm; according as it hath been heretofore accustomed.[1]

Prynne's elaborate attempt in 1643 to buttress the constitutional position of the Houses by earlier precedents in his *Soveraigne Power of Parliaments and Kingdomes* is ingenious but a distinct failure.

Popular sovereignty certainly rests on no valid precedents of the Tudor constitution, and the assertions of Charles I, in rejecting the jurisdiction of the court set up by the Rump to try him in 1649, were as crushing in historical accuracy as futile in effect, when he said,

The law upon which you ground your proceedings, must

---

[1] *Statutes of the Realm*, I, p. 189. It is doubtful whether even this statute and the ordinances it repealed had anything to do with the question at issue in 1643, the authority to make a law binding the people.

either be old or new: if old, show it; if new, tell what authority, warranted by the fundamental laws of the land, hath made it, and when. But how the House of Commons can erect a Court of Judicature, which was never one itself (as is well known to all lawyers) I leave to God and the world to judge. And it were full as strange, that they should pretend to make laws without King or Lords' House, to any that have heard speak of the laws of England.[1]

There remain to be compared the simple limited monarchy of Dr Ferne and the mixed monarchy of Hunton's *Treatise*. Whether one makes the comparison on the basis of logic or of precedent a decision between them is difficult, for they are not far apart in theory, and plausible historical precedents may be adduced for each. Since they are alike in practically everything but the one question of the possibility of a mixture of legislative authority in a state, the tenability of Hunton's theory on its theoretical side narrows down to a single consideration: are Bodin and his followers like Ferne, warranted in their denial that legislative authority can ever rest in any except a single individual or a body with a will as simple and undifferentiated as the will of one natural person? Hunton's own answer to the criticisms of his theory made on this basis is very acute, and to most of his opponents it is crushing. Those, he says in effect, who deny the possibility of "several incomplete independent powers concurring to make up one *Integral* mixed power", as King and Estates concur in the enactment of an English statute, are not excluding mixed monarchy alone; they are denying the possible existence of any simple aristocracy or simple democracy and reducing all legitimate forms of government in the world to the rule of one single individual. For the government of every aristocracy is a concurrence of individuals to make up one corporate ruling body, and in a popular state likewise there could be no government without a similar "concurrence" on an even wider scale. If King and Estates are unable to unite to perform a joint act of

[1] *The Constitutional Documents of the Puritan Revolution, 1628–1660*, edited by S. R. Gardiner (Oxford, 1889), p. 285.

sovereignty, how can the members of a simple aristocracy do it? Yet all Hunton's chief opponents, of whatever complexion, admitted the legitimacy of aristocracy and democracy while denying that of mixed monarchy—with one exception. Sir Robert Filmer was alone consistent, for he admitted no gradations of power between complete anarchy and the arbitrary rule of one. It is plain, he says, "1. That there can be no Form of Government, but Monarchy alone. 2. That there is no Monarchy, but Paternal. 3. That there is no Paternal Monarchy but Absolute, or Arbitrary. 4. That there is no such thing as an Aristocracy or Democracy."[1] Even Hobbes would have been caught on the horns of Hunton's dilemma if he had been interested at all in right instead of might. There seems in fact no logical escape from the acceptance of Hunton's mixed monarchy as a possible form of government along with the others, unless we are ready to reject every form of corporate action whatsoever as impossible among men; and few students of the history of law or institutions would venture to do that.

Filmer's assertion that Hunton was "the first and only man" who had given a description of limited monarchy before 1648 is not to be lightly disregarded, and I know of no facts to controvert it if we confine our attention to England; but on the Continent mixed monarchy had been the subject of considerable discussion, and from various angles, before 1643. A single example must suffice here, but it is one of an earlier political writer who accepted and expounded a theory of mixed monarchy which in its central principle seems precisely the same as Hunton's. In 1606 Henning Arnisaeus of Halberstadt published his first political work with the title *Doctrina Politica in Genuinam Methodum, quae est Aristotelis, Reducta*, and in it occurs the following passage:

There remains therefore a third mode [of mixture in a republic] when the rights of sovereignty are separated and different ones

[1] *Observations upon Aristotle's Politiques, The Freeholders Grand Inquest*, pp. 151–2.

attributed to different estates. As to Bodin's objection that sovereignty must be undivided, it is false, unless he means only the
highest and most perfect sovereignty. For there are several heads
and rights, the mingling of which makes a perfect sovereignty,
of which, though as an integral whole it may not be shared by
more than one, there is nothing to prevent the parts from being
separated and attributed to several. So that, while a portion of
the sovereignty inheres in the parts, the highest and completest
sovereignty rests in the whole body, from a concurrence of parts
which merges their several sovereign powers in one.[1]

But a refutation of the theoretical objections of critics was
only a part, and not the larger part, of Hunton's task. In
addition he had to bring some proof that the English monarchy
from time immemorial and up to 1643 had been in reality a
mixed and not a simple form of government. This was the
most difficult and remains one of the most interesting of the
parts of his *Treatise*. Whether Philip Hunton or Henry Ferne
is the better interpreter of earlier English constitutional development is a very nice question indeed, which depends for
its answer on the character of the English Constitution itself
in the Middle Ages and in the equally obscure period of fundamental change in the reigns of the Tudors; but difficult though
it is, this is a question which one cannot wholly ignore who is
serious in his attempt to form a true estimate of the value and
importance of Philip Hunton's thought. During the later
Middle Ages, as I have attempted to show at greater length in
another place,[2] in England and elsewhere in Europe, ideas of
limitations to the legitimate scope of monarchy prevailed
which conform pretty closely to the limitations accepted by
both Ferne and Hunton. The ruler had a *liberum regimen*, an
unhampered control of the administration which was legitimately his as king, and as king the subjects' goods and rights
were therefore his, but his only *quoad protectionem seu adminis-
trationem*. In the crucial matter of the promulgation of law this

---

[1] *Doctrina Politica* (Amsterdam, 1651), cap. viii, pp. 174–5.
[2] *The Growth of Political Thought in the West*, pp. 186–200, 364–94.

resulted in a difference between royal *edicta* on the one hand, necessary to administration and wholly within the monarch's free discretion, and on the other a body of rights inhering in the subject by ancient custom which the King at his coronation had sworn to maintain and could therefore neither take away nor abridge. There is thus a considerable distinction between the *consensus* of the Council to mere administrative orders, which the King was free to disregard if he chose, and consent to the official promulgation or affirmation of immemorial custom defining the subjects' rights and property, such for example as constitute most of the substantive provisions in Edward I's great statutes. It was no doubt the experience or the knowledge rather than the authority of the counsellors which had originally made their "consent" advisable in the one case and indispensable in the other, but there is a real difference between the two kinds of enactment, and in the course of time it gave rise to the application of the term *ordinatio* to one and *statutum* to the other. Nor is it strange in such circumstances that the distinction between ordinance and statute should not always have been entirely clear to the minds of men at the time. If it had been, historians to-day might be able to define a medieval statute with greater confidence, and a decision would also be easier on this great question in dispute between Hunton and Ferne, whether the King can promulgate such a statute, or only the King *in Parliament*.

Undoubtedly one great cause of the ambiguity of medieval precedents on this point was the late and the gradual development of the English bicameral assembly. Another was the difference between medieval promulgation and modern legislation, the former conforming to the prevailing medieval conception of law as custom, the latter consisting in the expression of a will to which obedience is legally due.

By the sixteenth century, it is true, the composition of Parliament was definitely fixed and the transition in enactments from affirmation to the creation of law was far advanced, but some of Parliament's functions still remained uncertain in the Tudor period, and the making of new law was too recent a phenomenon to attract general attention before the closing years of the sixteenth century.[1] Much of the ambiguity inherited from the earlier obscure period of growth, therefore, still clung to the institutions of the Tudor monarchy. Legislation in our modern sense was then a thing so new that it should not surprise us to find men uncertain whether to classify it with the older *edicta* which kings could freely make unaided, or with ancient customs "*quas vulgus elegerit*", defining the subjects' property which it was admitted the King could never take in ordinary circumstances without their consent, there being little practical difference in such a case between a power to take property and a power to determine what is property.

In 1587 the judges declared in the case of Cavendish that they were compelled by their oath to obey the law instead of an express command of the Queen depriving a subject of his proprietary rights, and there are several other like cases in the law reports of the reign. But the unenforceable commands in these cases have not the formality of a statute. In their uncertainty regarding the latter the controversialists turned for confirmation of their respective contentions to the words in the enacting clauses of the Acts themselves. All supporters of prerogative pointed to the fact—which was undeniable—that many, if not most of the earlier statutes were enacted, either in the name of the King alone, or by authority of the King and Council, at least with no mention of the Commons; while Hunton was easily able to show in reply that in modern

---

[1] As late as 1566 even Bodin seems still to be unaware of it. In his *Methodus*, published in that year, he considers the determination of and appointment to judicial office as the highest act of sovereignty. Ten years later, in the *République*, the giving of law to citizens and subjects has become the focus of it all. So far as I know, the latter doctrine was unheard of before 1576; a generation later it had become practically universal among the learned, though Loyseau notes incidentally in his *Treatise on Seigneuries*, published in 1608, that sovereignty and judicial authority are still synonymous—*en commun langage*, ch. iii, sec. 30.

times by the customary phrase "and by the authority of the same" "The King, Lords, *and Commons*" are always expressly referred to.

Such a change as this in the words of enactment is only a formal one, it has no legal significance, Ferne contends. The evidence of earlier ages is clear in its indication of the King as the sole enacting authority, and if he had such exclusive power at any time, it was impossible ever afterward, either that the subjects should deprive him of it or that he should divest himself. If Kings in after times consulted the Commons, this was a delegation of royal authority made of mere grace; it carried no right. For Hunton, on the contrary, the constitution is much more responsive to the social and political development of the people. As the King's original rights were first created by consent and compact between King and people, so when a need for change occurs modifications may be made by a like consent, and this is often only a tacit consent. Thus the change of phraseology in the statutes marks a corresponding evolution in the constitution itself, and the authority of the Commons even if new is not a concession but a right, because it has arisen out of an agreement between King and people which is no less valid because it is only tacit.

Much of the argument on this point turned on the results of conquest and on the character and effect of such conquests in England. The opponents, therefore, submit summaries of English history illustrating their conflicting views and running back as far as the *Germania* of Tacitus. It is unnecessary to follow these, but Ferne, of course, considers every conquest a complete subjugation, while Hunton insists that in every case the new régime of the conqueror was accepted by his subjects before it could be considered legitimate. Even the conquest of William the Norman, the most important of all, he considers a conquest only in name, because the Conqueror succeeded to an earlier title and admitted the fact in submitting to an election by the Witenagemot.

On this difficult question of the legislative authority of the

Estates, the opinions of contemporaries between 1485 and 1643 should probably receive more consideration than arguments drawn from the indefinite precedents furnished by the obscure developments of the formative period in the Middle Ages; on Hunton's theory of development they undoubtedly should.

It would be no very difficult task to find such opinions in the Tudor period, and they would be somewhat conflicting ones, but I shall have to confine myself here to two or three important expressions which occurred after the accession of the first Stuart, who with his usual lack of judgment made of this historical question a grave constitutional issue.

The first is from a speech of Sir James Whitelocke, later one of the judges of England, in the House of Commons, during the great debate on royal impositions in 1610.[1]

The soveraigne power [Whitelocke says] is agreed to be in the King: but in the King is a twofold power; the one in parliament, as he is assisted with the consent of the whole state; the other out of parliament, as he is sole and singular, guided merely by his own will. And if of these two powers in the King one is greater than the other, and can direct and controule the other; that is *suprema potestas*, the soveraigne power, and the other is *subordinata*. It will then be easily proved, that the power of the King in parliament is greater than his power out of parliament; and doth rule and controule it.... So you see the appeal is from the King out of parliament, to the King in parliament; the writ is in his name; the rectifying and correcting the errours is by him, but with the assent of the lords and commons, than which there can be no stronger evidence to prove, that his power out of parliament is subordinate to his power in parliament: for in acts of parliament be they lawes, grounds, or whatsoever else, the act and power is the Kings, but with the assent of the lords and commons, which maketh it the most soveraigne and supreme power above all, and

---

[1] It was printed in 1641 and again in 1658. From the latter edition it was reprinted in Howell's *State Trials* (II, p. 477) as a speech of Yelverton. The Notes of the debate edited by S. R. Gardiner indicate that the speech was made by Whitelocke. *Parliamentary Debates in* 1610 (Camden Society), p. 103.

controulable by none.... Can any man give me a reason, why the King can only in parliament make lawes? No man ever read any law whereby it was so ordained; and yet no man ever read that any King practised the contrary. Therefore it is the originall right of the Kingdome, and the very natural constitution of our state and policy being one of the highest rights of soveraigne power.

The words of Sir Matthew Hale may seem a little more ambiguous perhaps, but they are scarcely less striking.

No good Subject that understands what he Says can make any Question where the Soveraigne Power of this Kingdome resides. The Laws of the Land and the Oath of Supremacy teach us, that the King is the only Supreame Governour of this Realme.

He then enumerates six powers included within his sovereignty, and under the sixth he says:

In him resides the Power of makeing Lawes. The Laws are his Laws enacted by him.

These are the greate Jura Summi Imperii that the Laws of this Kingdome have fixed in the Crown of England, Butt yett there are certaine Qualifications of these Powers, especially of the two latter, vizt.... Though the Legislative Power be in the King, So that none but he can make Laws oblidgeing the Subjects of this Realme, yett there is a Certaine Solemnitie and Qualification of that Power, namely with the advice and assent of the 2 houses of Parlem^t, wthout which no Law can be made. And therefore, Proclamations cannot make a law.... Itt is certain that the King without the Consent of the Lordes and Comons in Parlem^t neith^r by Proclamation nor by Ordinance, Act of Council or Ordinance cannot make a bindeing Law; and this is so known a truth that itt needes no Instances to confirme itt.... And as he cannot make a Law without Consent of Parliam^t, Soe neither can he Repeale a Law without the like Consente.[1]

But one of the most interesting statements of all on this subject was made officially in the King's name in answer to

---

[1] *Reflections by the Lrd Cheife Justice Hale on Mr. Hobbes his Dialogue of the Lawe*, printed by Sir William Holdsworth in his *History of English Law*, v, pp. 500–13.

The humble Petition and Advice of both Houses of Parliament, with Nineteen Propositions sent unto his Majesty the 2ᵈ of June, 1642[1] which is aptly called by S. R. Gardiner a new edition of the Provisions of Oxford[2] and in Clarendon's opinion involved "the disinherison of the crown of all its choice regalities, and left only the shadow and empty name of the King".[3] In "his majestys' answer", "tending towards a Peace", the following statements occur:

We call God to witness, that as for our Subjects sake these Rights are vested in Us; so for their Sakes, as well as for our own, We are resolved not to quit them, nor to subvert (though in a parliamentary way) the ancient, equal, happy, well-poised, and never-enough commended Constitution of the Government of this Kingdom; nor to make our Self, of a King of *England*, a Duke of *Venice*; and this of a Kingdom, a Republick.

There being three kinds of Government among Men, Absolute Monarchy, Aristocracy, and Democracy: and all these having their particular Conveniences and Inconveniences. The Experience and Wisdom of your Ancestors, hath so moulded this out of a mixture of these, as to give to this Kingdom (as far as humane Prudence can provide) the Conveniences of all three, without the Inconveniences of any one, as long as the Balance hangs even between the three Estates, and they run jointly on in their proper Chanel (begetting Verdure and Fertility in the Meadows on both sides) and the overflowing of either on either side, raise no Deluge or Inundation.... In this Kingdom the Laws are jointly made by a King, by a House of Peers, and by a House of Commons chosen by the People, all having free Votes and particular Priviledges. The Government according to these Laws, is trusted to the King.[4]

[1] Rushworth, *Collections*, iv, p. 722 ff.
[2] *History of England*, x, p. 196.
[3] *The Life of Edward, Earl of Clarendon*, Part ii.
[4] Rushworth, *Collections*, iv, p. 731. Many years later, in 1669, Clarendon recounted the circumstances of the issuing of the King's answer, and if his memory did not fail him his account throws valuable light on the authors of it and their political opinions. The Nineteen Propositions were issued by the Houses soon after Clarendon had withdrawn from Westminster to join the King at York, leaving Culpepper

If Hunton's ideas, then, were an evidence only of confusion, it was a confusion shared by many; and one wonders, in light of the uncertainty of earlier precedents, whether such a "confusion" may not, after all, be an evidence of sounder political thinking than the extremer assertions made with such confidence by men like Sir Robert Filmer. Henry VIII had declared in Ferrer's Case, "We at no time stand so high in our estate royal as in the time of parliament; when we as head and you as members, are conjoined and knit together into one body politic."[1] In contrast Charles I had struggled desperately to supersede parliament altogether and might have done so indefinitely but for the Scottish war. Political conditions in England in 1643 were indeed vastly different from those of

and Falkland to look after the King's interests. The King's reply was thus apparently drawn up by Culpepper and Falkland, before their own departure for York, which followed soon after, then sent to Clarendon, who did not issue it till the arrival of his two colleagues, and later printed and formally issued at York in the King's name by all three. When he first saw the paper Clarendon objected strongly to the phrase "the three Estates", which he found in it, "and for this reason Mr. Hyde did not advance the printing it," "since in truth the *bishops* make the *third estate*, the King being the head and sovereign of the whole". Falkland, finding on his arrival that the paper had been suppressed, "appeared much unsatisfied", and intimated that Clarendon "therefore disliked it, because he had not writ it himself". Whereupon Clarendon "immediately procured the King's consent, and sent it to the Press that night, with order to lose no time in the impression". Falkland, he tells us, was later "much troubled when he knew the reason; and imputed it to his own inadvertency, and to the infusion of some lawyers, who had misled Sir John Colepepper; and to the declarations which many of the prelatical clergy frequently and ignorantly made, that the bishops did not sit in parliament as the representatives of the clergy, and so could not be the *third estate*" (*The Life of Edward, Earl of Clarendon,* Part II). It is to be noted in this that Clarendon's objection to the wording of the King's reply and Falkland's objection, if he had any, were solely to the mention of the King as one of the three Estates of Parliament instead of the bishops. There is no hint of any disagreement with the statement that "the Laws are jointly made by a King, by a House of Peers, and by a House of Commons". Clarendon's views on this matter, expressed at the end of his life in his answer to Hobbes's *Leviathan,* are no indication of his opinions in 1642.

[1] *Parliamentary History*, I, p. 555.

Henry VIII's time, and the fatuity of the first two Stuarts is one important cause. But it is not the sole cause, as the later years of Elizabeth clearly show. By 1643, as Sir George Prothero says, "the nation had outgrown the tutelary stage".[1] Whatever the causes, King and Parliament were no longer "knit together"; while all the constitutional precedents which either could cite presumed that they were closely "conjoined".

Where law and precedent can be properly and honestly cited by two powerful and uncompromising antagonists, the struggle between them cannot by any possibility be kept within constitutional bounds—a revolution is inevitable. The men of the Tudor period had in mind a commonwealth of which the King was a member. "King in Council" had not yet been arrayed against "King in Parliament". They had not anticipated the case of a divergence, between the elements of which Parliament was composed. But that divergence at length came, and the very closeness of the tie between King and people under the Tudors served to make the rent between them the wider under the Stuarts.[2]

Before his death Sir Walter Raleigh foresaw that

If the House press the King to grant unto them all that is theirs by the Law, they cannot, in Justice, refuse the King all that is his by the Law. And where will be the Issue of such a contention? I dare not divine, but sure I am, that it will tend to the Prejudice both of the King and Subject.[3]

It is evident that some change in the constitution was inevitable, and on Hunton's theory, as we have seen, it was not impossible; "The years that revealed the splendour of English

---

[1] *Select Statutes and other Constitutional Documents Illustrative of the Reigns of Elizabeth and James I*, Introduction, p. xxix.

[2] C. H. McIlwain, *The High Court of Parliament*, p. 343. In the volume just cited (p. 369 ff.), published in 1910, some general conceptions touching sovereignty are set forth or implied, which I have been led by further study and more mature consideration to review and in part to discard.

[3] *The Prerogative of Parliaments, Harleian Miscellany*, v, p. 208 (edition of 1745).

literature, that gave us Shakespeare and Ben Jonson, Richard Hooker and the King James' version, gave us in politics a new kind of Commons that was by and by to make inevitable a new constitution."[1] But if Charles I from his accession had observed the principles he admits in the reply to the Nineteen Propositions the change might have required no civil war to bring it about. In 1642, and conceivably even in 1643 when Hunton wrote, if men had been convinced of the entire good faith of the King, a peaceful outcome might not have been wholly out of the question. It is, therefore, scant justice to Hunton to assume that it was mere confusion of mind that led him and so many others with him still to retain some hope of a restoration of the old harmony, and to propose, almost in the very words of the King himself, the ancient constitution as a basis for the reconciliation. His solution is valid, of course, only if his interpretation of that constitution is not unsound.

Filmer cites Bodin at length to disprove both Hunton's mixed and his limited monarchy, quite properly for the former, totally without warrant for the latter. Bodin had asserted in his *République* that the royal monarchies of France and England were essentially alike in that the monarchy in each case was limited in scope, absolute in authority, and mixed in administration only, not in power. In this statement Hunton agreed with all but the last part as true of the monarchy in England, and it is pertinent to inquire whether there were not in the English political system some unique features, some differences from the French constitution, on which he might reasonably ground the reservation he thus makes in holding that the English sovereign is a corporate one even in respect of power or authority.

In considering this it is important to remember that for Bodin, for Hunton, for all Hunton's critics, such as Filmer and Ferne, and in fact for practically every theorist of importance at the time, the crucial element in determining the seat of

[1] Wallace Notestein, "The Winning of the Initiative by the House of Commons", *Proceedings of the British Academy*, 1924, p. 53.

sovereignty was the authority to make a binding law; legislative power was *primum ac praecipuum caput majestatis* to which all other governmental powers were merely incidental. In the second place, one must not forget another of Bodin's political maxims, not so generally accepted as the former, but admitted by many, including, apparently, Hunton and Ferne, though, of course, not Filmer; namely, that supply is properly no part of sovereignty at all; unlike the making of law it is a voluntary grant by subjects, and therefore a ruler may be truly "sovereign" though he cannot tax his people without their consent, provided his authority is "absolute" in administration, of which law-making is the principal part. For Bodin it is in fact this very inability to take property which marks out a ruler as a *royal* monarch, instead of a *seigneurial* one who rules over slaves instead of subjects.

If these two points of Bodin's political formula are kept in mind, the first of them especially, it becomes evident that the usual comparison drawn between the working systems of England and France between 1500 and 1643 is somewhat misleading when applied to this problem of sovereignty. The greatest difference between them, as is usually noted properly enough, is the regularity and comparative frequency of the meetings of the Estates in England and the almost complete suppression of them in France in the same period. But in France, and in the theory of Bodin based largely on actual conditions in France, this could have little to do with the seat of sovereignty, because the Estates there when they rarely met, met not to assist in the promulgation of law, but only to grant a supply or to tender petitions to the King; they had no regular part in legislation. If, then, one is to make a valid comparison of France and England *on this matter of sovereignty* in dispute between Hunton and Ferne, it is not the *États Généraux* that should be contrasted with the Parliament in England, but the French *Parlement*; for in legislation proper, the real point of comparison in locating sovereignty, the French Estates have no such part as the English Estates have. In France, the royal *ordonnances* which correspond to English statutes are registered and must be registered in the *Parlement* of Paris; in England, to become binding law, a similar rule must be formally enacted "by the advice and consent of the King, the Lords, and the Commons in this present Parliament assembled and by the authority of the same".

It is not strange, therefore, that Bodin should say:

> Si le Prince souverain est suget aux estats, il n'est ny Prince, ny souverain: & la Republique n'est ny Royaume, ny Monarchie,

or that he should add with special reference to England:

> Nous conclurons donc que la souveraineté du Monarque n'est en rien alteree, ny diminuee pour la presence des estats.... Par ainsi on voit que le poinct principal de la majesté souveraine, & puissance absoluë, gist principalement à donner loy aux sugets en general sans leur consentement.[1]

Nor is it surprising that Loyseau should declare

> que le Royaume de France est la Monarchie la mieux établie qui soit, & qui ait jamais esté au monde, estant en premier lieu une Monarchie Royale, & non pas Seigneuriale: une Souveraineté parfaite, à laquelle les Estats n'ont aucune part[2].

But neither of these writers makes so definite a statement regarding the *Parlement*, and their contemporary, Guy Coquille, says,

> Les loix & Ordonnances des Rois doivent être publiées & verifiées en Parlement, ou en autre Cour souveraine, selon le sujet de l'affaire; autrement les sujets n'en sont liez.

adding, significantly,

> Ces Parlemens sont établis par forme de contrats faits par le Roy avec le peuple, & pour le soulagement d'iceluy.[3]

My purpose in this discussion, is merely to show that the

[1] *Les six livres de la republique*, liv. I, ch. viii (edition of 1577, pp. 100–1, 103–4).
[2] *Traité des seigneuries*, ch. 2, sec. 92.
[3] *Institution au droit des François*, p. 2, *Les œuvres de Maistre Guy Coquille*, tome II (Bordeaux, 1703).

customary parallel between the frequency of Parliaments in England and the infrequency of meetings of the French Estates is a matter which has very little to do with the issue between Hunton and his opponents. I am not here concerned further in the interesting problem of the true relation of King and *Parlement* in the enactment of *ordonnances*. For it is certainly clear enough that no man living in England in 1643 could remember a time when it was not universally admitted that no statute could command the obedience of subjects, as a matter of fact, if it were not assented to by Lords and Commons, whatever one's theory of this assent might be. The difference between the two systems was momentous, for the High Court of Parliament included the people's elected representatives, the *cour souveraine*, none but lawyers; the "glorious revolution" was a success, the *Fronde*, a failure; and when revolution finally came to France, the *Tiers État* swept the monarchy away altogether.

Hunton's corporate sovereignty, or mixed monarchy, is the theoretical formula for the actual authority of the English "King in Parliament", and a consideration of the historical importance of his theory, if not of its general adequacy, would be incomplete if it did not take brief account of the part played by his idea of corporate sovereignty after the Restoration. But it requires no proof to show that the Whig theory of sovereignty which triumphed at the Revolution and is incorporated in the Revolution settlement is, on this question of mixture, the sovereignty of Philip Hunton; though some of its later exponents, such as Lord Mansfield, no longer believed, as Hunton did, that the supreme authority if mixed was *ipso facto* limited. It is by that time an accepted principle that the English monarchy is a mixed one and that the supreme authority legally rests in the King, and the two Houses jointly. True, the leading member of this corporate body is no longer the King as in the older time, but the Estates; yet sovereign action was for a time after 1689 in actual fact their joint action only, and in strict law it has remained only such even to our

own day. Since the reign of Queen Anne a more republican
principle than Hunton's has prevailed in the convention that
the monarch shall not withhold assent to a bill to which the
Lords and Commons have agreed, but no act has ever been
passed but by the King in Parliament. At the Revolution,
political *power*, in the sense of actual supremacy, shifted from
the King to the aristocracy, as it was later to shift to the
people; but the *sovereign* remained, and still remains, the King
in Parliament.[1]

In the latter part of the eighteenth century a new contention
arose concerning sovereignty, separating Englishmen both in
England and in North America, but the division of parties
was on the question whether the sovereignty was a limited or
an arbitrary authority, not whether it was vested in the King
alone or only in King and Parliament. Throughout it all
Hunton's mixed monarchy was never questioned in law and
a republican advance beyond it was always tacitly assumed in
practice.

[1] In proof of the importance of Hunton's theories after the Restoration,
and particularly at the time of the Revolution, the following examples
might be cited among others: "The Judgment and Decree of the University of Oxford against certain Pernicious Books and Damnable
Doctrines, Proposition 3, that The sovereignty of England is in the three
Estates, viz. King Lords and Commons. Lex Rex, Hunton of a limited
and Mixed Monarchy, Baxter, H. C. Polit. Catech." ([1683] (*State Tracts*
(London, 1692), p. 154); *State Tracts* (London, 1693), p. 447; *A Collection
of State Tracts* (London, 1705), I, pp. 153, 169, 254, 283). But probably
the best evidence of the influence of Hunton's *Treatise* on the Revolution,
aside from its republication twice in 1689, appears in the *Bibliotheca
Politica: or An Enquiry into the Ancient Constitution of the English Government.... Thirteen Dialogues* (London, 1694). The fifth dialogue (pp. 307–
72) deals specifically with mixed monarchy, and of the seven "Authors
made use of" in the list of books which precedes it one is Hunton's
Treatise of Monarchy. The dialogue itself, however, is a better indication
of Hunton's influence than this list; from beginning to end it is saturated
with Hunton's ideas often expressed in Hunton's exact terms. The book
was written by the Whig historian, James Tyrrell, and contains probably
the most elaborate and extensive collection of citations ever made in
justification of the Revolution.

For the reasons recited above I venture to put in a modest plea for reconsideration of any judgment which condemns Philip Hunton's theories of the state as "extraordinary confusions" that "naturally gave the absolutists an easy triumph", or asserts that Sir Robert Filmer's *Observations* on Hunton's *Treatise* "contains an annihilating criticism".

Hunton's is a theory of a government which must be precarious because it is based on harmony, and harmony, unfortunately, never lasts long unbroken among men. His ideal, therefore, could probably never have remained actual for long without some change from its original form, a fact to which Hunton was less blind than his opponents. Of necessity it was short-lived, because the times were transitional. Yet if England's political development since 1660 has on the whole been a peaceful evolution instead of a bloody overturn, some part of the credit cannot be denied to minds like Hunton's, which endeavoured "a thanklesse Moderation 'twixt two Extremes". In its own time his theory played its part and no unimportant part in the unique development of English constitutionalism. Nor is this all. I cannot escape the conviction that in the entirety of Philip Hunton's theory of the state, erected upon the solid foundations of Bodin's *Rechts-staat*, we have on the whole a nobler and truer ideal for any peaceful commonwealth than Filmer's fantastic patriarchal power; or Hobbes's sovereignty of might which hangs once more like a cloud over the earth, with its psychology of fear and its assumption that our primitive state, if not even our natural one, is the "war of every man against every man"; or even Austin's present-day variety of the latter, which concedes to any ruler able to exact habitual obedience from "the bulk" of a people, an unlimited authority touching all to override the rights of any—despotism by plebiscite, our modern form of "popular" sovereignty.

X

THE TRANSFER OF THE CHARTER TO NEW ENGLAND AND ITS SIGNIFICANCE IN AMERICAN CONSTITUTIONAL HISTORY

"Neither the Short nor the Long Parliament at their assembling in 1640 contained a single Republican." Such is the statement of a competent modern historian of the period, Mr G. P. Gooch.[1]

It is probably true, but it is one of those truths of which we are aware but do not know, for we seldom consider what it means. And yet it has a profound meaning for American history as well as English, for it was before 1640 that the foundations of Massachusetts were laid. If there was no republican elected to Parliament in 1640, how many presumably came to New England between 1630 and 1640? In 1661, Governor Endecott declared to Charles II:

Our wittnes is in heaven that wee left not our countrie vpon any dissattisfaction as to the constitution of the civil state....If it were in rebellion or schisme that wee wittingly left our dwellings in our owne, or continew our dwellings in this strainge land, saue vs not this day[2].

If Mr Gooch's statement is true, possibly we are warranted in accepting Governor Endecott's with fewer reservations than some modern historians have insisted upon.

But what has all this to do with the transfer of the Charter and its importance for later American history? Possibly the

[1] G. P. Gooch, *Political Thought in England from Bacon to Halifax* (London, 1914–15), p. 78.
[2] Ebenezer Hazard, *Historical Collections* (Philadelphia, 1794), II, pp. 580, 582; *Records of Massachusetts* (Boston, 1853), IV, Part I, pp. 450, 452.

connection may briefly be made clearer by the following propositions:

First. The Charter granted by Charles I in 1628/29 to the Governor and Company of the Massachusetts Bay in New England is, on the whole, the most important of all our colonial charters in its constitutional results. This I hope later to illustrate, if not to prove.

Second. This Charter of 1628/29, in form and legal effect, differs in no essential way from a number of other American charters of the same period. This is probably too obvious to need proof.

Third. If the Massachusetts Charter is significant, and this significance is not owing to its form, we must look for that significance in something else. We find it, in fact, in the use made of the Charter by the corporation—its transfer to America and the manipulation of it after the transfer.

Fourth. If Governor Endecott is accurate in saying that these things were done "wittingly", we may assume that some of this manipulation of the Charter was foreseen and intended by the incorporators before their migration. As Professor Osgood says, they "were in a pre-eminent sense self-conscious".[1]

Lastly. These intentions must have been formed and coloured, in part, by the conditions ecclesiastical and constitutional existing in England not after 1640, but before; and before 1640 not a single republican had ever been elected to Parliament, not one was chosen even in 1640. The incorporators of Massachusetts likewise were "wittingly" planning neither schism nor rebellion, as they defined these, and in 1661 they still considered their own former actions as neither schismatic nor seditious.

Clearly, if we are ever to understand the influence of the Massachusetts Charter on later American constitutionalism, we must first know what it actually was. If later American

[1] Herbert L. Osgood, *The American Colonies in the Seventeenth Century* (New York, 1904), I, p. 200.

theory depended on the views and purposes in regard to Church and State of the incorporators of the Company, then the substance of those views and purposes can best be found by a study of English history, particularly English intellectual history, before the year 1640. No small part of the attacks made in recent books upon the founders of New England are the result of inadequate knowledge or understanding of the constitutional and intellectual history of England in the earlier part of the reign of Charles I and before.

It is a significant fact that the critical years in the forming of this Colony are also the years between the Petition of Right and the Long Parliament, that period of eleven years in which no Parliament was summoned, the longest in all English history. It is in the ideas, the fears, the convictions, the constitutional views of this period in England that we must find the background of the Massachusetts Charter.

In 1641 Henry Martyn declared to Edward Hyde, afterward Earl of Clarendon, "I do not think one man wise enough to govern us all", which, Clarendon says, "was the first word he had ever heard any man speak to that purpose".[1] The founders of Massachusetts were not radicals, levellers, or antimonarchists. They were, in most respects, conservatives in both Church and State. They favoured neither schism nor rebellion. They were Nonconformists, it is true, but this to them did not mean unorthodoxy, schism, or sedition. James I had called the Puritans "novelists"[2], but this they denied. The real innovators, they insisted (with some truth), were not they but their Laudian opponents. Mr Keith Feiling, himself a high Anglican, has admitted in his history of the Tory party that the very founders of Anglicanism, Archbishop Parker and his fellows, would themselves have been called

[1] [Edward Hyde, First Earl of Clarendon], *The Life of Edward, Earl of Clarendon* (Oxford, 1827), I, p. 92.

[2] Charles H. McIlwain, ed., *The Political Works of James I* (Cambridge, Mass., 1918), p. 274. James I used this expression in the speech opening his first Parliament, in 1603.

Puritans if they had lived in the seventeenth century instead
of the sixteenth. Before the Savoy Conference following the
Restoration, men with such ecclesiastical views as John
Winthrop's might, and often did, consider themselves the
truest members of the Church of England. Governor
Endecott was speaking truth when he said the founders of
Massachusetts were not wittingly schismatics.

But it is the secular side of their views that mainly concerns
us here. Governor Endecott also said they were in no sense
rebels. He denied that they had taken an active part against
the King in the Civil War. "Wee are not seditious as to the
interest of Caesar." These statements have sometimes been
dismissed as the words of flattery or even deceit, used merely
to save the Charter. This is more than doubtful. England
before 1640 was not anti-monarchical, neither was Massachusetts. The views of a Hampden and a Hyde were not so far
apart before 1640. I doubt very much whether John Winthrop
and Falkland, if they had ever chanced to meet, would have
found much to quarrel with in each other's political or constitutional views. Even Sir John Eliot, the martyr to free
speech in Parliament, wrote a book, *De Jure Majestatis*, which
is one of the strongest of all the defences of monarchical
government written in the seventeenth century.[1] His biographer, John Forster, has garbled it outrageously in his frantic
attempts to make his hero a Whig. In New England John
Winthrop remained scarcely more of a parliamentarian than
Eliot had been. In 1641, he says, the leaders in Massachusetts
rejected offers of help from the English Parliament "for this
consideration, that if we should put ourselves under the protection of the parliament, we must then be subject to all such
laws as they should make or at least such as they might impose
upon us".[2] There is reason to believe that the founders of

---

[1] Sir John Eliot, *De Jure Majestatis, or Political Treatise of Government*
(Alexander B. Grosart, ed., London, 1882). But see p. 79 for a slight
correction.
[2] James K. Hosmer, ed., *Winthrop's Journal* (New York, 1908), II, p. 24.

Massachusetts held views not unlike this when they first came to America, and probably before they came. It was as early as 1632 that Winthrop tells us how he quieted the scruples of the men of Watertown against paying a tax imposed upon them, with the assertion "that this government was rather in the nature of a parliament" than of that of a mayor and aldermen.[1] In 1646 the Presbyterians charged the leaders of the Colony with just such views as these. They were said to consider the Colony "rather a free state than a colonie or corporation of England".[2] The answer of the General Court is remarkable. It does not deny that these are its views. It reiterates them and openly defends them. In England, it is admitted, "the supreame authoritie" may be in the high court of Parliament, but "The highest authoritie here is in the general court, both by our charter and by our owne positive lawes". And to hold this involves no breach of the oath of allegiance, since "our allegiance binds us not to the lawes of England any longer than while we live in England".[3]

These are remarkable statements, and other like ones might be added. But they are not usually regarded as expressing the normal and habitual view of Massachusetts on these questions. For my own part, they seem both normal and habitual, a fair expression of a constitutional view firmly held by some of the leading founders of this Commonwealth probably before they migrated, one of the main reasons why they determined to bring their Charter over with them and to treat it as afterward they did, as a true instrument of government. It is most important to bear in mind, in this connection, that the incorporators left their mother country before the quarrel in England between King and Parliament had passed from a controversy over law into a life and death struggle for mastery. The history of these critical years before 1640 has in general been given too strong a Whig flavour by later historians. They

---

[1] James K. Hosmer, ed., *Winthrop's Journal* (New York, 1908), I, p. 74.
[2] *The Hutchinson Papers* (The Prince Society, 1865), I, p. 219.
[3] *Ibid.* pp. 230–31, and Hosmer, *Winthrop's Journal*, II, p. 301.

have thrown back the ideas of 1689 into the period of the Petition of Right and sometimes with little discrimination. The principles of the Bill of Rights, however, are at bottom revolutionary; those of the Petition of Right, are still constitutional. The founders of Massachusetts belong, in thought and action, to the constitutional epoch of the Petition, not to the revolutionary epoch of the Bill. They regarded an American "free state" under the prerogative compatible with the constitution, in a way impossible for English revolutionary Whigs of the next generation. The incredible folly of Charles I had not yet divided his subjects into the two irreconcilable groups, one holding doctrines of divine right and unlimited obedience, the other, a republican, or even a democratic, theory of the state.

There is evidence that the constitutional view thus held by the founders of the Colony existed in Massachusetts nearly a century and a half later. It is one purpose of this paper to inquire whether this later view is connected in any way with the doctrines of 1632.

The principle that allegiance to the English King involves no obedience to the English Parliament, as everyone knows, is the accepted political, if not legal, principle in all English self-governing colonies to-day. I have contended elsewhere that it was also the final and the strongest of the American constitutional contentions before the American Revolution.[1] Here we are concerned only to ask whether it was not in a rather special sense a Massachusetts doctrine, held here from the first planting of the Colony, revived after the Declaratory Act of 1766, and transferred from here about 1774 to the other colonies.

With one important exception (the Resolves of the Assembly of Virginia in 1765) it is a noteworthy fact that the earliest clear statements of the constitutional position of America to be found in the continental colonies between 1771 and 1776—the theory that they were subject to the King of England but

[1] Charles H. McIlwain, *The American Revolution* (New York, 1923).

not to the Parliament of England—all seem traceable, more or less directly, to Massachusetts. The colonies retain allegiance to the King but they reject the authority of the Parliament in England because they have parliaments of their own in their colonial assemblies. But how does this differ in any essential way from what Governor Winthrop told the men of Watertown as early as 1632, when he showed them that the General Court of the Massachusetts Bay was "in the nature of a parliament"? If we find such statements as this earlier and oftener in Massachusetts than elsewhere in the colonial period and later find in the years from 1771 to 1776 these same statements coming again from Massachusetts earlier, more clearly, and more frequently than from the other continental colonies, it is not unnatural to conclude that this is not altogether an accident. We may even be justified in saying that this American constitutional doctrine probably came in large part from the conditions existing under the first Charter of Massachusetts Bay.

Aside from the reference in Virginia referred to above, the earliest statements of this doctrine that I have met with after the Stamp Act occur in the writings or speeches of Benjamin Franklin. In 1766 he told a committee of the House of Commons in England that "the colonies are not supposed to be within the realm; they have assemblies of their own, which are their parliaments", almost the very words of Governor Winthrop in 1632.[1] Other similar expressions occur elsewhere in Franklin's writings. But Franklin was born here, grew up here, and here received all the formal education he ever got, to say nothing of the informal—which was more important. He did not leave Boston till he was seventeen, a remarkably mature young man for his age. It does not seem a very wild guess to say that there was probably a real connection between the words of Governor Winthrop in 1632 and those of Franklin one hundred and thirty-four years later.

[1] William Cobbett, ed., *The Parliamentary History of England* (London, 1806–20), XVI, column 156.

If you will move on another five years to the year 1771, we shall find another statement of the same constitutional view and one in some ways even more striking. It was the custom for a number of years after 1770 to celebrate the so-called Boston Massacre by an oration delivered in the Old South Meeting-House. The first of these annual orations was delivered in 1771 by James Lovell. One of its periods was as follows:

The declarative vote of the British parliament is the death-warrant of *our* birthrights, and wants only a Czarish king to put it into execution. *Here* then a door of salvation is open. Great Britain may raise *her* fleets and armies, but it is only *our own king* that can direct their fire down upon our heads. He is gracious, but not omniscient. He is ready to hear our APPEALS in their proper course: and knowing himself, though the most powerful prince on earth, yet, a subject under a divine constitution of LAW; that law he *will* ask and receive from the twelve judges of ENGLAND. These will prove that the claim of the British parliament over *us* is not only ILLEGAL IN ITSELF, BUT A DOWN-RIGHT USURPATION OF HIS PREROGATIVE as king of *America*.[1]

To James Lovell, George III was "King of America" as well as King of England, and he had parliaments in America as well as in England, of which he was an integral part. Therefore, if the Parliament in England interfered in the business of the parliaments of America, it was exceeding its authority and trampling not only on the rights of the colonists but of their King. Again, one is tempted to ask, where did this Massachusetts man get these ideas, and how far does this striking expression of them differ essentially from the constitutional doctrines of 1632 voiced by Governor Winthrop?

Moving on again, this time about a year and a half, to the well-known proceedings of the Boston town meeting in 1772, we find them complaining that "the British Parliament have *assumed* the power of legislation for the colonists in all cases

---

[1] Hezekiah Niles, *The Principles and Acts of the Revolution in America* (New York, 1876), p. 19.

whatsoever", and have "exerted *that assumed power*".[1] From this time on expressions of this idea become so frequent here in Massachusetts that I can mention only a few of them. Between 1774 and 1776 you can find similar statements in Pennsylvania, Delaware, and Virginia, but in Massachusetts they are more frequent and they began much earlier. In fact, they are almost continuous here from 1772 on.

The next expression to be noticed came in March, 1773, an answer to a speech of Governor Hutchinson made by the Massachusetts Assembly and probably written by Samuel Adams: "Our ancestors", they declare, "considered the land, which they took possession of in America, as out of the bounds of the kingdom of England, and out of the reach and extent of the laws of England; and that the king also, even in the act of granting the charter, considered the territory as not within the realm." So it follows, they say, that our ancestors here in Massachusetts believed that "the right of being governed by laws, which were made by persons in whose election they had a voice, they looked upon as the foundation of English liberties. By the compact with the king, in the charter, they were to be as free in America as they would have been if they had remained within the realm; and, therefore, they freely asserted that they 'were to be governed by laws made by themselves, and by officers chosen by themselves'."[2]

We now come to the next year, 1774, to the adoption of what I venture to call the Massachusetts doctrine, in the famous declaration of the Second Continental Congress at Philadelphia, and to the important part played by Massachusetts in its preparation. On 17 September 1774, there were laid before the Congress certain resolutions of delegates from towns in the county of Suffolk in Massachusetts drawn up shortly before in meetings held at Dedham and Milton. These resolutions declare that George III is "justly entitled to the allegiance

---

[1] Samuel E. Morison, ed., *Sources and Documents illustrating the American Revolution,* 1764–1788 (Oxford, 1923), p. 91. The italics are mine.
[2] Niles, *Principles and Acts,* pp. 90–91.

of the British realm, and agreeable to compact"—a reference
to the Charter—"of the English colonies in America". But
they complain of recent acts of the British Parliament as
breaches of "the laws of nature, the British constitution, and
the charter of the province", and assert "that no obedience is
due from this province to either or any part of the acts above-
mentioned". These resolutions were spread on the minutes of
the Continental Congress;[1] then the delegates proceeded to
draw up their own famous resolution. The first draft of it was
made by Major John Sullivan of New Hampshire;[2] it asserts
in principle the old Massachusetts doctrine—a fact scarcely to
be wondered at, since New Hampshire was mainly settled by
colonists from Massachusetts, during the latter half of the
seventeenth century was practically a part of Massachusetts,
and drew its constitutional views from the same sources as
early Massachusetts Bay. But Major Sullivan's draft was not
quite strong enough, so the Congress ultimately accepted an
amendment made by John Adams of Massachusetts, and the
famous provision as finally agreed on was his work. In part
it reads as follows:

Resolved, 4. That the foundation of English liberty, and of all
free government, is a right in the people to participate in their
legislative council: and as the English Colonists are not represented, and from their local and other circumstances, cannot
properly be represented in the British parliament, they are entitled
to a free and exclusive power of legislation in their several pro-
vincial legislatures, where their right of representation can alone
be preserved, in all cases of taxation and internal polity, subject
only to the negative of their sovereign, in such manner as has
been heretofore used and accustomed.[3]

This provision was adopted by the Congress on 14 October
1774, and about two months later the question was reopened
in Boston in the papers of *Massachusettensis* answered by John

[1] Worthington C. Ford, ed., *Journals of the Continental Congress*,
1774–1789 (Washington, 1904), I, pp. 32 ff.
[2] *Ibid.* p. 63 n.   [3] *Ibid.* p. 68.

Adams under the name of *Novanglus* in the most powerful and comprehensive statement ever made of the doctrine of the Continental Congress. It is the old doctrine of John Winthrop that the assemblies of the colonies are their parliaments and their only parliaments.[1]

No time remains to develop in detail any of the positive contributions of the transferred Charter to our later institutions, state and national, or even to mention more than one or two of the most important; yet they are scarcely less significant than the negative ones already referred to.

The first Charter of Massachusetts Bay was not strictly a popular constitution, because it was in form and legal effect a royal grant, but in its practical operation after the transfer, it approximated a popular constitution more closely than any other instrument of government in actual use up to that time in America or elsewhere in modern times. It seems no accident, then, that what Charles Borgeaud has termed "the first American constitution accepted by the people" and "the first written constitution of modern democracy"[2]—namely the Fundamental Orders of Connecticut of 1639—should have been the work of men who migrated to the Connecticut River from Watertown, Newtowne, and Dorchester. Its provisions of greatest historical importance came, no doubt, in part from the actual situation of the settlers, in part as a reaction from the narrowness of the Boston government, but they owe fully as much to the actual self-government in which Thomas Hooker and the other leaders had been active participants here. The first American constitution was an outgrowth of the self-government under the first Massachusetts Charter.

In closing, let me turn to a much later example of the

[1] The letters of *Novanglus* and *Massachusettensis* were reprinted together in John Adams and Jonathan Sewall [*sic*], *Novanglus, and Massachusettensis: or Political Essays* (Boston, 1819). Daniel Leonard, not Sewall, was the author of *Massachusettensis*.

[2] Charles Borgeaud, *The Rise of Modern Democracy* (London and New York, 1894), p. 123.

influence of the early government under the Charter—but one scarcely less significant. Massachusetts was not the first state to adopt a constitution after independence, but she has the greater distinction of being the first to reject one, and she has been rejecting them almost ever since. It is difficult now, after a century and a half of experience of written constitutions, to appreciate how novel they were just after our independence. The people were eager to control them and make them really "popular" constitutions, but as they had no experience they did not know how. John Lilburne and the Levellers about 1648 apparently thought the best way would be to have the people actually subscribe to the document, as had been done occasionally to petitions addressed to the King.[1] In the American states before the nineteenth century it was deemed enough to secure popular control if a constitution were made by an assembly elected by the people for that express purpose. None, therefore, was submitted to the people for ratification except in Massachusetts and New Hampshire, which naturally offered the only opportunity of rejection. They were submitted in Massachusetts and New Hampshire—the local institutions of which were practically the same in origin—because the local institutions were better suited to this purpose than the machinery of government elsewhere—except in Rhode Island and Connecticut, where no new constitutions were proposed. But the institution of the town meeting in which Massachusetts rejected the first constitution proposed, was influenced, I need not point out, at every step of development by the ideas and practices obtaining under the first Charter.

If ratification is the chief security for the popular character of a state constitution, certainly its formulation by an assembly chosen for that particular purpose is the next in importance. Mr Hoar has shown in his book on the constitutional convention that the first distinct assertion of this principle, also, came

[1] Samuel R. Gardiner, *The History of the Great Civil War* (London and New York, 1905), III, p. 388.

from Massachusetts, in a resolution of the Concord town
meeting on 21 October 1776.[1]

All these things have become so much a matter of course
to us that we appreciate with difficulty the boldness and the
novelty of some of these expedients which have since spread
all over the constitutional world. If you will take the trouble
to enumerate the most important of them, you will find that
a disproportionately large number come either from Massachusetts or from other colonies which were early subject, like
her, to the influence of political ideas and political expedients
which the founders of this Commonwealth brought with
them—or devised soon afterward under authority of the
Charter granted by Charles I in 1629 to the Governor and
Company of the Massachusetts Bay in New England.

[1] Roger Sherman Hoar, *Constitutional Conventions* (Boston, 1917),
p. 7.

XI

THE FUNDAMENTAL LAW BEHIND THE CONSTITUTION OF THE UNITED STATES[1]

It is a very curious and interesting fact that in ordinary language we usually speak of a constitutional monarchy as a "limited" monarchy. The characteristic that distinguishes this kind of monarchy from others for us is a negative, not a positive characteristic. We think first of all of what the monarch may not do, not of what he *may* do. The whole history of modern constitutionalism proves the soundness of this instinct. A constituted authority is one that is defined, and there can be no definition which does not of necessity imply a limitation. Constitutional government is and must be "limited government" if it is constitutional at all. Whatever its form may be, whether monarchical, aristocratic, or democratic, in any state that we may properly call constitutional, the supreme authority must be defined and defined by a law of some kind. That law may be unwritten and entirely customary, as it has been for the greater part of its history; or it may be set forth in a single official document as in our state and federal constitutions, but in every case it is a law that puts bounds to arbitrary will.

It is true that in such of our early state constitutions as made a formal distinction between the "bill of rights" and the "frame of government", the latter usually took up more space than the former; but this should not blind us to the fact that in any concession of "enumerated powers" such as most of these were, the very enumeration means a limitation. In

[1] A paper read on 29 December 1937 at the annual meeting of the American Historical Association held Philadelphia, Pennsylvania on the one hundred and fiftieth anniversary of the Constitutional Convention of 1787.

many ways the non-enumerated powers are more important practically than the enumerated, for they establish the boundaries of any government that can be called legitimate.

In creating this government of enumerated powers the founders of our state were merely setting forth in explicit form the essential principle of all historical constitutionalism. For most of the past it was the arbitrary power of princes which was hemmed in by these rights of subjects. In a popular state such as we think ours is, it is the arbitrary will of the government to which the rights of the citizens form a barrier. But the principle is the same. A safeguard is provided in our state by the fundamental law of the Constitution; it is an appeal from the people drunk to the people sober. If we have made any contribution to modern constitutionalism, it lies in the effectiveness of these constitutional limitations, in the sanction of individual freedom, in withholding from government what belongs to the citizen.

It is the earlier history of bills of rights, of this negative feature of our constitutional system, that I should like briefly to trace, for it is this negative feature, and not its positive provisions, that constitutes the chief bulwark of liberty, as well during the whole history of modern constitutionalism as in our existing government. It is our most precious heritage from the past constitutional struggles of our race.

The framers of our Constitution—the Constitution as finally adopted—were under the constant fear of an arbitrary rule such as they thought they had suffered under as colonists. Therefore they incorporated in our fundamental law the express negative checks of the bill of rights, whose historical background I propose briefly to trace, and further restricted the legitimate sphere of the federal government by withholding from it powers of which some have been shown by later developments to be necessary for the public welfare. But not content with these precautions, in their dread of despotism, they added a dissipation of authority in the form of positive checks imposed by one organ of government upon another, and carried to what I must regard as a dangerous extreme, a separation of powers which could only have the effect of rendering the government they set up both feeble and irresponsible. As one foreign observer puts it, in their fear of the government's doing harm, they incapacitated it for doing much good.

These positive checks, I am bold enough to say, are proof that the founders of our state had not thoroughly learned the lesson of all past constitutionalism—that the really effective checks on despotism have consisted not in the weakening of government, but rather in the limiting of it; between which there is a great and a very significant difference.

And even to-day, in the protests that have recently arisen against the "regimentation" of our times, I find a demand for the restoration of all our former "checks and balances", usually without much discrimination between these and the older historic process of putting dangerous powers entirely beyond the government's sphere of legitimate action.

"Medieval history", as Professor Pollard observed in his *Factors in American History*, "not only contained the germs of what was made explicit in modern England, but much of what has been made explicit in the history of the United States." In the historical outline which follows I may have to start further back even than the Middle Ages. The outline will include only "modern" history, but for the growth of constitutionalism specifically the tracing of modern tendencies can hardly begin much later than the second or third century B.C.

The Greeks of the pre-Hellenistic period apparently knew nothing of them. When we translate their word *politeia* by our word "Constitution", as we always do, we mistranslate it. There may be no other English word we could use, but it is none the less a very bad misfit, not so much in etymology as in actual content. Plato and Aristotle could think of an ideal of which an actual government must be an approximation if that government was to be considered good, but apparently they had no conception of a definite superior law to which a government must conform if it is to be treated as legitimate. They thought of law in terms of politics, we moderns think of politics in terms of law. This I take to be the most fundamental of the differences between ancient and modern conceptions of government.

As moderns, therefore, we tend to fix our attention on the legitimacy of an act of government where the ancients looked merely to its desirability or expediency. Such an idea of legitimacy could only arise after men had come to think of a universal law which had more coercive power than mere universal reason, but like reason was coterminous with mankind, and what is more, coeval with man himself. Since states are obviously the creations of men in time, this means therefore that these states are not as old as this law of nature. And granted that there was such a pre-existent law, it became inevitable that governments and their acts should be judged by their conformity to it rather than to reason alone. As St Thomas says, those conditions must also be observed which are of the essence of a law. From such a law of nature, there was a further and obvious inference of rights defined by such a law, and if the law antedated the creation of actual states, so these "rights of man" were older, more fundamental, more universal, and therefore more binding than the merely "civil" law of any particular state. It is but a step further to say as St Thomas Aquinas did in the thirteenth century that a state may promulgate a civil law beyond this law of nature but never a binding law contrary to it, that a civil law flatly violating the rights of man is void.

In brief, for the ancients, the state makes the law; for moderns, the law makes the state. The first known extension of the latter idea was in the Hellenistic period by the Stoics, but the fullest surviving expression of it was by the Romans and the *locus classicus* is in the writings of Cicero. 'What is a state', he asks, "except a society (or sharing) in law" (*juris societas*)? "Law is the bond of civil society" (*civilis societatis vinculum*).

The newer, more constitutional idea, is expressed at Rome, under the Principate and afterward, in the *lex regia* by which the people conferred on the Emperor an authority defined in very broad terms, yet certainly defined. With the gradual growth of absolutism earlier restrictions disappear, and by the sixth century the authors of Justinian's Institutes can say that in this *lex regia* the *populus* concedes to the Emperor not a part but the *whole* of its authority. Throughout all these changes, however, the basic conception of a fundamental law is never entirely absent, and in the legal sources it survived the encroachments of despotism and the fall of the Empire, eventually to influence new races for centuries to come.

These new races in turn brought with them and added the new—or rather the very old—conception of law as the immemorial custom of the tribe, and when their wanderings were finally over and their boundaries permanently fixed, this tribal custom became the common custom of a local community. The last of these stages, this returning phase of territorial law, we characterize by our word "feudal", and from it we are able to trace the growth of constitutionalism up to our own times as a continuous development.

In a peculiar sense, therefore, feudal institutions and ideas may be said to furnish evidence of the beginnings of our distinctive modern constitutionalism. And if it be true, as I have maintained, that constitutional government is essentially limited government, feudalism assumes a special importance, for one of its most striking features is the prominence of the negative check on government inhering in the rights of feudal vassals which no lord, not even a king, may lawfully infringe. For the Middle Ages the validity of my thesis of limitation, not dissipation of government, depends on the existence of evidence clearly showing that contemporaries drew a distinction between two things that we now usually confound, autocracy and despotism. Autocracy is unmixed government; despotism, lawless government. Under modern conditions they tend in practice to merge—we have startling instances in almost every morning's news—and we habitually treat the two—unfortunately I think—as practically identical. In feudal times and after, this was not so in either practice or theory. Unmixed government and lawless government were quite different things, and well recognized as such. Autocracy was always accepted as legitimate, despotism never. The King, in other words, was never controlled but always limited. If such a limit existed, we should look for it in a period of customary law primarily in custom, and in a feudal period in the custom of fiefs. If the law defining and protecting the fiefs of his vassals is beyond the King's authority to define or abridge in the Middle Ages, we may say that it constitutes a true limitation of his governmental power. It may be only a feudal and scarcely yet a constitutional limitation, but it is a real and a legal limitation. In France, even down to the Revolution, as Viollet notes, the King's ordinances seldom touched the "private law". In feudal England it was felt that they could not legally do so, if this meant arbitrary definition or diminution or transfer of private rights. There is a curious illustration in a side remark of the author of the *Dialogue of the Exchequer* written in the reign of Henry II, indicating the nature of the current theory and also the difficulty of enforcing it against an unwilling King. Among the royal revenues enrolled in the Exchequer, the master in the *Dialogue* had mentioned chattels of fugitives from justice which were forfeited to the King. "I am amazed at what you have said", the pupil replies. "It is surprising in the case of a lord who has rights over both the person and the goods of a delinquent and has himself committed no offence for which he should be deprived of his possession. It would seem just that an edict of the King should inflict punishment for an offence on the person of the wrong-doer but should relinquish his goods and even his lands for the use of the lord."

"What disturbs you has disturbed me too", the Master answers.

"I think we are wasting time on these things which are

aside from our original topic, but if you must know why this is so, it is solely on account of the edict (*assisa*) of the King. For there is no one who would presume to resist a royal edict which was made for the good of the peace. As I have said it is the King's edict alone, in a case of urgent necessity, made for the good of the peace, that furnishes an answer to this important question."

This reply is very significant, but the pupil's amazement is not likely to have been any less after hearing it. "I see that it was not without a cause," he says, "Now, if you please, let us go on to something else."

An even more interesting example in an actual case, and a remarkably early one, occurred some years before, during the reign of Stephen, as recorded by the chronicler of Battle Abbey.

In one of the manors on the south-east coast granted by William the Conqueror to the Abbey of Battle, an ancient custom prevailed under which all vessels wrecked on the coast and not repaired within a certain time should belong to the abbot. Henry I, "hating that custom", by an exercise of royal power, issued an edict under which a single living survivor of a wreck should have it instead of the lord of the manor. But, as the chronicler says, "when the new King died, the new law died with him". On Henry's death the magnates quashed his edict and restored the ancient custom. Soon after this a ship sailing from lands of the Archbishop of Canterbury was wrecked on this coast, and the abbot's men by force seized it and the cargo, pursuant to "the maritime customs and the royal dignities of the Church of Battle". The archbishop at once appealed to the King's curia and the abbot was summoned to defend the acts of his men. In his defence he asserted that a King might at will change the ancient rights of a district for his own lifetime, but only by consent of the barons of the realm could this change be treated as legitimate afterward. Therefore he said he would concede this claim if the barons should now declare that it was lawful. This the barons denied "with one voice", although the King himself was present and favoured the archbishop's cause; and in the end they decreed that the abbot had maintained his right and that no further complaints of the archbishop were to be heard. That was in the year 1139. Have we heard it said that judicial review was a thing undreamt of yet in the constitutional convention of 1787?

Here in this case is the same question that disturbed the master and the pupil in the *Dialogue*. No one will dare oppose an administrative order of the King, but if against private right, it cannot be maintained as law, at least after that King's death. There certainly is limitation here—some royal acts are *ultra vires*. But there is no hint of positive compulsion, or control, or parcelling out of royal authority *intra vires*. There are no "checks and balances".

If we look carefully through the famous assizes of the next reign we find further confirmation of these same views. In this general period, rights embodied in ancient custom are never spoken of as "made". In the *Summa de Legibus* of Normandy, they are said to be "held" from ancient times, "approved" by the prince, and "preserved" by the people; they are "established" and "promulgated" by the King, and "defined" by his Council, as Bracton says. But Henry II's assizes are "*made*" (*facta*), and they turn out on examination to be administrative edicts, not definitions of rights. In the preamble of the Assize of Clarendon in 1166, it is said to be "made" with the assent of the magnates, but its last section declares that it shall be in force as long as the King pleases. It is clearly concerned with government rather than law, and it is a temporary thing totally unlike the definition of an immemorial customary law which from its nature must be permanent. The King, it implies, can at any time quash his own edict, but a custom enjoyed by his subjects is beyond his power. This earlier difference between a temporary governmental order concerned with administrative procedure, and an official determination of immemorial custom, is the precedent for the later distinction between ordinances and statutes which we find in the Rolls of Parliament in the fourteenth and fifteenth centuries. The latter are always distinguished in the same way by their temporary or their permanent character. But all are acts of the King, and the King alone can give binding effect to any of them. All government is the King's government, there is no other; and any act which is strictly governmental he may legally do alone and unaided. Even for a period as late as the fourteenth century, Professor Tout declares, "The great fact, never to be forgotten, is that the King governed the country, and, whatever advice he took, was ultimately responsible for all executive acts."

In administration the King, as Bracton says, is without a peer, much less a superior. Within his legal sphere he is "absolute" in the medieval sense of that term. And yet that sphere is legally limited; a royal act may be *ultra vires*. The King may be legally an autocrat but he is no despot. Bracton puts it all, both sides of it, into a single sentence in his famous line: *Rex non debet esse sub homine, sed sub Deo et lege*: The King is without control, but he is limited by law. Here we find essentially the same constitutional doctrine that Sir Edward Coke makes his own in the seventeenth century in the famous "Case of Proclamations", and he accepts both parts of it: "...it is a grand prerogative of the King to make proclamation (for no subject can make it without authority from the King, or lawful custom) upon fine and imprisonment." And yet: "...the King by his proclamation, or other ways, cannot change any part of the common law, or statute law, or the customs of the realm...the King hath no prerogative but that which the law of the land allows him."

When we come to Magna Carta, "the palladium of our liberties", we see as before the same absolute administration within a legally limited sphere. If we took the trouble to trace the quarrel between John and his barons from its beginning to the issuance of the Charter, we should never find a single challenge of the King's sole right to make and to direct a "foreign" war, or, in fact, any part of the royal administration. That is the King's business. What we do find is a stubborn resistance to his attempts to compel by force the attendance of his feudal tenants of English fiefs in a campaign in defence of his other dominions across the Channel. The latter involved no question of royal administration, but a disputed point of feudal law, touching the rights and obligations of the tenants themselves. The determination of such rights could never be legally "made" by the King arbitrarily and alone and enforced by arms; they could be only "defined", and defined by a judgment of peers which "found" what the customary law actually was. In Magna Carta we find much legal limitation, but no strictly governmental checks. Even the committee of twenty-five, in its final section, was no committee for government; it was nothing but a temporary committee for enforcement of the terms of the document, and it was never revived in any of the subsequent reissues of the Charter.

For the long reign of Henry III it may be enough to cite the interesting example of the Provisions of Oxford and their aftermath, and the classic exposition of our distinction in Bracton's great book on the laws and customs of England.

The Provisions of Oxford of 1258 might be considered an early indistinct anticipation of modern English cabinet government, for under them Henry III reigned but did not rule; but one would search in vain for any balances. There was neither diminution, nor splitting of royal administration. All that was done was to transfer it whole to a committee of barons. There was as much solidarity in their rule as in that of a modern cabinet. But even this was without precedent, and when barons and King agreed to submit to the arbitration of Louis IX of France, his decision was clear and unambiguous and wholly in favour of the King. Committee government was illegal. The King in person had a right to a *liberum regimen*, that is, an autocratic rule in matters properly belonging to government. There is no denial of the legal limits, but within these limits the King must be free of all restraint. We have seen that Bracton's constitutional doctrine was the same, but there is one passage in his book, much quoted by parliamentarians in the seventeenth century, which seems to contradict it. It is the famous passage which reads: "Moreover the King has a master, namely God. Likewise the law under which he was created King. Likewise his curia, to wit the earls and barons; for the earls are so-called as a kind of associates of the King, and one who has an associate, has a master; and so if the King is without a bridle, that is, without law, they ought to put a bridle on him." But as Maitland has said, this doctrine is flatly contradicted "by at least five statements found in all parts of the book", and the passage is lacking in most of the best manuscripts. He concludes that it was "no part of the original text", but an addition by a later hand. Nevertheless it is repeated in full by the author of *Fleta*, written in the reign of Edward I; but even this statement, it should be noted, is no defence of checks and balances or of a division of authority; at most it merely advocates the substitution of the will of the majority of a single committee of barons for the will of the King in the royal administration.

In the Year Books, which begin in Edward I's reign and cover the whole remaining medieval period, I know of no references to checks and balances, but the discussions of legal limits to the prerogative are many, and in them all the King's legal rights are invariably treated under the same ordinary feudal definitions that apply to any fief in the hands of a subject. Prerogative is a right of the King standing beside, but not above the rights of his vassals. These same facts constitute the true interpretation of the famous books of Sir John Fortescue, consideration of which may bring the medieval part of our survey to an end. In 1932 I suggested that Fortescue's well-known phrase *dominium politicum* meant merely medieval limitation, and not modern control as it had always been interpreted. Since then the brilliant studies of a young English historian on English constitutional ideas of the fifteenth century seem to me to have demonstrated the soundness of this thesis beyond a reasonable doubt.

It is notorious that the Tudor period was a period of concentrated administrative authority so far as the central government was concerned. What is not so well understood is the fact of the persistence of the old limits of law which still remained to protect subjects from an exercise *ultra vires* of governmental power. It is true that this power occasionally broke through these barriers, and the cases are dramatic, but, after all, such cases are comparatively few. No better summary of the general situation was ever made than by Sir Francis Bacon when he said, "although the King in his person, be *solutus legibus*, yet his acts and grants are limited by law, and we argue them every day". In the third year of Elizabeth this doctrine was laid down in the Court of Common Pleas, when it was said that "the common law has so admeasured his [the King's] prerogatives, that they shall not take away nor prejudice the inheritance of any.... The King's prerogative by the Common Law cannot prevail against such a Custom as stands with the Right of Inheritance of another." But the most striking case of all in the Tudor period is Cavendish's Case in 1587, which I have often cited, but must cite once more. The late Professor Thayer considered it important enough to print in his case-book of American constitutional law. The Queen by letter patent had granted to a hanger-on of Leicester's the lucrative office of writing the writs of *supersedeas* in the Court of Common Pleas, and by letter commanded the justices of that court to admit him to the office. Since it was legally the property of another, the justices ignored the command. It was repeated in a second sharper letter which the justices also ignored. They were then ordered to appear and explain their disobedience. In so doing they said

that they must needs confess that they had not performed the orders; but this was no offence or contempt to her Majesty, for the orders were against the law of the land, in which case it was said, no one is bound to obey such an order. And they said that the queen herself was sworn and took an oath to keep her laws, and the judges also, as regards their willingly breaking them. As to this matter, so far as it concerned the judges, they answered again that if they obeyed these orders they should act otherwise than the laws warranted, and merely and directly against them; and that was contrary to their oath, and in contempt of God, her Majesty, and the country and commonwealth in which they were born and lived.

To the end of the Tudor period there was no balance of control, but a very real limitation of law. As Justice Crawley put it later in the Ship-money Case, "In the King are two kinds of prerogative *regale* and *legale*", a statement in which was much truth, although Crawley's interpretation of it was probably as politically dangerous as his grammar was bad. Crawley's is essentially the same distinction made by Sir Edward Coke between the "prerogative indisputable", and the "prerogative disputable" concerning *meum et tuum* and founded by law; or by James I himself when he contrasted a judicial decision affecting only his "private prerogative"—in which "I will as humbly acquiesce as the meanest man in the land"—and one touching "the absolute prerogative of the Crowne", which "is no subject for the tongue of a lawyer, nor is lawfull to be disputed". Probably no clearer statement of these constitutional views could be found than the following extract from the instructions of Sir Orlando Bridgeman to the jury for the trial of the Regicides in 1660:

Though this is an Absolute Monarchy, yet this is so far from infringing the people's rights, that the people, as to their properties, liberties, and lives, have as great a privilege as the king. It is not the sharing of government that is for the liberty and benefit of the people; but it is how they may have their lives, and liberties, and estates, safely secured under government.

Between the Conquest and the present many have beaten against these legal bulwarks protecting our "lives and liberties and estates"; but in the Anglo-Saxon race they have never yet beaten them down. In the Stuart period the disputes and the conflicts did not touch directly this legal aspect of prerogative; that was assumed. They were concerned more with what Crawley called the regal, "the *absolute* prerogative of the Crowne"; they began to turn on the King's discretionary powers, "matter of polity, not of law", in the apt words of Hobbes; control and not mere legal limitation was becoming the new centre of a new debate and ultimately the cause of a great civil war. Subjects were beginning to dispute the indisputable.

With the growth of this new quarrel, with the new *formulae* under which it was finally composed, and its modern outcome in cabinet government of a democratic state, I shall not deal—they are to be dealt with in part in the valuable paper of Dr Pargellis; but no one who knows anything of modern English cabinet government would venture to say that it is a system of checks and balances, and what little check survived to the beginning of this century was in large part swept away by the Parliament Act of 1911 in taking from the Lords the legal right permanently to block an action of the cabinet approved by the House of Commons. What is more vital for us here in America is the bearing on our own present constitutional problems of this history of the past, and above all the history of the last twenty-five years. Since the English civil wars of the seventeenth century there has been no challenge to constitutional government such as we have witnessed in this last decade and face at the present moment. There is a tidal wave of despotism sweeping over the world. On this anniversary of our Constitution we find constitutionalism itself threatened everywhere as it has never been threatened since the founding of our government. We are meeting in Philadelphia this year in circumstances as critical as those the framers of our Constitution faced here in 1787. Do we realize as fully as they realized the crisis we have to meet? Does the history of constitutionalism suggest any cause of that crisis? Above all, can past experience furnish any help in finding a remedy?

I have attempted the analysis above because I believe this past history does indicate one important cause, and also the one possible line of defence. The cause, in a word, is the feebleness of government. It must be strengthened. The present danger is despotism. It must be prevented, and by legal limitations on government. If weakness is the cause, no true remedy can lie in increasing that weakness; it can lie only in making government effective, in removing such "balances" as prevent prompt and decisive action; but also in seeing to it that such action can never jeopard the just rights of any. We must preserve and strengthen those bounds beyond which no free government ought ever to go, and make them limits beyond which no government whatever can ever legally go. We must make *ultra vires* all exorbitant acts of government. If the states which are still constitutional hope to remain so for the future, they must make their governments strong enough to defy the despotisms which now threaten their destruction; but above all, as the whole history of constitutionalism also shows, they must never let this strength become the lawless usurpation, divorced from right, under which individual liberty is trampled under foot before our eyes in so many parts of the world to-day, and may in time become only a memory even here.

XII

LIBERALISM AND THE TOTALITARIAN IDEALS[1]

When President Dennett did me the great honour of asking
me to make this address and I tried to collect such thoughts
as it might be fitting to express on an occasion like this, one
thing above all others kept coming to mind—the uncertainty
and the instability of the times in which we are living. To one
who is in constant contact with young men just beginning
their careers it ought to be, it is, a very sobering thought that
the young men leaving here to-day have never known what
it was to live in a world that was stable. Twenty or thirty years
ago we were reading books and papers on the subject of the
idea of progress. I have not noticed many of them lately.
Those books all assumed that we were on a steady gradual
upward curve of development that would go on indefinitely,
keeping what we have won and making further gains. Since
the Great War our feeling is probably better expressed by
Robert Burns—"An' forward, tho' I canna see, I guess an'
fear." The most striking thing about our life at the present
time is its instability. How different these conditions are from
those that some of us faced when, armed with our new sheep-
skins, we left our *alma mater* to conquer the world, twenty, or
forty, or was it fifty years ago! We knew, of course, that there
might be some changes, but we never even dreamt of a
catastrophe. We assumed that the basic conditions of life
would remain about as we had always known them, and we
made plans for the future in full confidence that those conditions were permanent, never for a minute suspecting that they
could be anything else.

[1] An Address at the Williams College Commencement, 1937.

At times, I must confess, I do look back with some longing to that distant past when fifteen miles an hour was "speeding", and one might cross a country road without giving an imitation of a chicken chased by a hawk. But for good or ill those times are gone and probably gone for ever, and we have now learned by sad experience that much of that earlier bliss was nothing more than ignorance. We cannot go back to that. It is for us to see what we are going to do about it—now; but none of us can fully appreciate the change that has come over us all if he cannot remember something of those old care-free days, and if he is not now in close personal contact with the newer generation and has not seen their unrest, their feeling of insecurity and uncertainty for the future. Is there anything, then, that we can do about it? To put it in a more practical way, are there any remnants left of the old security worth keeping, remnants that we ought to try to preserve?

One thing seems sure: we must be clear as to our common objective, and we must present a solid front against all those forces that may stand in its way when once we have found it. The experience of a more stable epoch may possibly enable some of the older of us who still think in terms of evolution instead of mechanics, to contribute something toward that common object—something, but by no means everything. The idealism of the younger must furnish the drive to carry it through. But carried through it never can be if older liberals and younger idealists can find no common ground, and form no solid front. From one end of our line we must drive away the hopeless selfish reactionaries, from the other we must throw out the self-seeking demagogues. Thus united I firmly believe we may be able to achieve something of that just equilibrium, which alone can make our world a better place than it is now, a world in which the younger men at least might look forward both to a greater social justice and to more economic and political security than we know now.

In the past, reform of abuses usually meant a defence of individual rights against despotic government. Curiously enough reform has apparently come to-day to mean for most reformers an increase of the power of government against the individual. The world's present trust in the benevolence of despotism is tremendous if not tragic, sometimes in the face of confiscations, imprisonment and even death itself. Slowly but surely we are drifting toward the totalitarian state, and strange to say many if not most of the idealists are either enthusiastic about it or unconcerned. For the time they have left the protection of the individual entirely to the selfish reactionaries whose only real care is for their own particular pockets. Many liberals seem to have accepted at its face value the philosophy of these cynical exploiters that the only rights that need protection are the rights of property, and thus in their proper desire to free "the forgotten man" from economic exploitation they seem willing now to leave every man helpless against a political exploitation more ruthless than modern times have ever seen before. Our sole danger is not from "economic royalists". In the past we have suffered too much at their hands, but the present threat is from "political royalists" who would have us believe that the only cure for economic slavery is political slavery. That surely is homœopathic treatment. A really intelligent liberal wants no slavery of any kind, economic or political. But what alarms me most of all at this present time is that those old traditional allies the social reformer and the liberal constitutionalist have parted company. They are no longer presenting a united front against any and all exploitation of every kind, economic or political. We who ought to be united have allowed ourselves to be divided. The foes of progress must be laughing in their sleeves to see us thus disunited. This means that if they are to win, liberals must become more constitutional and constitutionalists more liberal. When they have fought successfully before, they have fought side by side. It must be done again, but this can never be, if constitutionalism becomes reaction or reform turns into despotism. On one side selfish men are always trying to accomplish the former, under vague promises of reform we are now in grave danger of the latter. There is little need to point out the danger from the reactionaries. They have always been with us and we know them. The chief threat at present is from the other side, for the wolves there wear sheep's clothing. It is in the name of a "healthy public sentiment" that German men and women are being sacrificed to-day. In this world struggle of our day for liberty —for that is what it is—if we who profess to love liberty do not patch up our little differences we shall lose it all. This is why I am pleading to-day for constitutionalism. Past victories of reform have never been made lasting save where they were clothed with legal and constitutional guarantees. It is the only way to consolidate and to keep our gains, short of the constant application of physical force. With the history of past struggles before me I dare to say that we are living in the midst of the greatest danger to human liberty and human welfare that any living man can remember, and I am afraid many of us either do not see it or are unwilling to make the sacrifices necessary to meet it. It might be worth our while to review briefly one or two of those past struggles.

It was chiefly economic exploitation in the later fifteenth century in England that led the people to support the despotic measures of the early Tudors; it was the opposition of constitutional liberals—and some of them pretty conservative ones —that finally upset that despotic rule in the seventeenth century. Must we again go through all the stages of that same dreary cycle to clinch our liberties? It would be a good thing if those English constitutional struggles could be studied in every American college just now, and I could almost wish that the study were made compulsory. Such a study might lead liberals to see that they must also be constitutionalists if they ever hope for an accomplishment of their ends that has any promise of permanence. Ship-money was conceded even by the extreme royalists to be against precedent. It could not be levied without Parliament in ordinary circumstances. To levy it was not an ordinary but an extraordinary power, a

power to be exercised only in a national emergency. But—
and this is always the important "but"—the King was the
sole judge of the existence of such an emergency. No man
should be arrested and imprisoned without due process of law.
Of course not, *but*, said the royalists—political, not economic
royalists—no court can inquire into this if the arrest is at the
King's own order, *per speciale mandatum domini regis.*

And such things as this are by no means ancient history.
Consider the defenceless position of an accused person in
Germany at this day. There courts are instructed to punish
offences not punishable by any existing law, provided they
are contrary to the Nazi idea of what the law ought to be;
"healthy public sentiment", and you can easily guess whose
sentiment. In view of such things can anyone light-heartedly
weaken our constitutional safeguard against an *ex post facto*
law? And if one should think that such things as these could
never happen here, let me ask him if he believes that any man
in Germany could have dreamt ten years ago of their ever
happening there. We are all too familiar in these days with
concentration camps and blood-purges, and wholesale execu-
tions by firing squads, too familiar to be even shocked. Yet
these things are all done in the name of the people. I want to
plead here against any weakening of our constitutional
limitations of power, even the power of the people themselves; in the interest of individuals or minorities among the
people. For the people have now succeeded to the power of
the benevolent despots of the eighteenth century, and in the
exercise of it they are often swayed by special interests or
crafty demagogues as their predecessors were by favourites.
I frankly want to rely on the earlier, the sounder, yes the
medieval principle, that there are some individual rights that
even a people's government can never touch. There are many
powers that for our own good we should concede to our
government, and some of these it does not now possess; there
are some abuses of power that we should expressly forbid it
ever to exercise; there may be a few that we should actually

take away from it. We do need a strong government, but a government so limited that it can always help but never harm us. The greatest delusion of the modern political world is the delusion of "popular sovereignty". It is the fiction under which all the dictators have sprung up and now thrive. The people is not the sovereign; the government is. If the people sets up a sovereign government, they must in their own interest also set up or keep up all the necessary barriers against its despotic action, and the only effective barrier short of actual resistance is the barrier of law. The only impartial interpretation of that law lies in the courts of justice, not in "healthy public sentiment" with a dictator as its mouthpiece.

You are wondering now, perhaps, what all this has to do with our own present constitutional crisis, the question of the proposed legislation touching the Supreme Court of the United States. Anyone interested in the constitutional guarantees of religious belief, free speech, immunity from arbitrary arrest or imprisonment, to mention no more, must be alarmed by any proposal that might touch these guarantees; and the liberal most of all. The long painful history of the securing of these safeguards ought to make him of all men most fearful of any proposal that could enfeeble them. He should be afraid that any judge compliant enough to read into our constitution a beneficial power patently not there, might at another time be compliant enough to read out of it any or all of these guarantees of his liberty which are there; for a judge willing to take orders from a benevolent despot might be equally subservient to a malevolent one. More than any other man, the liberal, even in his own interest, ought to strive for the maintenance of an effective judicial review by an independent judiciary. This is the lesson of the whole history of modern constitutionalism if I read that long history aright. If so, let us forget our little differences and unite to get our needed reforms by constitutional means. Let us remember that to have our rights defined by existing law not by "healthy public sentiment", is far more important for us than the temporary prejudices of one or two judges, or even the temporary postponement of some much needed reforms. If we can get these reforms in this way, we shall know when we have them; they will not be dependent on the changing whims of any *duce* or *führer*. There are undoubtedly strong arguments for improving our judiciary, but these are not arguments for weakening it. Let us discriminate.

I was struck a few days ago by an interview on the subject of the court proposals between a newspaper correspondent and a member of Congress. The latter was reported as saying, "I would be willing to vote against these proposals, but only the thinking people of my district are opposed to them. The great bulk of the people either do not know anything about it or do not care."

It is not too much to expect that you will constitute a part of "the thinking people" of your districts wherever they may be. If these do not outnumber the ones who do not think or do not care, then we are all lost together. You may come to particular conclusions far different from mine on this fundamental issue of the court. That is not the important matter. It is that you should care and should think about it. If it is actually true, as this representative said, that the bulk of the people who determine our destinies "do not know anything about it or do not care", then God help us. We need have no fear of the decisions of those who think and care, but if your future and mine and that of our children depends on the decisions of the thoughtless or the careless, despotism could be no worse; in fact despotism is almost sure to result. To prevent that should be our common aim, and on it we must unite. Democratic government is on its trial here as well as elsewhere. If we allow it to fall into the hands of leaders chosen and controlled by those who "do not think or do not care", then the great American experiment must end in failure, and with it democracy itself. Here is a challenge fit to call out the best in any real man.

XIII

GOVERNMENT BY LAW

I

The one great issue that overshadows all others in the distracted world to-day is the issue between constitutionalism and arbitrary government. The most fundamental difference is not between monarchy and democracy, nor even between capitalism and socialism or communism, tremendous as these differences are. For even in any socialistic or communistic régime, as now in every bourgeois democracy, there will be rights to be preserved and protected. Deeper than the problem whether we shall have a capitalistic system or some other enshrined in our law lies the question whether we shall be ruled by law at all, or only by arbitrary will.

The prevailing system of private ownership is so old and has in the course of centuries become so entwined in most existing systems of positive law that it is a natural mistake to identify private property with law itself, and opposition to it with lawlessness. The agitator for a communist revolution, like the capitalist, is in danger of forgetting that law does something more than merely protect vested rights of property: in capitalistic states it is law alone that leaves the agitator free to preach capital's overthrow. If, then, we give an economic definition to conservatism and to radicalism, as is commonly done, it is not legitimate to identify constitutionalism with either. Under an arbitrary government, the radical agitator is as likely to find himself in a concentration camp as the capitalist, and under those arbitrary governments which are now fascist it is he oftener than anyone else who feels the brunt of government by arbitrary will.

The problem of constitutionalism, then, is everybody's

problem, whatever economic or social system he may prefer. It is law alone that gives protection to rights of any kind in any individual, personal as well as proprietary, whatever form the state may take and whatever the nature of social control. In this world struggle between arbitrary will and settled law, it is true that liberalism and democracy are deeply involved. The triumph of will over law must mean the end of both. But our present crisis is not merely the crisis of liberalism or of democracy; it is a struggle for every human right against despotism.

II

Down to the eighteenth century political theorists usually drew a distinction which we in later times have slurred over— the distinction between despotism and tyranny. The former might be a legitimate form of government in which will was supreme; the latter was always to be condemned because its end was the good of the government, not of the governed. In the eighteenth century there were kings who were, or who thought themselves to be, "benevolent despots". The surge of democracy since the French Revolution has tended to destroy this distinction. To the average man the terms "despot" and "tyrant" have for a century meant practically the same thing. No government, we have thought, could be a good government if it was not "self-government". Now we seem to be reviving the old distinction. In the disillusionment of the war and its aftermath, and with the shipwreck of the nineteenth century's high hopes in *laissez-faire* democracy, the world seems to be turning in despair to despotism as the only solution for the problems with which democracy has suffered us—or, as some would say, has *caused* us—to be overwhelmed. There is probably no one who would not now admit that the hopes of the nineteenth century were far too high. To-day the "idea of progress" seems to be nearly as extinct as the dodo. According to the late Professor Bury, this "idea of progress" is linked with secularism and has grown in proportion as a sincere belief in a world to come has faded. If this is true, then we may probably expect, as some of our religious leaders now do, a return to supernatural religion as one ultimate outcome of our present pessimism. But the immediate political outcome of that pessimism is a return to despotism. The former blind faith that democracy would bring the millennium, like the conviction so recently and so loudly preached that economic depressions could never recur, has been rudely shattered; but with a faith even more blind our world is now desperately trying to persuade itself that despotism is always benevolent. The amazing thing is that so large a part of the world seems to have succeeded in the attempt, in the face of examples of confiscation, persecution of religious belief, suppression of the press and free speech, and even murder. It may require further bitter lessons to prove the truth of Plato's conviction that after all a lawless autocracy is worse for mankind than even the feebleness of democracy.

This is no new issue, but probably never before in the history of the world has the fate of the race been so involved in its outcome as now. That it is at bottom an issue between law and will was never more clearly shown than in a startling dispatch from the Berlin correspondent of the London *Times*, dated 5 July 1935, which I quote in part:

A principle entirely new to German jurisprudence has been introduced by the Penal Code Amendment Law, which was one of the batch of laws published by the Reich Cabinet on June 26 and is promulgated today in the official *Gazette*. It is that the Courts shall punish offences not punishable under the code when they are deserving of punishment "according to the underlying idea of a penal code or according to healthy public sentiment (*Volksempfinden*)". If no penal code applies directly, such an offence is to be punished according to that law the underlying idea of which best fits it....

The principle that an act could be punished only if it was an offence punishable under the code was enshrined both in the penal code and in the Weimar Constitution. As a principle of German law it was centuries old. The result was that *ad hoc* laws or decrees had to be passed from time to time to meet new offences.

Dr Hans Frank, Reich Minister without portfolio and former Reich Commissar for Justice, explains in a newspaper article that the new principle does not mean that anyone against whom a charge is brought in future in Germany is to be regarded from the outset as guilty, or that the rights of the defence will be impaired. The National Socialist State, he says, knows very well how to distinguish between criminals who are of thoroughly evil character and a pest to the community and small, harmless, everyday sinners. The Judge is not given unrestricted powers to condemn all and sundry in every case; he is invested with a proud power of decision which confers on him as representative of the National Socialist world-outlook and the healthy German public sentiment the rôle of a people's Judge in the finest meaning of the term. Dr Frank declares the new law to be a landmark on the road to a National Socialist penal code.

Let there be no mistake as to the meaning of this. The principle "that what was not prohibited was allowed" is condemned and repudiated as a "Jewish liberalistic principle". Even where no penal code "applies directly" to an offence, that offence is nevertheless to be punished "according to that law the underlying idea of which best fits it". "The National Socialist State... knows very well how to distinguish between criminals who are of thoroughly evil character and a pest to the community and small, harmless, everyday sinners"! In other words, in order to be punishable an offence need not be against any law, and punishment for it requires no warrant of law. It is enough if it is against "the idea". Whose idea? How can anyone take seriously the explanation that this "new principle does not mean that anyone against whom a charge is brought in future in Germany is to be regarded from the outset as guilty, or that *the rights of the defence will be impaired*"? Doubtless no rights will be impaired, for from now on no rights exist.

It is probably fortunate that the unashamed frankness of the present German leaders has made the issue so plain to all the world. We may appreciate how galling this pronouncement must be to many liberal Germans when we remember how great a contribution Germany has made in the past to the theory of the *Rechtsstaat*. This is the repudiation of everything for which Germany has stood since the Thirty Years War. However, the present silence of Germans in Germany is easy enough to understand. What is harder to account for is the apparent acquiescence of the outside world. Startling as this repudiation of law is, it seems to have startled nobody. I have seen little comment on it, favourable or unfavourable. We are no longer even surprised at events or at political doctrines which would have been shocking if they had been thinkable in the western world a bare score of years ago. This easy complaisance is the measure of our common danger.

Pronouncements like the one quoted above bring into stronger relief the opposing doctrine which underlies the recent decision of the United States Supreme Court in the Schechter case, and they enable us better to understand the true significance of that case and the principle on which it is based. Surprise has been expressed that the "liberal" justices joined with the rest of the court to make the decision unanimous. To some it has seemed strange that a judge who sincerely believes that only a federal authority can effectively perform the essential services involved in this case, should nevertheless join in a judgment which denies it the power to do so. Such critics overlook the fact that it is not merely the specific power to regulate commerce which this case involves, nor the definition of what is and what is not interstate commerce. The ultimate question is far deeper than that. However necessary, however beneficial such a power may be, if *ultra vires* it must be disallowed.

Reformers are naturally irritated when comprehensive plans of social betterment are thus wrecked, apparently on the rocks of mere legalism; but in their irritation they may be overlooking what the alternative means. Government without or beyond law is despotism, and it is none the less despotism because it is benevolent. As St Augustine declared, judges may not judge *of* the law, but only *secundum legem*. The laws may be those of "the horse and buggy era", but, as Lord Bacon said, "Judges ought to remember that their office is *jus dicere* and not *jus dare*." The justices of our Supreme Court have remembered it. When judges cease to do so it will be but a short step further to say, "If no penal code applies directly, such an offence is to be punished according to that law the underlying idea of which best fits it." In order to prevent that it may be worth while *temporarily* to forego even needed reforms. I say "temporarily", because obsolete laws should be changed, and that right speedily, but the judges have no commission to do it. Present criticisms of our highest court, and proposed constitutional amendments affecting its authority to review legislation, call to mind the case of Chief Justice Herbert at the time of the English Revolution. Unlike our American judges, he had upheld a discretionary and arbitrary power instead of denying its legality, but the underlying principle in the two cases is identical. No more dangerous power could easily be imagined than the dispensing power which the court had upheld in this case, and none was ever more outrageously exercised than this had been by James II. Yet the reply of the Chief Justice to his critics seems unanswerable: "When we were to give judgment in Sir Edward Hales's case we could neither know, nor hinder if we did, any ill use the King might make of this power; we were only to say upon our oaths, whether the King had such a power or no." Readers of Macaulay need not be reminded that this, as well as my interpretation of it, is the rankest heresy. This may not be the only part of our orthodox historical creed needing revision in the light of recent developments in continental Europe.

The modern school of sociological jurisprudence have done a very great service, but there is very great need to limit their teachings to their proper sphere. The only alternative to despotism is constitutionalism. Call this mere legalism if you

will, and admit to the full the unfortunate obstructive delays
that legalism sometimes involves. But let us not close our
eyes to the alternatives. We must choose one or the other.
Dr Frank and the Nazi leaders in Germany have seen these alternatives more clearly than we, and they have deliberately made
their choice for will against law. Dare we make the same?

To make all this perfectly clear, allow me to quote one or
two further paragraphs from Dr Frank's article in the *Zeit-
schrift der Akademie für deutsches Recht*, referred to above in the
dispatch of the London *Times* correspondent:

National Socialism, conscious of its creative power in all
spheres of the iron laws of national life, racial theory, and authoritarian government, practically found no formulated ideas or
generally recognized conceptions of organization in the field of
law. Law, for many decades, had been a subject of rationalist
thought exclusively treated on the principle of technically
polished logic. It was the school of Roman Law jurisprudence
that had replaced direct service to life with service to abstractions,
with the result that the substance of juridical thought and science,
no less than the personalities professionally connected with law,
led a life of isolation, hardly understood by the people and rarely
regarded with respect, never with sympathy....

The German Academy of Law, consequently, is the corporative
representative of the German conception of law which considers
the common weal the sole standard of its work, definitely doing
away with former schools: the schools of natural law, of historical
law, of the sociological theory of law whose destructive materialist
tendencies it regards as least fitted for German justice. Service to
the vital necessities of our people, not service to theories, is the
ideal of the German guardians of law. In this sense the Academy
of German Law will develop the Aryan conception of justice, thus
contributing to the progress of our entire European civilization.

Thus German, or "Aryan", justice is something different
from what the world has known since the time of Plato and
Aristotle and the Roman lawyers, and something vastly
better, based not on universal reason or "polished logic" but
on the will to serve tribal ideas. This is indeed, as *The Times*

correspondent says, a breach of the Weimar Constitution and of all German conceptions of law held for centuries. It is more than that. With a relentlessness that may remind some of us of German methods in the Great War, the Nazi leaders have broken with the cultural development of two thousand years and more, with Jewish and Christian morality as well as with Latin law and tradition. In all these, "racial theory and authoritarian government found no formulated ideas or generally recognized conceptions of organization". So all must go, law must be remade, and a new history written.

To see what this would mean for us it is necessary to remember how long and how difficult has been the "struggle for law"—to use the words of the title of one of von Ihering's books—the struggle between despotic will and constitutionalism. Juries not answerable for their verdicts, writs of *habeas corpus*, the condemnation of *ex post facto* laws, judges with independent tenure, strict definitions of treason, rigid enforcement of the rights of accused persons—every one of these would require a volume to trace its history, and in some cases that history would extend backward for hundreds of years, through revolution and civil war. Yet not one of them is compatible with the Nazi ideal. If it persists they must all go, and much more with them. Are we willing to give up these hard-won gains in return for the "direct service to life" of a despotic *Führer*, benevolent or otherwise? This is the question. All others are insignificant in comparison.

But if we ever hope to give a true answer to such a question, we must try to understand why it has been asked. I have made no effort to conceal my own preference for constitutionalism and even for democracy. Nevertheless we must not condemn unheard this deliberate repudiation of them both. When a great cultured nation like modern Germany suddenly turns its back on the principles it has been among the foremost in teaching for hundreds of years, there must be a cause and it must be a cause lying far deeper than the mere mentality of the present German leaders.

III

To President Wilson in 1917 the problem was whether the world could be made safe for democracy. Now it seems to be whether democracy can be made safe for the world. It is even more fundamental than that. As I have tried to show, it is a question whether constitutionalism itself can or should persist, or whether we shall turn away from the political teaching of two thousand years and welcome a revolution which would make the French Revolution pale in comparison. Can liberalism, can democracy, can even constitutionalism, be made safe for the world? If a poll had been taken on that question as recently as fifteen years ago it seems probable that the answer would have been in the affirmative. It is doubtful if it would be to-day.

Democracy on a great scale is a relatively new thing in the world. It has not yet reached its two hundredth birthday. Practically no great statesman or political theorist ever had a good word to say for it before the French Revolution. Its vogue began with that revolution, yet it now seems to many to have failed in its first great test; they are tempted to throw it over for an older and more effective form of state organization, for a despotism which they pray may be benevolent. To some of these men one proof of the failure of liberalism, democracy, and even constitutionalism lies in the social dislocation which has followed the Great War; to others liberalism and democracy are unacceptable because they were unable to avert the war itself. On any other basis than this it is hard to account for the acquiescence of thousands if not millions of intelligent and liberal men in many recent acts and policies, unspeakably arbitrary and oppressive in character, on the part of their national governments. Faced with the hateful alternatives of disorder or despotism, they have chosen the latter as the lesser evil. It is not the first time in the history of the West.

To one who looks on the whole of that history since

medieval times it does not seem strange—whatever may have been the form of our governments—that we have failed thus far in solving the unprecedented problems of our new world. Such an observer knows that to-day the population of a single European country like France or Germany is probably larger than that of the whole of Europe less than three hundred years ago. He recognizes that the wholesale industrialization of this huge mass has inevitably brought forward problems unthought of before in the ancient, medieval, or modern world, problems to which old formulas can never be fitted. But the average man takes little account of these things. He is rightly impatient with existing conditions, and it is his voice that counts. However liberal he may be, he is influenced by the apparent failure of liberalism as a solution of his problems, and may even be willing in the long run to entrust his fortunes to King Stork instead of King Log.

Those who still cling to a belief in the essential soundness of democratic institutions and who hope for their future cannot afford to ignore these ugly facts. It will not do any longer to wave them aside, or to treat them lightly as the results of an economic depression soon to pass. The future historian will smile at so shallow an explanation of the history of the last dozen years or more in Italy, Germany, the Balkans and Spain, or even in the United States and England where democracy is not an exotic. The causes of these things did not arise suddenly in 1918 or in 1914. The crisis of the war and its aftermath of dislocation undoubtedly brought them to an issue, but their true causes are older, deeper, and more lasting. It is plain that if democracy is to persist it must become more effective and less corrupt than it has been for a long time past. Those who believe its feebleness and graft are only incidental and not essential must lose their case if they are unable to point to some means of purging these evils short of revolution or despotism. For purged they must be.

From ancient times the standing objection to democracy has always been its ineffectiveness, and it is still its greatest defect. An arbitrary government may permit corruption, but a feeble government invites it. The lessons of history are not to be hastily drawn, and most so-called "historical parallels" are dangerous. It is not strictly true that "history repeats itself". Yet a student of history may be warranted in thinking that in the past weakness has probably caused the fall of more governments than wickedness. An unjust ruler is hated by his subjects, but they usually tolerate him longer than one incapable of preventing injustice in others. The King must have an abundance of power, says a great political writer of the thirteenth century, if he is to maintain peace and justice. Machiavelli believed that it was less dangerous for a government to be bad than to be contemptible. One need not be a fascist to admit that fascism would very likely never have gripped Italy if the preceding parliamentary régime had not become contemptible.

Probably no form of political and social control ever tried in Europe has embodied higher ideals than the feudalism of the later Middle Ages. Yet it was replaced by strong monarchies many of which became despotisms.

In times of disorder men care more for order than for liberty. In this respect the transition from fifteenth- to sixteenth-century Europe seems to show a parallel to conditions existent to-day in at least some European nations. There was then for a time the same indifference to liberty but a passionate desire for order and a willingness to render unquestioning obedience to the only authority capable of maintaining it. In France the despotism of Louis XI can be explained only by the feebleness of the rule it replaced. In England we cannot account for the sufferance of "Tudor absolutism" except in the light of the feudal anarchy of the fifteenth century. From 1215 to the present we hear constant appeals to Magna Carta, the "palladium of our liberties"—save in one period alone, the era of the Tudors. From 1485 to 1603 there is scarcely a mention of it, and even at the end of the period Shakespeare wrote his *King John* without a reference to it. To Simon Fish, writing in

1529, the barons of 1215 were simply rebels fighting against "a rightuous Kinge", "forbicause that he wolde haue punisshed certeyn traytours". Since the sixteenth century it has not been usual to regard John as a "rightuous Kinge". It seems strangely true that each age will reconstruct the past in its own image: if so, we may expect some peculiar history to come out of Germany in the near future.

Thus we have foreshadowed the most pressing problem of modern government—the preservation of the delicate balance between order and liberty, so that the former may not turn into oppression nor the latter into licence. Can it be done? One thing at least seems clear from both recent and earlier history. The democracies of the present world, if they are to succeed, must become less contemptible than they have been; that is to say, they must become more competent. Disorder in the past has always been overcome by a concentration of power. It can be overcome by no other means now. At his coronation the medieval King swore to preserve order and maintain justice. It was his comparative success in doing so that explains the long continuance of monarchical government since feudal times; and he could never have succeeded in it if the statement accredited to Louis XIV had not in some sense always been true: *L'état, c'est moi*. But by the eighteenth century the strong constitutional monarchy in France had degenerated into the personal one which resulted in the Revolution. The serious problems of to-day require the same concentrated power that enabled the medieval King to enforce his peace in times of disorder; but as that King was "under the law that made him King", in Bracton's phrase, so our modern governments must also have their legal bounds. We must have power; but we need safeguards against its wrongful extension or abuse if it is to remain constitutional and not become despotic, as it became in France before 1789 or as it is now in the German Reich. The powers of our governors should be great, yet they must be limited. If so, *Quis custodiet ipsos custodes?* Who is to have an eye on those governors themselves? Who shall determine when they have overstepped the bounds of the law which at once confers and defines their authority? Who, if not those technically qualified and duly constituted to interpret that law?

IV

Two historical fallacies have obscured the answer to this important practical question. One is the unwarranted notion that we here in America were the first discoverers of judicial review. The other is the theory so brilliantly set forth by Lord Bryce, and especially by Professor Dicey, that in England, the main source of our political conceptions, there was no constitution which the sovereign parliament could not override. Neither of these assumptions will bear the light.

As to the first: judicial review, instead of being an American invention, is really as old as constitutionalism itself, and without it constitutionalism could never have been maintained. In France, for example, the long history of the Parliament of Paris is a struggle for judicial review against arbitrary government. True, it was a losing fight—if it had not been, the Revolution would not have come on in 1789—but it is none the less important for that. When Louis XI cowed his Parliament by force it was felt to be a usurpation, and all the great French constitutional lawyers in the next two centuries admitted the fact at least by implication. If the Parliament refused to register a royal ordinance, as it frequently did, there was always the same reason for this refusal: the qualified interpreters of the law considered the act as *ultra vires*. They were merely putting into practice the same fundamental theory of constitutional government recently applied in the Schechter case by our Supreme Court, or asserted in England in the early seventeenth century by Sir Edward Coke when he reminded James I that the King in person could pronounce no judgment in his courts even though they were his courts.

All such facts seem to rest on three necessary assumptions: first, that there is a fundamental constitution; second, that its interpretation rests with the judiciary; and third, that judges have an authority only, in the words of Lord Bacon, "to interpret Law, and not to Make Law, or Give Law".

Our own American judges who thought to avert civil war by political *obiter dicta* certainly did not make a notable success of it; and Clarendon tells us that it was similar *dicta* concerning the royal prerogative in the Ship-money Case which stirred up the popular discontent resulting in the English civil wars of the seventeenth century, rather than the mere decision in favour of the King. In 1788 or 1789, by ratifying a written constitution which reserved all unenumerated powers "to the States respectively or to the people" and in a "bill of rights" expressly forbade certain governmental infringements of individual liberty, we in America merely made our fundamental law more explicit. We added nothing really new. The fact that judicial review was not debated in the constitutional convention of 1787 means little. Judicial review was taken for granted, and as soon as settled government was established under the new constitution, it inevitably emerged, as it always must if a constitutional régime is to persist at all.

But judicial review implies a fundamental constitution to be reviewed, and this means a set of rules not made by the sovereign authority subsisting under that constitution, nor subject to his will. Such rules have existed and must exist in any state worthy of the term "constitutional". It is true enough that statesmen have not always clearly grasped this fact. Misinterpreting the real nature of the English Revolution, a few misguided ones in the eighteenth century tried in the case of Englishmen overseas to violate political traditions which they would never have dared touch at home. The loss of a great colonial empire was the result. The fictitious character of the doctrine of the omnipotence of parliament is now explicitly admitted by the recent Statute of Westminster in imperial matters, the only important field in which it has ever been exploited. In internal matters, in England itself, there are many fundamental rights of the subject that parliament in modern times has never dreamt of infringing and could only infringe at the cost of revolution.

The true glory of England's institutions lies not in her representative parliament, but in the fact that through it she has preserved her ancient liberties and made them more secure and more general. It has been her unique good fortune that her traditions of free government are so old and so firm that they have never been overturned or seriously interrupted. Thus no formal written constitution has ever been needed, as on the Continent or in North America; the possibility of revolution remains the only sanction of constitutionalism. Our amendable constitution offers a milder alternative. Of course it would be absurd to say that modern English parliaments have never exercised an arbitrary power over subjects. National crises always breed popular hysteria. The treatment of the so-called "delinquents" by the Long Parliament smacks suspiciously of Dr Frank's "healthy public sentiment" rather than of law; and such things did not end at the Restoration or the Revolution. On the whole, however, they became progressively fewer, so few in recent times, in fact, that one likes to think they never can recur. Like some legal fictions, the political fiction of the omnipotence of parliament may possibly serve some useful purpose. It is dangerous only when it is mistaken for a fact. Among free peoples such fictions persist only so long as they are unreal enough to be harmless.

V

The limits of a single article are too narrow to permit further historical illustrations, and I must be content with a rather bald résumé of a few of the practical conclusions which seem to me to be deducible from the history of constitutionalism. If, as I have insisted, the problem consists in making constitutionalism safe for the world, one method is suggested by the recent tendency toward autocracy. It must fit itself to "serve the vital necessities" of the people, in Dr Frank's phrase, and to compete successfully with dictatorships in so doing. Otherwise dictatorships are likely to replace it. To serve these necessities democratic government must have something of the strength, the decision, and the independence that a dictator enjoys.

In the United States such a concentration of power as this implies would of course be legally impossible without some amendments to the Federal Constitution; and the reformers are justified in demanding such amendments. These would strengthen the authority of law, for they would provide legal means of securing what men believe that justice demands. Under our vast new industrial system it is felt that the old guarantees of "life, liberty, and the pursuit of happiness" must include more than they did under the simple rural economy of 1776 or 1787. They must protect men against peonage as well as against prosecutions; they must do more than merely make them equal before the law. These things are so necessary that they will be done somehow. True liberty will be conserved if they can be done constitutionally and within proper limits. If our exaggerated system of checks and balances stands in the way, then that "system" should be altered by amendment.

In his recent book our ex-President has advocated a wholesale return to all those time-worn checks as a cure for our present "medieval" regimentation. To make such a proposal in all seriousness one must be almost as oblivious of the causes of our present miseries as of what actual conditions were in the Middle Ages. We have indeed been illegally regimented in some cases, and fortunately the Supreme Court has so found; but we must devise legal means to end the abuses which provoked this regimentation, or worse is likely to follow. And it is under the shadow of these very checks and balances that some of the worst of these abuses have sprouted and flowered. When, for example, we see one branch of our government, under pressure from a selfish minority, passing a bill they know to be vicious in the secret hope that another branch may nullify their action, we have the very *reductio ad absurdum* of all government and an end of all true responsibility. Where responsibility cannot be fixed, corruption will inevitably spread and the interests of greedy minorities are sure to supplant the common weal. But there can be no responsibility without power and there should be no power without responsibility. Government, if it is to be honest and impartial and effective, needs to be restricted; but it must not be weakened. The principle of the separation of powers, valid and necessary if restricted so as to mean merely the independence of the judiciary, when extended too far into the spheres of legislation and administration becomes a menace and an open invitation either to illegal usurpation or to actual revolution.

True constitutionalism, from medieval times to our own, has never meant government enfeebled by divisions within itself; it has meant government limited by law. None but reactionaries will insist that this law shall remain for ever fixed and immovable regardless of economic and social development. The true conservative will admit the need of changes if they are sound and constructive. Indeed, he should welcome them, because they will heighten and not lessen respect for law itself. The one thing he can never safely tolerate is to see law undermined, even under the guise of Dr Frank's "healthy public sentiment". Against such insidious encroachments of despotism our chief reliance must remain what it has always been: a fearless and impartial interpretation of law by a free and independent judiciary. Our problem to-day, in a word, is to make needed changes in the laws, but always to keep them law.

XIV

THE RECONSTRUCTION OF LIBERALISM

The Good Society. By WALTER LIPPMANN. Boston: Little, Brown, 1937, 402 pp.

The present generation is rightly concerned, and concerned far more deeply than its immediate forbears ever were, in the ending or mending of the monstrous economic and social inequalities and iniquities which permit and even foster the distress we see about us in the midst of plenty. In sharp contrast with the older notions of an inevitable progressive development that had best be let alone, or even with the recent naïve belief that depressions were a thing of the past, there is a determination among men of the present day, particularly the younger ones, to do something about this; and some would even go so far as to threaten the very existence of plenty itself, in their hatred of the glaring unevenness of its distribution. There is a divine discontent in the air, a discontent which may lead us on to reform if it is wise, or to chaos if it is misdirected. Which shall it be? This is the burning practical question; and it must have an answer very soon, for we are now in the dangerous state of readiness to accept and to act on any suggestion whatever, bad or good, rather than not act at all. Unquestionably one cause of our confusion and bewilderment is the suddenness with which events have thrust this question upon us. We have been faced unexpectedly with the necessity of making a quick decision which may in all likelihood involve the fate of our race, and we have had no time to think the question through.

One thing is clear enough: the world in its present mood will never put up with a mere "muddling through" as an answer. The preservation of the *status quo* is a solution that can satisfy none but the contented; and just now most men are not contented. Whether the answer to be made shall be for reform or for annihilation of our institutions, that answer will be given by those who are dissatisfied with existing conditions. These are the ones whose decisions and actions will either mend or end the ingrown abuses of our present social and economic system, will make or mar any system replacing it; and these are the ones therefore to whom all arguments, to be effective, must be directed. The quietists and reactionaries, though they are always with us, have become, for the time at least, practically negligible. Meantime an increasing number of us have grown conscious that these imminent decisions and actions are likely to determine for us and our children no less a question than whether we shall be freemen or slaves in the times to come—and times not far distant. We are becoming more and more concerned that no decision be made that could enslave us all, and, with the present state of Europe in mind, we fear that some present proposals might have that effect.

It is a principle of equity that he who seeks a remedy must come with clean hands. Now we "liberals", advocates of reform, but a constitutional reform, do not come with hands entirely clean. Among our fellows there are doubts of our sincerity, and not altogether without reason; so any cautions or suggestions that may come from us are likely to be received with some suspicion. Why did suspicion of this kind arise? Is it a justifiable suspicion? If not, can we do anything to remove it and thus get a fair hearing for warnings that we believe might, if heeded, save us all from disaster? These are some of the preliminary questions to which the liberal of to-day must make answer as best he can. I take it, the sum of all the answers, to be effective, will be a plea in confession and avoidance: a frank and full confession of wrongs and blunders past and present—but the wrongs and blunders of liberals, not of liberalism.

If he believes this, it is the liberal's business—or his duty rather—to try to demonstrate it to a discontented, impatient, and hostile world; no easy task, for past mistakes have laid upon him a heavy burden of proof.

Liberals do not differ from others in their conception of the true end of the state, for to all parties at all times the end, actual or professed, has been the good life of the whole; the differences come in determining what is "good" and how this is to be attained. True liberalism can never countenance, even if some "liberals" have, the sacrifice of individual well-being to "reasons of state". There can be no good life for any state whose members live in wretchedness and misery, material or spiritual. National glory or national wealth at the cost of individual welfare is the mark of no true commonwealth, but of a tyranny. The well-being of any state—the common weal—can only be a weal that is common to all. For a state, in the only proper sense of the term, as Cicero said long ago, is not any chance aggregation of men but a multitude united in the common purpose of securing this common good, and that can mean nothing less than the individual good of all, not some, of its members.

But Cicero did not stop there, nor does liberalism stop there. He also said that this multitude must be joined together in consent to law (*juris consensu*), and by law he meant no mere fiat of government. These are his words, among the most memorable in political literature: "True law is right reason consonant with nature, diffused among all men, constant, eternal; which summons to duty by its command and hinders from fraud by its prohibition.... To make enactments infringing this law, religion forbids, neither may it be repealed even in part, nor have we power through Senate or people to free ourselves from it."

This, of course, is an idealistic statement to which the sober facts of human life can never fully reach, yet reduced to the level of actual experience its central principle still holds good. It means that "what pleases the prince" may temporarily "have the force of law", but is not law; for the common good for which the state exists requires a stronger guarantee than the nod of any prince or any government. Now this is liberalism pure and simple. For, stripped of all its husks, liberalism is constitutionalism, "a government of laws and not of men", a common weal of individual rights that neither prince nor magistrate nor assembly has any authority to impair. In a word, liberalism means a common welfare with a constitutional guarantee. I maintain that not one part, but both parts of this definition—in essence, Cicero's definition—must be translated into working fact if we mean to live in a true commonwealth and hope to keep it in being. So-called liberals have ignored the first part of the definition and have fouled the nest by invoking the guarantee for privileges of their own, conducive only to the destruction of any true common weal. None have ever prated more of guarantees than these so-called liberals; but they have forgotten, if they ever believed, that these guarantees must secure the rights of all, not the selfish interests of a few. They are the traitors within the gates who have probably done more than all others to betray liberalism to its enemies and put it to its defence. Of all the errors of "liberals" theirs seems the worst; for it is largely the result of greed, and a principal cause of man's recent inhuman exploitation of man.

It is unlikely, however, that this exploitation could ever have reached the proportions it did without more protest, had really liberally minded men not been beguiled by the extreme doctrine of *laissez-faire*, surely one of the strangest fantasies that ever discredited human reason. Thus the self-seekers and the doctrinaires were drawn together into an alliance to maintain the *status quo*, and all its abuses and inequalities were made sacrosanct. This pseudo-liberalism usually exhibited itself in the ineffectiveness of legal guarantees for almost every human right except the right of property, and the acceptance of an unhistorical definition of contract under which the sanction of the law could be obtained for almost any enormity to which men could be induced to agree.

A contract is "an agreement" to do or not to do a particular thing, according to a definition once laid down by Chief Justice Marshall. According to the Roman jurists, a contract is a bond of the law (*vinculum juris*) which the state sees fit to attach to agreements of which it has no reason to disapprove. Between these two definitions the practical difference may not seem great, but in theory and emphasis it is profound.

Under *laissez-faire* and our distorted notions of contract, a lunatic may be protected against the results of his agreement, but of economic inequalities the law can never take notice— *De minimis non curat lex*; there is little or no safeguard for the weak against the strong; protection of the public against an adulterated product would be unthinkable—*Caveat emptor*.

Now this is a return toward Hobbes's "war of every man against every man", without the equality that Hobbes premised. Yet, we are told, the state cannot and should not do anything about it. State interference in such matters would be a violation of a sacred right. What a caricature of liberalism! Few illusions have been more disastrous than the one arising from an uncritical acceptance of Sir Henry Maine's sweeping generalization that human progress has been a development from status to contract.

No doubt conditions such as the ones mentioned above have long been accepted as "natural", or normal, or even desirable by liberals without number. It is equally true that this belief has often led to a callous indifference on their part to many forms of human misery. The indictment that might be drawn against them is a long one, though in fairness it ought to be remembered that this indictment would have been against the great majority of us all, if it had been drawn before the Great War and the awakening caused by that event. The number certainly included more than the justices of the Supreme Court of the United States.

Two wrongs do not make a right; no more do two errors make a truth. The question before us now, the decision we shall have to make before long, is whether we shall renounce these errors and remove these abuses that liberals have allowed to grow up, or whether, once and for all, we shall level with the ground all the bulwarks of our liberty, because some traitors have crept in behind them. This is what the decision we must make really means, for between constitutionalism and despotism there is no tenable middle ground. Of that the recent history of Europe leaves no reasonable doubt for any intelligent man who chooses to look into it.

The men in a hurry are trying to tell us that the only cure for economic inequality is political slavery. They would have us believe that regimentation is the only practical form of liberty. Stripped of all its idealistic phrases, their creed is a creed of pure despotism, and these dreamers could not believe in it if they had not persuaded themselves somehow—honestly enough, no doubt—that despotism will always be altruistic and never selfish. They are willing to entrust to a government without legal limits, and only imperfectly responsible, not only their own present welfare but their children's future fortunes. What a sublime faith in human benevolence! What an opportunity for an adventurer! Much of the bloodshed and misery that history records has been the direct result of this kind of honest, idealistic, but impractical, wishful thinking.

That it should crop up again in this twentieth century is one of the disastrous results of our unfortunate divorce of history and politics. Our public men and even our professed students of government are woefully ignorant—shall I say "blissfully" ignorant?—of the historical "struggle for law", and what it has meant; and they seem equally blind to what it means now. Almost any day they might read in the newspapers of confiscations and banishments and concentration camps and castor oil, of blood-purges and "liquidations" (what a polite term!), of the imprisonment of religious leaders and the beheading of "traitors". But these everyday horrors slip over their minds like water over a duck's back. Terrible as the crimes of liberals have been, are they as bad as these? "You must trust me", this is the whole sum of the "constitution" under a dictatorship. And we are now asked to accept it in place of our bills of rights! With the past and the present before us, dare we then accept as our guides men who thus show that they are unable or unwilling to face the ugly facts, in human nature, in history, and in our world to-day?

An acceptance might, of course, be not quite irrevocable. History shows cases where such despotic governments have been finally overthrown. But seldom has it been done without distress and bloodshed following a period of intolerable oppression. Would the cost of redressing the wrongs of liberals be likely to be as great as this?

If we look at our present situation, its most ominous aspect is in the cross purposes, the divisions, and even the conflicts we find among those who ought to be presenting a solid front against the forces of reaction. The faults of our liberals and the blindness of our reformers have thus broken up the historic alliance of reformer and constitutionalist through which alone we have gained and kept what little of liberty we still enjoy. And we underrate the present strength of the forces of greed, corruption, and the lust for power, if we think we can hold what we have won from them, to say nothing of winning more, while our own forces are thus divided and weakened. Before we advance to new positions we must secure the ground already won; we must consolidate our gains, and to do it we must restore the old winning combination of reformer and constitutionalist. In the past the reformer may have made these gains, but the constitutionalist enabled him to hold them. The economic and political rights wrested from oppressors have been rendered secure by making them *legal* or constitutional rights, by adding to them the sanction of the law. Only one of two other sanctions is ever possible: physical force, or the acquiescence of the government. The former amounts to a permanent state of civil war, or at best, of armed peace; the latter is a benevolent despotism. Can we then, dare we, exchange our constitutionalism for either of these?

Constitutionalism is more a method than a principle. It is the method of law as contrasted with force or with will. If this law has perpetuated some abuses, it has also preserved all our liberties. The abuses are eradicable and in no way essential to it; without it, the liberties are ours only on sufferance. The moral seems to be that we should guard our legal rights, but see to it that they shall never be economic wrongs. To strip of legal sanction all such wrongs as still exist, to add this sanction to all reforms our times require, this is a programme that should enlist the support of every forward-looking man; not half this programme, but the whole of it. Before such a programme can be realized we must scrap much of the current nonsense about "popular sovereignty". We must discard our traditional notions of sovereignty itself, derived from Hobbes and Austin, and substitute sounder ones. We must strike at the corruption that is eating at the vitals of our body politic. We must modify some of our so-called "checks" that only enfeeble government and make it responsible to selfish minority groups instead of to all the people. But in it all, and above all, we must retain those legal limits of governmental action which now exist in our bills of rights to protect the personal as well as the proprietary rights of the humblest and even the most hated of our citizens. Not only must we retain them; we must revive and revise, we must clarify and even extend them, for only so can we ever hope to give permanence to our needed reforms themselves. If they are to last, these reforms must have a better guarantee than the passing whim of any dictator; and the only guarantee that men have ever been able to devise, short of actual physical force, is the guarantee of constitutional limitations.

Much of our thinking on these points has been confused, and this has been and is one of the greatest obstacles to sound practical progress. Among the confusions is our conception of what we choose to call "popular sovereignty".

We live under a government in which the "sovereign" is limited by a superior law, a constituent law, made directly by the whole people themselves, not made and not alterable by the "sovereign" who exists only by virtue of that same constituent law. This is the system which the founders of our state deliberately established and this we think we are trying to preserve. And yet there are many among us to-day who would emasculate that system by destroying the only means by which it can work or endure, namely, a judicial review which makes sure that no act of the "sovereign" shall exceed the legal authority conferred upon it by the people in the constituent law, or constitution.

In the main, this destructive attitude is not a reasoned one, but in so far as it has any basis at all in thought or theory it seems to come from the common acceptance of the delusion of "popular sovereignty". Popular sovereignty, at bottom, is an identification, contrary to fact, of the government and the people. Now "We the people" do not govern ourselves; we have established a government to do it, and it does it. If the people really governed, it would, of course, be both absurd and impossible to try to limit governmental action by any law. The notion that our government *is* the people, therefore naturally leads to the conclusion that the government has no limits. The logic is sound, the premise is utterly untrue. This unwarranted belief, necessarily destructive of all constitutionalism and of all bills of rights, has been fostered by a strange unhistorical conception of "sovereignty". We are only able to accept "popular" sovereignty, because of our peculiar notions of what sovereignty itself is. Blind followers of the blind have persuaded us—mostly lawyers who have taken Blackstone literally and uncritically—that sovereignty is might, not right, and that this might could not conceivably be the might of any true sovereign if it had any legal limits whatsoever. These men have hopelessly confused authority with power, and apparently have been entirely oblivious of the fact that their conception of political supremacy, fathered by Hobbes and nurtured by John Austin, is completely subversive of the constitutional system under which we all live and to which they themselves have usually paid the most extravagant lip service.

This is not the place to try to expose the fallacy of Austinianism and its incompatibility with past constitutional development or with the present safeguarding of minority and individual rights, but I do believe that this kind of crooked and dangerous political thinking, though the extent of its influence is hard to estimate, has been one potent cause of our "present discontents".

The generation now at the height of their political activity have been called by Mr Walter Lippmann "the lost generation". They certainly have no monopoly of the errors and confusions that I have tried to outline above, but it is true that upon them in a peculiar sense has fallen the accumulated burden of these traditional abuses, prejudices, and heresies. They are truly a "lost generation". And not the least interesting aspect of Mr Lippmann's remarkable book, to a student of contemporary politics, is its autobiographical character. It is nothing less than an *apologia pro vita sua*, the life story of one of the most thoughtful members of this lost generation; an idealist, perplexed and appalled by the present outcome, so sadly different from his earlier confident hopes and expectations, groping for an explanation of this debacle, and finally finding it, not in the defects inherent in liberalism, as some other present-day idealist reformers have, but in the perturbations which have thrown liberalism out of its only true orbit, the fulfilment of the "good life" for all.

The brief summary which I have given above does not follow Mr Lippmann's discussions very closely, but I hope it contains the gist of his political arguments and conclusions. On the other hand, it conveys no idea whatever of his treatment of the economic aspects of his subject. Much of his book deals with the economic side of the degradation of liberalism and the economic aspect of the changes necessary to restore its integrity. To assess the value of this important part of Mr Lippmann's work would require the knowledge of a trained economist, to the possession of which I lay no claim. The general inference seems to be that the recrudescence of authoritarianism in our time comes in large part from the belief "that the new machine technology requires the control of an omnipotent state", a belief based on the prior assumption that the concentration of control in modern industry is the result of technical change. The history of industry, however, completely disproves this assumption. "Concentration has its origin in privilege and not in technology." It is "a creation of the state through its laws". As for the rights with which legislatures and courts have gradually invested the modern business corporation, they are conditional only and are subject to alteration by the state. "There is no reason whatever for the assumption, made both by individualists and by collectivists, that corporations must either be allowed to enjoy all their present rights or be taken over and administered by the state." "There is only one purpose to which a whole society can be directed by a deliberate plan. That purpose is war, and there is no other." Hence, "a directed society must be bellicose and poor. If it is not both bellicose and poor, it cannot be directed.... A prosperous and peaceable society must be free. If it is not free, it cannot be prosperous and peaceable."

For reactionaries whose liberalism is only protective colouring, there will be scant comfort in this book. It is addressed to sincerely forward-looking men. If these remain deaf to the appeal presented here with such telling force, then the victory of autocracy seems assured. And let the reformer bear in mind that a victory for autocracy, if not coupled with complete responsibility, is in our day a victory for reaction in the end.

THE TENURE OF ENGLISH JUDGES[1]

At the meeting of the Political Science Association last year, in the general discussion, on the subject of the recall, I was surprised and, I must admit, a little shocked to hear our recall of judges compared to the English removal of judges on address of the houses of parliament.

If we *must* compare unlike things, rather than place the recall beside the theory or the practice of the joint address, I should even prefer to compare it to a bill of attainder.

In history, theory and practice the recall as we have it and the English removal by joint address have hardly anything in common, save the same general object.

Though I may not (as I do not) believe in the recall of judges, this paper concerns itself not at all with that opinion, but only with the history and nature of the tenure of English judges, particularly as affected by the possibility of removal on address. I believe a study of that history will show that any attempt to force the address into a close resemblance to the recall, whether for the purpose of furthering or of discrediting the latter, is utterly misleading.

In the history of the tenure of English judges the act of 12 and 13 William III, subsequently known as the Act of Settlement, is the greatest landmark. The history of the tenure naturally divides into two parts at the year 1701. In dealing with both parts, for the sake of brevity, I shall confine myself strictly to the judges who compose what since 1873 has been known as the Supreme Court of Judicature.

Few subjects so important in English legal or constitutional history have been treated more vaguely than this. In

[1] A paper read in 1912 at the ninth annual meeting of the American Political Science Association, and reprinted from The American Political Science Review, vol. VII, No. 2, May, 1913.

one well-known constitutional history it is said that "until 1701 the judges held office at the royal will", and even Maitland says that judges of the Stuart period "all along...held their offices *durante beneplacito*". Both these statements are very wide of the mark.

Judicial office in England before the Norman Conquest was communal in general character. The courts were not yet the king's courts and it could not be said the judges were his: in fact there were no judges in the modern sense. In the Norman and earliest Angevin period all this was changed. Separate manorial jurisdictions, franchises, liberties, of course, continued to exist; and the old communal courts of the hundred and shire were retained; but the latter were now linked with the central *curia*, which in all its varied functions was in a real sense the king's court. The king's judges who replaced the old suitors were now his deputies acting by virtue of his commission, and causes were determined under his writ. The king had become the fountain of justice.

These are royalist and anti-feudal tendencies, and may even be called national, for they shaped the common law.

But in addition there is a feudal element of the tenure, which enters into and affects judicial tenure in all its history. This is the feudal conception of an office. The grant of an office, in mediaeval England, was, in effect, the same as a grant of land: it conferred on the grantee an estate in the office, and (usually more important) in its emoluments. In both lands and office the rights vesting in the grantee were, of course, strictly determined by the terms of the grant, unless some rule of law supervened. A freehold of office, for example, was not essentially different from any other freehold. The balancing of these two elements, of royal control and feudal tenure, and the addition later of a popular element exercised through parliament, really make up the history of judicial tenure in England from its beginning to the present time.

The great offices of the king's household, such as that of seneschal or constable, early became hereditary in this way and thus less useful. Their place was taken by newer offices, such as that of justiciar and of chancellor, held by *novi homines* of lower birth but greater power than the older nobility. These new officials furnished the core of the king's *curia* which performed all the functions of the central government of whatever kind, including of course much judicial business. Their tenure was naturally at the king's pleasure.

As the business and problems of government became more complicated, a division of labour and a specialization of function became inevitable. By the thirteenth century the separate judicial machinery had become fixed, the courts of king's bench and common pleas had acquired a definite organization, and we may speak more definitely of judicial tenure in its strict sense. Fortunately, from about that time also, the rolls of the king's letters patent by which the grants to judicial office were made, become available, and I shall summarize briefly the material in them affecting the tenure of the judges.[1]

It will not take long to dispose of the early history of the judges of the king's bench and common pleas. From the earliest patents down to the Long Parliament, their tenure was practically invariable—during the pleasure of the king. Though grants for life, even without a limitation as to good behaviour, are sometimes found in the patents of the Welsh and Irish judges, the grant to the English judges is in this period always a grant by the king to hold and occupy the office with its proper fees and emoluments "*quamdiu nobis*

---

[1] Though it is impossible to make particular reference to these unprinted rolls in this brief paper, all the specific statements included here concerning the tenure of the judges, especially before the seventeenth century, have been taken from them; and all the more general ones are based on an examination of practically all the surviving patents for high judicial office between the thirteenth century and the seventeenth.

placuerit"—it is, in fact, an estate in the office terminable at the will of the king. This continues until 1641.

The tenure of the barons of the exchequer is a more difficult matter, and it is concerning it that most of the mistakes have been made.

It is probable that in the earlier time, in the exchequer (as elsewhere) no clear distinction was made between ministerial and judicial offices, and in fact no real distinction even between the various barons of the realm who were summoned by the king to assist him, now in the exchequer, now elsewhere, as his curia. But in time both distinctions arose. It becomes possible after a while to see a difference between ministerial exchequer officials, such as the treasurer, and the chancellor of the exchequer, who often have a freehold in their offices: sometimes an estate for life, sometimes one in fee simple, in tail male, etc.; and what may be called the judicial exchequer officials—the *barones scaccarii*. The very use of the word *barones* in this narrower connection shows that they had also become a wholly different order of beings and a far lower one than the barons of the realm.

The ministerial exchequer offices, from the nature of their tenure, being often in incapable hands, were frequently filled by deputies. It is probably in this way that such offices as vice-chancellorships, etc., first arose. There are many complaints in the rolls of parliament of the incompetence of these deputies. The barons of the exchequer were on a very different footing. In the earliest patents their grants are always during pleasure. An early example is found in 4 Edward I, where the king makes the grant "*quamdiu sibi placuerit*".

The statement is sometimes made in modern histories that the barons of the exchequer held during good behaviour till the time of the Stuarts. This is unfounded. Until the middle of the fifteenth century they seem invariably to have been appointed during pleasure—*quamdiu nobis placuerit, quamdiu Regi placuerit, quamdiu nostrae placuerit voluntati; exercendum ad voluntatem Regis*, or the like. Not until the reign of Henry

VI are any barons of the exchequer appointed during good behaviour. Those appointed at the accession of Edward IV had this tenure. In that year, however, the commons pray that the various commissions made by the Lancastrians and afterward may continue in force. The answer is: "It is agreed, so that the Barons of the Exchequer exercise their Offices at the Kynges pleasure, as the Judges doon." Notwithstanding this, Edward IV did afterward make grants during good behaviour. There is one interesting one in reversion during good behaviour in 1467. When Henry VI returned to the throne in 1470 all grants to the barons of the exchequer were during pleasure.

This was soon changed once more, and it seems probable that practically throughout the Tudor period these grants were uniformly made during good behaviour—*habendum tenendum et occupandum...quamdiu se bene gesserit.*

So it continued until the year 1628. Then an interesting thing happened. Sir John Walter had received his patent as chief baron of the exchequer *quamdiu se bene gesserit*, but Charles was dissatisfied with his opinion in the case of parliament-men imprisoned for alleged seditious speeches in parliament, and ordered him to surrender his patent. He refused to do so, on the ground that his grant was for good behaviour, and that he ought not to be removed without a proceeding on a *scire facias* to determine "whether he did *bene se gerere* or not", as Whitelocke puts it.

This was embarrassing. Charles could not risk another unpopular trial. He, therefore, had to allow the Chief Baron to retain his office and his revenues, and Walter retained them until his death about a year later; but the king did command him to stay away from the courts and not to perform his functions as judge, and he never appeared again in the court of exchequer to the day of his death.

Something somewhat like this had occurred when Elizabeth sequestered Archbishop Grindal in 1577 at a time when it would have been inconvenient to deprive him; and the precedent became useful later to Charles II. The same precedent may also, possibly, have influenced Lord Holt in 1690, when he advised the Council that the King might appoint a governor of Maryland in violation of Lord Baltimore's charter without first vacating it, provided the grantee's profits were secured to him.

The view that a great judicial office is just the same as its emoluments, is an interesting survival of feudalism the effects of which can be seen in several ways in the law reports. An interesting parallel to it is found in the opinion of the author of the *Mirror of Justices* that a freeman of the realm denied the rights promised in Magna Carta ought to recover damages by an assize of novel disseisin. But the idea was extremely dangerous to liberty in the seventeenth century. The next patent to a baron of the exchequer, granted after 1628, I need hardly say, read "*durante bene placito*". And so they all remained till the Long Parliament.

In the meantime there were troubles in the king's bench and common pleas also. Richard II had struck one of his judges for refusing to comply immediately with his demands and had even "trampled him under his feet". But it is James I who must bear most of the blame of beginning the interference with judicial tenure and functions which were so prominent in the civil troubles of the years following. His interference to procure the shameful divorce of the Countess of Essex, his part in the trials resulting from the murder of Sir Thomas Overbury, his pretensions of omniscience and claims to exercise judicial office in person, but above all his transfer and final removal of Sir Edward Coke, the most learned lawyer of his time, make some pretty black pages of history. I feel at times almost like agreeing with the rather vigorous language of Mr Horace Round who calls James " perhaps the most unseemly monster that has ever sat on the English throne".

Charles I unfortunately saw fit to follow this policy of interference with his judges. Even before he removed Baron

Walter from the court of exchequer, he had put out the chief justice of the king's bench, Sir Randolph Crew, in 1626, because he refused to sanction the king's forced loans. This was easier to do than in Walter's case, for the tenure was during pleasure. In 1634, the chief justice of the common pleas, Sir Robert Heath, followed, Sir John Finch being appointed to fill his place. And four days after the appointment, the writ for ship-money was issued.

To make possible such things as arbitrary imprisonment, forced loans, and ship-money, Charles within ten years had removed the heads of three great courts. It is little wonder that parliament took action.

In the Long Parliament, on January 11, 1640–1, the lords appointed a committee to consider the tenure of the judges. This resulted in the drawing up of a petition to the king praying that tenure during good behaviour be substituted for that during pleasure. On January 15 the king's reply was reported to the house—that "his Majesty is graciously pleased to condescend", and on June 5, Charles begged parliament to remember, among the concessions he had lately made, "that the judges, hereafter, shall hold their places, *quamdiu se bene gesserint*".

Apparently Charles kept his promise faithfully, and all his appointments after this, of which there were several, were made during good behaviour.

During the Interregnum the judicial office was not a bed of roses. The judges had to uphold by precedent a government based solely on force. Though apparently their tenures were all during good behaviour, Whitelocke records in 1655 that "Baron Thorpe and Judge Newdigate were put out of their places, for not observing the Protector's pleasure in all his Commands", and in the same year Chief Justice Rolle resigned because of friction between Cromwell and himself.

For a few years after the Restoration, possibly owing to Clarendon's influence, the tenure remained during good behaviour and a number of judges were so appointed. The pressure on the king, however, eventually became too great. In 1672 he tried to remove Sir John Archer from the common pleas, but Archer held during good behaviour and refused to surrender his patent without a *scire facias*. Charles then followed his father's example and ordered him to forbear to exercise the office of a judge either in court or elsewhere, appointing another judge to fill his place, though, as Rushworth wrote, Archer "still enjoys his Patent...and received a share in the Profits of that Court, as to Fines and other Proceedings by virtue of his said Patent, and his name is used in those Fines, &c. as a judge of that Court". It is probable that only his fees, not his salary remained to him.

Succeeding judges appointed to all the central courts held during pleasure for the rest of Charles's reign and through that of James II, and the transfers and removals were many. In the four years of James' reign alone some thirteen were removed; the law reports usually noting in a matter of fact way that on a certain day justice so and so "received his *quietus*". In 1680 the commons resolved to draw a bill providing that thereafter judges should hold their places and salaries *quamdiu se bene gesserint*, and also to prevent the arbitrary proceedings of the judges; but nothing came of it.

The removals of James's reign passed all precedent and all decency, and the number necessary proves that the judges were not all as bad as has sometimes been said. Four were removed in one day in 1686 for refusing to decide for the dispensing power, and two in the next year for declining to transfer the execution of a convicted deserter from the county where he had been tried to Portsmouth where his execution would have a greater effect on the troops.

In the debates in the Convention Parliament judicial tenure was discussed, and the evicted judges were examined at length as to the cause of their removal; but in the Bill of Rights no mention of the subject is made. Nevertheless all the patents under William and Mary and William III ran during good behaviour and there were no removals.

In 1691–2 a bill passed both houses for ascertaining the commissions and salaries of the judges, but it failed of the royal assent, and Burnet says this was due to the advice of some of the judges themselves that "it was not fit they should be out of all dependence on the court". In 1696, however, a statute was passed to extend the judges' commissions for six months after the death of a king.

But the principal statute on this subject in modern times, and the one substantially followed ever since, is the Act of Settlement of 1701. It was limited to take effect after the death of the king and the Princess Anne and in default of issue of either. The important provision was that "Judges' Commissions be made *quamdiu se bene gesserint* and their salaries ascertained and established but upon the Address of both Houses of Parliament it may be lawful to remove them".

The original draft of the bill in the commons provided for removal on address of either house, but on motion it was amended to read, "both houses". Motions were also twice made and lost to omit the whole provision for removal altogether.

Subsequent acts were passed in 1760, 1873, 1875 and 1876 on this subject, but they merely re-enact or supplement that of 1701, and I shall not retail them. After 1760 the death or the reigning king no longer put an end to all judicial patents. Before that, even after the Act of Settlement became effective, in 1714 and 1727, a number of judges failed of reappointment on the accession of the new king.

The net result of it all is that to-day an English judge holding by patent *quamdiu se bene gesserit*, like any other official so holding, may lose his office by judicial process under a writ of *scire facias*, if it appear that the conditions of the patent have not been fulfilled. Second, he may be impeached and removed from office by sentence of the house of lords, though this has not occurred for over a century. Third, the Crown may remove him without any cause shown, after a joint address of the houses of parliament requesting it, but not otherwise.

The address provided in all the acts from 1701 on is a most interesting thing. Its history is inseparably bound up with the whole great question of parliamentary and popular control of judicial tenure, which I dare not enter upon. Enough to say that as early as 1244 parliament demanded a control over both removal and appointment of judges greater than either the laws or the conventions of the constitution allow even to-day, and something very like the address is described by Matthew Paris for that year. An almost perfect example of a joint address for the removal of the Chancellor is narrated at length in Knighton's Chronicle for 1386.

All I shall say is that in 1701 the address was a perfectly well known form of procedure. The name "address" had gradually superseded the name "petition" for a communication from one or both houses to the Crown, while "petition", since the Restoration, had come to be applied almost exclusively to requests coming from individuals or bodies outside parliament. Such addresses had been frequently employed in the years just preceding 1701, and they had even been used to request the removal of a great officer of the Crown. There was absolutely nothing new or strange in this use of them in 1701. It was the ordinary method. But it is well to remember also that this parliamentary joint address was and is a procedure of extreme formality and great solemnity, never resorted to except in matters of national concern. It is the method of communication adopted by parliament, for example, in case of a death in the royal family. This is no mere resolution of both houses.

No case of any importance requiring the interpretation of the act of 1701 arose for over one hundred years. The first was the case of Luke Fox, an Irish judge, in 1804. Only once has a joint address for removal actually occurred, and that was in the case of Sir Jonah Barrington, a judge of the court of admiralty in Ireland, in 1830. Another great case was that of Baron Smith, another Irish judge, in 1834, though it stopped short of an address.

In these and other cases where the conduct of judges became the subject of parliamentary discussion, a number of interesting questions have arisen as to the proper interpretation of the words of the act of 1701: "but upon the address of both houses of parliament it may be lawful to remove them".

In this long history that I have tried to summarize, you will notice that there is no statutory action in modern times until 1696. Even in 1641 the lords only petitioned the king for an act of the prerogative. And it is my belief also that these words of the Act of Settlement, and even the act of 1875, confer no power upon the houses of parliament which they did not have before, of interfering with judicial tenure. All any of them does is to limit the royal prerogative, and that in a purely negative way, by permitting removals by the Crown only after an address. Not one of these statutes gives the houses power of removal. Not one forces the king to remove or even gives the houses authority to force him to comply with their request for removal.

The houses may address the king, and so they have been doing for some hundreds of years. But he is no more under the legal necessity of complying now than Charles I was in 1641. So far as parliament's power goes, the words of 1701 seem merely declaratory of existing law.

Were they, then, put there merely as a mitigation or exception to the general command to the Crown to grant all judicial patents during good behaviour? Or were they really intended also to give an additional power of interference to parliament? The late Professor Hearn held the latter view, and believed that parliamentary control of judges as well as judicial independence of the Crown was aimed at—on the ground that if independence had been the sole object, the address would have been omitted entirely from the statute as it was later from the constitution of the United States. If, however, parliamentary control was really intended, the words chosen to convey it were about as ill suited for their purpose as possible; for they give the houses no power not already theirs and they in no way affect the power of impeachment which already existed for cases of a serious character.

A second question is of a more practical kind. Are the preliminary investigations of the houses on motion for an address judicial in their character, or not? This involves in many ways the most fundamental question connected with the English form of government. If you examine every real dead-lock occurring within the last 200 years, in most cases you will find that it arises from the undefined and possibly indefinable boundary between the *lex terrae* and the *lex parliamenti*. Lord Auckland in Judge Fox's case, for example, denied that the clause in the act of 1701 could be construed "to take the judges from the general protection of the law of the land, in order to place them in a situation of disadvantage and dependence, which does not affect any other individual, or any other class of men". Lord Hawkesbury, on the other hand, pointed out that it was not a judicial matter at all—the house was merely exercising "that inquisitorial authority with which they were vested by the constitution", and urged that if it were improper in this case then they could neither address for the removal of a secretary of state, a first lord of the admiralty or the governor of a colony.

The difference disclosed here is fundamental. It has cropped up in almost every case that has come before parliament. In an investigation of judicial conduct, is the house merely ascertaining in a judicial proceeding whether a judge's conduct warrants a removal under the law? If so, then the accused is entitled to be heard, he may employ counsel, the laws of evidence should be strictly observed—in short, the procedure is governed by the *lex terrae*. The other view is that the whole procedure is purely discretionary with the houses. They may under the act vote for an address for any reason or for no reason. It is an act of power, and the procedure is entirely under their own control—a part of the *lex parliamenti*. On this rock most of the cases have split. Fox's case was dropped, after two whole years of wearisome talk had been expended on it, because the lords' preliminary discussions of it would be a prejudgment of the case if it came up to them later under impeachment proceedings. That set one precedent. Baron Smith's case was also dropped, in the commons, because they could not agree on the boundary between their powers of control and criticism and their judicial functions. Barrington's case alone issued in a joint address, and that only after months of discussion, in which the accused appeared both in person and by counsel, cross-examined witnesses, produced papers, made formal objections to evidence, and was in general given all the privileges of an accused person allowed under the *lex terrae*.

I want to close with one or two observations with which you may agree or not:

1. That, owing to the change by which the king's ministers have passed under the control of parliament—or more properly the commons—and now seem to be passing under the more direct control of the electors themselves, the power of parliament to put a sharp question to the government in regard to the conduct of a judge—a power in no way due to the act of 1701, and one successfully employed many times in the last century—is sufficient safeguard against judicial incompetency or minor lapses of conduct, to which experience has shown the address cannot in practice be applied; and that for serious offences impeachment is always possible.

2. That the procedure by address has proved to be very unsatisfactory in operation. Actually applied only once, and that as far back as 1830, failing of operation several times, rendered ineffectual and uncertain because it involves the most unsettled point in the English system—the line between the law of parliament and the law of the land—I think we

are to be congratulated that James Wilson's thorough understanding of the English constitution prevented its incorporation into our federal Constitution.

3. Whether the procedure on an address, in cases serious enough to warrant it, be in strict contemplation of law a judicial procedure under the *lex terrae*; or an arbitrary one under the *lex parliamenti*; in every case *in practice* the legal guarantees and immunities of accused persons have been observed. And *therefore* to compare our political removal on a recall, by a simple popular vote without hearing or process of any kind, either to the *law* of the Act of Settlement, or to this slow, elaborate, painstaking, conservative *practice* invariably employed in England under that law, is in my opinion misleading to the last degree. The main purpose of the English Act of Settlement was to make judges independent of what in the seventeenth century had claimed to be the sovereign power in the state—the Crown; the avowed purpose of our recall is to make them dependent on a popular majority, the power to which the "sovereign" is politically answerable to-day. The two aims have very little in common. They seem to be almost as far apart as the poles.

INDEX

Act of Settlement, 294
Adams, John, 240 f.
Adams, Samuel, 43, 84 f., 239
Address, of Parliament, for removal of a judge, 302 f.
Allegiance to King, 236
Althusius, 212
Amendments, 281
Aquinas, St Thomas, 19, 247
Archer, Sir John, 301
Aristotle, 35, 39
   on supremacy, 48
Arnisaeus, 79
   on mixed monarchy, 215 f.
Assemblies, colonial, as Parliaments, Chap. x
Augustine, St, 27, 28 n., 271
Austin, 33, 39, 43, 61
   on sovereignty, 57
Authority, 26, 38
Aylmer, John, quoted, 5

Bacon, Francis, 255, 271
Barker, Ernest, on authorship of *Vindiciae*, 178
Beaumanoir, 50
Bellarmine, Cardinal, 19
Bentham, 59
Bill of Rights, 236
Bills of rights, in constitutions, 244 ff.
Blackstone, 59
Blackwood, Adam, 40 n.
Bodin, 26, 28, 31 n. 1, 34, 37, 39 f., 72, 205, 212
   on sovereignty, 52 ff.
Bouvines, 100
Bracton, 22 ff., 130, 135 f., 252, 253 f.
   on changes in law, 153
Bridgeman, Sir Orlando, at Regicides' trial, 256
Bryce, Lord, 30
Burns, Robert, 259

Camden, 43
Cavendish's case, 24, 80 f., 218, 255
Charles I, 62, and judges, 299 f.
Charles II, and judges, 301
Charter of Massachusetts 1628, Chap. x
Checks and balances, 246
Cicero, 28, 35, 247, 285
Clarendon, Assize of, 9
Coke, Sir Edward, 7, 186 f., 252
   statement on Magna Carta as Common Law, 128, 140
   removal of, 299
Commons, House of, in 1621, Chap. VIII
   consent required to Statutes, 156 ff.
   initiative of, 184 f.
   liberty of debate, 185 f.
   rôle in legislation, 218 f.
Committee of the Whole, 193
Connecticut, Fundamental Orders of, 241
Consent, in medieval law, 145 f.
Constitution, U.S., Chap. XI
Constitutionalism, Ch. XIII, 64, 290
   and Liberalism, 261 ff.
Constitutions, 279 f.
   as fundamental law, 176 f.
Consuetudo, 130 f.
Continental Congress, Second, 239
Contract, 286 f.
Corruption in democracy, 275
Counter-Reformation, fear of in England, 189
Court, county, 11
Creasy, Sir Edward, quoted, 12
Crisis, present, 1, 257, 259

Declaratory Act 1766, 57, 236
Democracy, 274 ff.
Despencers, 132, 134

Despotism, 267, caused by weakness of government, 257 f.
benevolence of, 261
Dialogue of the Exchequer, 249
Dicey, 48
Dominium, 47, 50 f.
Dort, Synod of, 20

"Economic Royalists", 261
Education, 46
Edward I, 17
Confirmation of the Charters, 127
Edward III, 133
Eldon, Lord, 57
Eliot, Sir John, 19, 62 f., 78, 234
Endecott, Governor, 231 ff.
Engelbert of Admont, 206
Exchequer, Barons of the, 297

Fascism, 33, 275 f.
Ferne, Henry, reply to Hunton, 197
Feudal constitutionalism, 248
Fictions, in English Constitution, 32
Filmer, Sir Robert, 39, 63, 70
on monarchy, 215
answer to Hunton, 179
Fleta, 130, 254
Floyd's Case 1621, 187 ff.
Forest, Charter of, 132
law, 14 f.
Fortescue, Sir John, 23, 254
Frank, Hans, 269, 272
Franklin, Benjamin, 237
Freeman, 9 ff.
French monarchy, compared with English, 228
Fuller, Thomas, 2

Germany, 263
Glanvill, 109, 111, 130 ff.
Gooch, on Hunton, criticized, 209
Government by Law, Chap. XIII
Great Charter, *see* Magna Carta
"Great Council", 11
Greek thought, absence of constitutionalism, 246
Green, T. H., 35, 45

Hale, Sir Matthew, 19, 62 f.
on sovereignty, 81 ff.

Hale, on English constitution, 221
Hamilton, Alexander, 65
Henry IV, accession declaration, 134
Historian's role, Chap. I
History, importance of, Chap. I
Hitler, 85
Hobbes, Thomas, 27, 40, 63, 75
on sovereignty, 55 f.
view of affairs in 1642, 199
Holdsworth, Sir William, 69
Hooker, Thomas, 241
Hoover, Herbert, 281
Hume, 29
Hunton, Philip, Chap. IX
on limited monarchy, 200 ff.
on mixed monarchy, 204, 212 ff.
revised estimate summarized, 209
differences from Bodin, 225

James I, 233, and judges, 299
James II and judges, 301
Jolliffe, J. E. A., 124
Judges, recall of, 294, 307
Judicial Review, 251, 264, 278 f.
Judicium Parium in Magna Carta, 91
Jury, trial, and *judicium parium*, 91
de Justa Reipublicae Authoritate, authorship of, 178 f.

Lancastrian constitution, use in 17th-century debates, 194 f.
Langton, Stephen, 96 ff., 103
Law, and State, 246 f.
Law as custom, 248
Law of nature, 247
Law of the forest, 14
Leges Henrici Primi, 123
Legislation, 217 f.
and participation of the Estates, 154
in a mixed monarchy, 205
Lex, 130
de Imperio, 26
parliamenti, 305 f.
regia, 248
terrae, 111, 307; meaning of, 92 f.; in Magna Carta, 108
Liber Homo, in Magna Carta, 88 f.
meaning, 122
Liberalism, Chap. XIV, 260 ff.

Liberalism, and Constitutionalism, 261 ff.
Lilburne, John, 242
Lippmann, Walter, Chap. XIV, 292 f.
Locke, 208
  on right of revolution, 37, 44
  influence of Hunton on, 203
Long Parliament, and tenure of judges, 300
Louis, St, 253
  and Provisions of Oxford, 16
Lovell, James, 238
Loyseau, 41, 44, 212

Macaulay, T. B., 271
McKechnie, 13
  on Chap. 39 of Magna Carta, 86
Magna Carta, 12, 276, Chap. V
  Chap. 39, means of interpreting, 104
  and Common Law, Ch. VI
  significance under Henry III, 169 f.
  as Common Law in 14th century, 172 f.
  confirmations of, 174 f.
  as fundamental law, 176 f.
Maitland, F. W., 8 ff., 61
Mansfield, Lord, 67 f., 69
Manwood, John, on forest law, 14
Marches, Scottish, 140
  Welsh, 115, 139
Marlborough, Statute of, 132
Maryland, tenure of governors of, 299
Massachusetts, early political positions, 232 f.
  Charter 1628, Chap. X
  Circular Letter, 43, 71
Merton, Statute of, 15 f., 135
Mirror of Justices, 137, 299
Mixed monarchy, theory of, 199
  Hunton's analysis, 204, 212 ff.
  Arnisaeus on, 215
Model Parliament, 17
Monarchomachs, 44
Monarchy, French, 228
  mixed, *see* Mixed monarchy
Montfort, Simon de, 17

Morton, Thomas, 179
Mussolini, 33

Nazism and law, 268
Normandy, Grand Coutumier of, 109
Northington, Lord Chancellor, 84
Notestein, Wallace, 183 f.
Novanglus, by John Adams, 241

Obedience, 27
Office, feudal conception, 295 ff.
Ordinances, 217
  regarded as temporary, 148
Oxford, Provisions of, 16, 253

Parliament, 146 (*see also* Commons)
  power over removal of judges, 304 f.
Parsons, Robert, 179 f.
  Theophilus, on limitations of sovereignty, 66 f.
Petition of Right, 236
Pluralism, 34 ff., 58
Politics, divorce from history, 288
Pollard, A. F., 62
Popular sovereignty, 264, 290 f.
Populus, limited to barons, 146, 154
Potestas, see Power
Power, 27, 38
  arbitrary, 72
Powicke, F. M., 117
Prothero, Sir George, 224
Prynne, 213
Pym, John, 62
  diaries of Parliament, 192

Radin, Max, 117 f.
Raleigh, Sir Walter, 224
Ranke, 4
Recall of judges, 294, 307
Rechtsstaat, 60, 74, 230, 270
Regicides, trial, 256
Representation, 37 f., 64 f., 146
Revolution, American, 68
  of 1688, 62 f.
Reynolds, William, author of *de Justa Reipublicae Authoritate*, Chap. VII
"Rossaeus", Chap. VII
Rousseau, 29, 31 n. 1, 34, 37, 39 f., 64

Rousseau, on representation, 32 f.
Runnymede, 102
Russell, Lord John, on government of Canada, 70

Salic Law, 54
Salisbury, Gemót of, 10
Schechter Case, 270
Ship-money Case, 211, 256
Sovereignty, Chaps. II, III, IV
    purely juristic, 30
    limitations, 42 f.
    origins, 51 f.
    as power to make law, 51 f.
    popular, 64
    and law, 73
    corporate, *see* Mixed Monarchy
Spinoza, 28 f., 42, 43
Stamp Act, 237
State, and law, 246 f.
Statute, 217, 251
    early use of the term, 141 f.
    distinct from ordinance, 161 ff.
    permanence of, 147 f., 165
    publication of, 168
Stenton, F. M., 9
Stoic theory of the state, 49
Story, Joseph, on Bill of Rights, 67
Stubbs, Bishop, 11
Sullivan, John, 240

Suspending power of king, 168 f.

Tenure of judges, 294
du Tillet, 42, 44
Tout, T. F., 5
Treatise of Monarchie of Philip Hunton, Chap. IX
Tudor absolutism, 18, 276
Twysden, Sir Roger, 79 f.
Tyranny, 43

Vindiciae contra Tyrannos, authorship, 178 f.
Virginia Resolves 1765, 236 f.

Wales, rights in the Marches, 115, 139
Walter, Sir John, 298
Wentworth, Peter, 24
Westminster, Statute of 1931, 70
    Statutes of under Edward I, 148 f.
Whig theory of sovereignty, 61 f.
Whitelock, Sir James, on English constitution, 76 f., 220
Williams College, address at, 259
Willion *v.* Berkley, 80
Wilson, James, 307
Wilson, President, 274
Winthrop, John, 234 f.
Wright, Elizabeth, on forest law, 14

CAMBRIDGE: PRINTED BY W. LEWIS, M.A., AT THE UNIVERSITY PRESS